4 Z8746 1991

.ul N.

The great reversal

DATE DUE

| | | | |
|---|---|---|---|
| FEB 13 1995 S | | | |
| | | | |
| | | | |
| | | | |
| | | | |
| | | | |
| | | | |
| | WITHDRAWN | | |
| | | | |
| | | | |

# The Great Reversal:
## Politics and Art in Solzhenitsyn

*Paul N. Siegel*

**The Great Reversal: Politics and Art in Solzhenitsyn**
By Paul N. Siegel
Copyright © 1991 by Paul N. Siegel

Library of Congress Catalog Card Number: 91-65815


ISBN: 0-929405-05-6 (Softcover)
ISBN: 0-929405-06-4 (Hardcover)


Manufactured in the United States
First edition, 1991
Walnut Publishing Co., Inc.
3435 Army St., suite 308
San Francisco, CA 94110

**OTHER BOOKS BY PAUL N. SIEGEL**

<u>Author</u>

*Shakespearean Tragedy and the Elizabethan Compromise* (1957)

*Shakespeare in His Time and Ours* (1968)

*Revolution and the Twentieth-Century Novel* (1979)

*Shakespeare's English and Roman History Plays: A Marxist Approach* (1986)

*The Meek and the Militant: Religion and Power Across the World* (1986)

<u>Editor</u>

*His Infinite Variety: Major Shakespearean Criticism Since Johnson* (1964)

*Leon Trotsky on Literature and Art* (1970)

*For Jessica,*
*who was not included with her sisters*
*and brother in a previous dedication*
*because she was not here yet.*

# CONTENTS

# ACKNOWLEDGMENTS

I wish to thank Cliff Conner, who with his usual generosity offered to do the typography for this book as a contribution to the Walnut Publishing Company and a favor to me. He enlisted, moreover, the aid of his fellow worker, Dennis A. Nelson, who does not know either the Walnut Publishing Company or me but worked with Cliff on this project out of esteem for him. Without Dennis' technical wizardry this book could not have come into existence.

During the many years of my friendship with Cliff, he and I have frequently read each other's manuscripts, rather like the women of a poor village who were said to eke out a living by taking in each other's laundry. Unlike the village women, however, I have genuinely profited both from what I learned from Cliff's papers and from his comments on my own. For this also I am grateful.

I wish to thank Dennis Edge, who did the cover design, and Alex Chis of the Walnut Publishing Company. Both have been unfailingly helpful and cooperative.

Finally, I wish to thank the editors of *Clio: A Journal of Literature, History and the Philosophy of History* and of *Jewish Currents* for permission to include material which first appeared in their pages.

# *Preface:* **What this Book Will Seek to Show**

Rarely has an author in his own lifetime achieved the kind of acclaim achieved by Aleksandr Solzhenitsyn. For a long time the world press was full of stories about how he, a single individual, was challenging a despotic regime, as Tolstoy had done in Czarist Russia. The subject of many adulatory books, he was hailed not only as a hero but as a novelist of the stature of Tolstoy and Dostoyevsky. By 1972 his works had been translated into as many languages as were those of Shakespeare. Since Shakespeare was translated into the multitude of languages of the Soviet Union, where publication of Solzhenitsyn was forbidden, the statistic is all the more startling. By 1976 thirty million copies of his books had been sold throughout the world. To use an image he himself made famous, his readers constituted a vast worldwide archipelago with the population of a large country.

For many years now, however, Solzhenitsyn has secluded himself on his estate in Vermont, working on an immensely ambitious lifetime project, a series of novels on the Russian Revolution. From a front-page celebrity, he became a remote presence. A number of political speeches he made damaged his reputation so that now he is seen by many in the United States as an inverted Stalinist or a kind of Russian Orthodox Jerry Falwell. His literary reputation also suffered when his *August 1914*, published abroad when he was still in the Soviet Union, was received respectfully but with a bewildered disappointment.

But in 1989 Solzhenitsyn once more entered the news. Dispatches from the Soviet Union told of how in the era of glasnost he has ceased to be a non-person. Finally, it was announced that *The Gulag Archipelago* was going to be published in full. In the United States the publication in English translation of his revised and expanded *August 1914* has made his name return to prominence.

However, the earlier disappointment in *August 1914* has been succeeded by dismay. "What has happened to Alexander Solzhenit-syn?" wrote Irving Howe in the lead review of *The New York Times Book Review* (July 2, 1989). The artist who "grazed moral sublimity"

i

in his earlier work has been replaced by "a shrill and splenetic polemicist."

This book seeks to analyze what happened to Solzhenitsyn. As its title indicates, it is concerned with both the politics and the art of Solzhenitsyn and with the relationship between them. The meaning of *The First Circle* and *Cancer Ward*, Solzhenitsyn's two great novels, cannot be fully apprehended, it is my claim, without an understanding of their political implications, which have not been properly perceived. A close reading of these novels shows that they imply that, while Leninism by itself is not a remedy for the problems in Soviet society created by Stalinism, in conjunction with other thinking, particularly Tolstoyism, it does provide such a remedy.

And yet in *August 1914*, published not very long after, there is a violent reaction against both Leninism and Tolstoyism. How are we to explain this sudden change? The evidence I shall present shows that Solzhenitsyn harbored doubts about communism during his imprisonment but did not definitely break with Marxism in his thinking. He suppressed these doubts after *One Day in the Life of Ivan Denisovich* was published with the approval of Khrushchev himself. Under the traumatic shock of the neo-Stalinist reaction, when Solzhenitsyn feared that he would be sent back to prison camp and that, in any event, his literary career was over with his ambitious project unrealized, his doubts became certainties, and he became strongly anti-communist.

It was during the period of shock at the recrudescence of Stalinism that Solzhenitsyn wrote *The Gulag Archipelago* and smuggled it out to the West. The three large volumes of this huge work have been received reverentially but with little critical analysis. It is, however, both an authentic and powerful account of the horrors of the Stalinist labor camp system and a very shoddy history of its origins that is tendentious, contrary to the verified facts, and self-contradictory. Yet it is this work that has been widely cited by those arguing that socialist revolution must lead to the Stalinist camps.

The final stage of Solzhenitsyn's political evolution is reflected in *Lenin in Zurich* and in the revised version of *August 1914*. *Lenin in Zurich* suggests that the Jewish financier-revolutionist Alexander Parvus, whom Solzhenitsyn gives the features of many traditional anti-Semitic stereotypes, was the behind-the-scenes figure of the Russian Revolution, standing secretly behind Lenin and giving him his opportunity. The revised *August 1914* suggests that the Jews were responsible for the assassination of Peter Stolypin, Russia's prime minister in 1911, which Solzhenitsyn makes the event that left the regime open to revolution and that decisively changed the history of the world.

Solzhenitsyn claims that his fiction is historically accurate and that his Lenin is a painstaking re-creation of Lenin as he actually was. My chapter on his portrait of Lenin establishes, however, that its main features are incompatible with what all serious scholars have had to say about him, with historical fact, and with the comments of enemies who had been his intimates as well as the comments of his friends.

The falsity of this portrait is of a piece with the shallowness and inaccuracy of his political pronouncements about the Soviet Union as a demonically evil power on the verge of defeating a soft and decadent West and conquering the world. Based on the immoral doctrine of Marxism, the Soviet Union, he alleged, is totally incapable of internal change. These pronouncements have been disproven by the crumbling of Stalinism, but I have thought it worthwhile to analyze the sources of Solzhenitsyn's political errors, which are relevant to his depiction of the approaching revolution in *Lenin in Zurich* and *August 1914*.

Finally, in my last chapter I discuss at length Solzhenitsyn's art and the effect upon it of his change of politics. Both *The First Circle* and *Cancer Ward* are polyphonic, containing a multitude of characters, with things being seen from the point of view of each one as attention is focused on him or her. Even when Solzhenitsyn condemns his characters, he is able to see what made them what they have become. His understanding makes possible both compassion for his characters and irony in the depiction of their rationalizations. Each novel is held together by an intricate network of contrasts, parallels, and ironic juxtapositions constructed in accordance with the novel's underlying theme.

*August 1914*, I find, is considerably less polyphonic, the soldiers especially being seen from the outside. Characters tend to be static, without a previous development being shown that might explain why they are what they are now, and are often the cardboard cutouts of the propagandist. Solzhenitsyn's research to gain the materials to give substance to his view of the Russian Revolution has not made history come convincingly alive but rather overloaded the book with technical material concerning the logistics of the military operations. The modernistic literary devices introduced into *August 1914* do not energize this inert material. Solzhenitsyn has, moreover, lost the compassion of previous novels, which enabled him to see even informers and prison camp officers not as stereotyped villains but human beings who have degenerated under difficult conditions, and the irony is heavily insistent rather than subtle, as before.

*Lenin in Zurich* presents conflicting views of Lenin as a theorist incapable of action and as a demonic force bringing disaster, each intended to denigrate him. Lenin's character is thus artistically incoherent. *Lenin in Zurich* and *August 1914*, therefore, make clear that Solzhenitsyn's fanatical anti-communism is stultifying his art.

# 1. Solzhenitsyn: The Man and his Work

Michael Scammell's thousand-page *Solzhenitsyn* is a fine biography of a remarkable man. Scammell labored prodigiously to go through the enormous amount that has been written on this controversial figure and to interview all those who have played a part in Solzhenitsyn's life. Solzhenitsyn himself for a long time cooperated with him—albeit hesitantly and with misgivings about working with a biographer not under his supervision and control—but then ceased to do so. "The termination of relations," says Scammell, "was friendly but final."[1] The book, judicious and scrupulously fair, gives a fascinating picture of a complex man who is full of contradictions.

However, although all Solzhenitsyn scholars must be indebted to Scammell's highly valuable book, it has two major shortcomings. The first is that Scammell, one of whose aims is avowedly to examine Soviet society "through the prism of one exceptional man's life and career" (p. 19), is inhibited in his understanding of that society by reason of the anti-Bolshevik bias he shares with Solzhenitsyn. He is, to be sure, aware of the extravagance of many of Solzhenitsyn's pronouncements such as his statement that *Russia Under the Old Regime* by the Harvard scholar Richard Pipes is a "pseudo-academic book," full of "mistakes, exaggerations, and perhaps premeditated distortions," a book influenced both by the Russian pre-revolutionary intellectuals' unbalanced criticism of Czarist society and the "hurricane" of propaganda let loose by "committed socialist circles." Concerning this statement Scammell comments tartly (p. 953) that Pipes "went on to become a personal adviser on Soviet affairs to President Reagan, not generally known for his softness on communism or a tendency to bow to the 'socialist hurricane.'"

Nevertheless, Scammell basically agrees, as is evident from his historical background descriptions, with Solzhenitsyn's thesis that Stalinism is simply a continuation of Bolshevism. The consequence of Scammell's implicit acceptance of this thesis, which I shall seek to

1

disprove in subsequent chapters, is that, failing to have a sufficiently analytical understanding of the origin and development of Stalinism, he does better at achieving one of his aims, "to illuminate and explain . . . a major figure of our era," than at achieving his other aim, "to come to grips" with the "phenomenon" of Stalinism "and to understand it" (p. 19) and the present neo-Stalinist society of the Soviet Union.

The other shortcoming of the book is its lack of analysis of Solzhenitsyn's work. Scammell has written that he is conscious of this inadequacy but that he couldn't add to the length of what is already a very big book. However, in failing to analyze Solzhenitsyn's work, Scammell all too frequently accepts at face value what Solzhenitsyn himself has to say about it. Examples are these echoings of Solzhenitsyn: "*The First Circle* [in the version translated in the West] was ultimately anti-Communist in content, but the political message was well-buried" (p. 561); the only purpose of Shulubin's "ethical socialism" in *Cancer Ward* is that Solzhenitsyn "found it interesting to make the best possible case for socialism through the medium of a sympathetic character" (p. 578); "*August 1914*, except for one chapter, was in many respects orthodox from a Soviet point of view, and certainly in comparison with Solzhenitsyn's previous novels" (p. 688). But Solzhenitsyn's comments on his work, to which these statements are indebted, are, as we shall see in the next chapter, utterly untrustworthy as guides to understanding it.

The consequence of Scammell's lack of analysis is that he does not answer or even raise important questions. How are the novels of this most political of novelists an expression of his political ideas? Are there significant differences between *The First Circle* and *Cancer Ward* on the one hand and *August 1914* on the other? How have Solzhenitsyn's politics affected his art? Did his politics affect the truthfulness of his celebrated *Gulag Archipelago*? These are questions that cry out for answers.

Relevant to these questions is the question of how we are to appraise the conflicting statements about Solzhenitsyn as an author seeking publication in the Soviet Union made by himself and by Vladimir Lakshin, the chief literary critic and editorial board member of *Novy Mir*, the liberal literary magazine through which Solzhenitsyn had published *One Day in the Life of Ivan Denisovich* and sought to publish *The First Circle* and *Cancer Ward*. Solzhenitsyn informs us in his memoir *The Oak and the Calf* that he kept secret from Alexander Tvardovsky, the editor of *Novy Mir*, and from the other members of the editorial board the fact that he was hostile not just to Stalinism but to the social system established by the October Revolution, from which he regarded Stalinism to be a logical development, not an aberration. Lakshin, however, takes issue with him and presents quite a different version of Solzhenitsyn's early career.

In an essay written in samizdat—despite its attack on Solzhenitsyn, its vigorous opposition to the regime would not permit it to be published in the official press—he describes Solzhenitsyn as a great writer who showed magnificent courage in combatting the Soviet bureaucracy but who has become a megalomaniac whose judgment and memory are not to be trusted.

> Solzhenitsyn seems to think that . . . at least since the day when he crossed the threshold of *Novy Mir*, he has not changed but has merely been putting his own secret plan into operation. That is not true. He has changed, and his plan has changed too. . . . [I]n 1962–4 he . . . was sincerely trying to "grow into" Soviet literature and public life . . . despite his highly critical stance. . . . Although unwillingly, he did make compromises in order to be published: he wanted to please (and did please) the country's top leadership; he attended receptions given by the Central Committee's Secretary for Ideology, and was prepared to accept a Lenin prize. . . . I sometimes think that if the leadership . . . had not prevented him from getting the Lenin Prize in 1964, if they had allowed *Cancer Ward* and *The First Circle* to be printed in the Soviet Union—we should today see Solzhenitsyn as a very different person.[2]

The mine of information in Scammell's book enables us to adjudicate between Solzhenitsyn and Lakshin: Lakshin is basically correct but not entirely so. Scammell points to the internal contradictions in *The Oak and the Calf* and concludes that Solzhenitsyn projected

> the thoughts, attitudes, and ideas of his later years back to a period when they existed only in embryo and when the public persona that later became famous was just beginning to take shape. . . . He claims to have seen through the

shams and deceptions of the literary establishment from the start, planning his campaigns against it with the vision of a prophet and the strategic cunning of a general. There is a kernel of truth in this picture. Solzhenitsyn did hold aloof from official literary circles and had always conducted himself as something of an outsider, but he was prepared to participate and make compromises. He joined the Writers' Union, attended meetings at the Kremlin and in Ryazan, made friends with "liberals" in the literary establishment and competed keenly for the Lenin Prize (Scammell, p. 540).

The compromises Solzhenitsyn made entailed constant revision to attempt to get past the censorship. "[I]n all my books," he told *The New York Times*, "I left out certain things and toned down my words."[3] The question is whether these compromises went so deep that they resulted, as he states in *The Oak and the Calf*, in a fundamental change in his meaning. In 1979 the YMCA Press in Paris published a 96-chapter version of *The First Circle* as against the 87-chapter version published in the West and thereby, he says, "saved" the book, the 87-chapter *First Circle* being only an "ersatz, truncated" version.[4]

But is it really true that *The First Circle* we know in English did not conform, at least in a general way, to Solzhenitsyn's intent at the time? He had tried desperately to have the "ersatz, truncated" *First Circle* published in the Soviet Union and then, as insurance that it would be published somewhere, had smuggled it out for publication in the West. Olga Carlisle, his American agent, says that, when he asked her to see to its publication in the West, he described it "as the one that mattered," "a big book—my life."[5] To be sure, Solzhenitsyn subsequently quarreled with her and called her "dishonest."[6] But if Solzhenitsyn regarded the 87-chapter *First Circle* as an "ersatz" production that needed saving, why did he smuggle it out without saving it? It would seem that the version the English-speaking world has was at the time dear to his heart as an expression of what he felt, not an inferior substitute.

An idea woven into the very fabric of *The First Circle* and *Cancer Ward* is, as we shall see in the second chapter, that the Soviet bureaucracy has betrayed Leninism. Are we to perceive the favorable way in which Lenin is regarded as a mere expedient to get by the censor? Is it likely that Solzhenitsyn, with his exalted sense of the function of the novelist, would so violate the integrity of his novel? It is one thing to omit prudently that which one would have liked to have said, another to include that with which one is in violent disagreement. He himself stated in challenging Sholokhov's authorship of *The Quiet Don*, which he charged was plagiarized from the manuscript of another author: "Over the years Sholokhov has given permission for numerous unprincipled corrections to *The Quiet Don*—political and factual. . . . Of the two mothers of the disputed child, the true mother was the one who preferred to hand the child over rather than have it mutilated."[7] Are we to believe that he himself "truncated" the child of his creation?

Not only does Solzhenitsyn allege that he did damage to his own brain-child; he alleges that critics, before he set them straight after coming to the West, did so. At a press conference in Stockholm he "reproached Western literary critics for wanting to identify him with socialist ideas. He pointed out, for instance, that contrary to their opinion even Shulubin [in *Cancer Ward*], with his ethical socialism, 'is entirely opposite to the author.' "[8] After Solzhenitsyn proclaimed his anti-communism, such statements by journalistic critics ceased and were forgotten, while academic critics have concerned themselves little with the precise political implications of his novels.[9]

The opinion that the need for ethical socialism is a central theme of *Cancer Ward*, not merely a concept of one of its characters, was not only held by journalistic critics of the West; it is held by Lakshin,[10] whom Solzhenitsyn had once called "a very gifted literary critic . . . who can stand comparison with our best nineteenth-century critics" (Scammell, p. 669). This opinion is profoundly correct. Although Solzhenitsyn at the time he wrote *Cancer Ward* and *The First Circle* was, according to Roy Medvedev and Lakshin, praising Lenin and early Soviet society to his friends,[11] he is not in these novels a simple Leninist. "Ethical socialism" is a modification of Leninism, and the implication of the two novels, as will be shown when we come to examine their political overtones, is that such a modified Leninism is the answer to Stalinism.

In them and in *One Day in the Life of Ivan Denisovich*, his Christian belief is manifest. In *The First Circle* and *Cancer Ward* this Christianity—in *Cancer Ward* it is most specifically indicated that it is the Christianity of Tolstoy—is blended with the Marxist socialism of Lenin into a curious mixture of Solzhenitsyn's concoction. In *August 1914* this mixture of Tolstoyism and Leninism is succeeded by anti-Tolstoyism and anti-Leninism, and the Christianity becomes that of the Orthodox Church rather than that of the excommunicated Tolstoy, the radical critic of Czarist society.[12]

This reading is confirmed by the documentary evidence we have of Solzhenitsyn's religious belief at this time. Solzhenitsyn claims that he gave up Marxism and became converted to religion during his stay in the sharashka, the special camp for prisoners with scientific knowledge that is the setting for *The First Circle*,[13] but this is not accurate. Peretz Herzenberg, a fellow prisoner there, told Scammell that Solzhenitsyn had refused to assert in the sharashka that he was a religious believer, saying that the question of religious belief is very complex and implying that he was not ready to answer it. Subsequently, after having gone to a labor camp from the sharashka, Solzhenitsyn wrote to Natalia Reshetovskaya, his first wife, that he accepted his imprisonment as part of his destiny, adding, "Perhaps this belief in fate is the start of religious feelings? I don't know. It seems I am still a long way from believing in god."[14] And in *The Gulag Archipelago* he tells us that it was not until he was in prison hospital, awaiting his operation for cancer, that he fully embraced religion. This account is confirmed by a letter to his wife on his release from the hospital. "He had been apprehensive before the operation, he wrote, but the faith 'in God's will and in God's mercy' that he had recently acquired had greatly eased his path" (Scammell, p. 303).

Solzhenitsyn's religious belief, however, did not take the form of unquestioning acceptance of the Orthodox Church. The religious Dimitri Panin, the original of Sologdin in *The First Circle* and the intimate of Solzhenitsyn at the sharashka,

> welcomed Solzhenitsyn's return to Christianity, but in 1959 he wrote him a long letter saying that faith was not enough and that before Solzhenitsyn could regard himself as a true Christian he would have to submit his will to the church (Scammell, p. 374).

As for Solzhenitsyn's relinquishment of Marxism, it is clear that this did not take place in the sharashka either, although it was here too that the process of evolution in his thinking about it began. Lev Kopelev, the original of Rubin in *The First Circle*, who was then a

Stalinist believer and the other intimate of Solzhenitsyn, writes of their fierce intellectual debates,

> In skirmishes like this [against Panin, an anti-communist] Solzhenitsyn and I were allies. But when we were left alone, he opposed my dialectical-materialist arguments with stubborn disbelief. In those days he considered himself a skeptic, a follower of Pyrrho, but he already hated Stalin— "the ringleader"—and was beginning to have doubts about Lenin.[15]

He also "began having more and more doubts about Marxism itself," for, he stated, "even the greatest" Marxists, "Marx and Lenin," were "wrong in their predictions."[16]

There is, in fact, no evidence in the form of letters or assertions by intimates that Solzhenitsyn had definitively broken with Marxism at the time of his writing of *The First Circle* and *Cancer Ward*, as there is for his conversion to Christianity. Even the memoirs of his first wife, Natalia Reshetovskaya, tendentiously edited though they were by a Soviet publisher (she protested against the doctoring), make no mention of it.

He did, however, give literary expression to the doubts he voiced to Kopelev about Marxism and Leninism in a play, *Victory Celebrations*, that he composed in camp in 1951 and seems to have gone beyond those doubts to a repudiation of the October Revolution in another play, *Prisoners*, composed in 1952–1953. Prison conditions did not permit him to write them down so he carried them in his head in a stupendous feat of memory and only committed them to paper in exile. They were published for the first time in 1981. These plays and another early play, *The Love-Girl and the Innocent*, were, as Scammell says (p. 349) a "release of all" Solzhenitsyn's "frustration and bitterness" and "an essential catharsis . . . , enabling him to clear his mind and work his way through to the themes that the mature artist was to take up and transmute into works of literature."

In *Victory Celebrations* Captain Nerzhen, the skeptic in *The First Circle* whom Solzhenitsyn based on himself, does not report to the authorities a sympathetically drawn woman who is working for the Vlasovites, the Russian ex-prisoners of war serving under the Nazis, telling her, "Not to be an enemy doesn't mean being a friend." Concerning her anti-communist politics, he says: "I do agree with a lot of what you say. Most of it is true. But nothing is all black in nature."[17] At another time he ruminates: "I feel sometimes that the very core of the Revolution, its very structure had a fatal flaw. But where and in what way? I scratch about for the truth, like a pig digging for truffles."[18]

In *Prisoners*[19] there is continuous argumentation among the many characters, some of whom express ideas such as the alien character of the Bolshevik revolution, the decadence of the West, and the messianic mission of Russia, whose spiritual strength has been developed through suffering, that were to be expanded upon in Solzhenitsyn's political works. Vorontyntsev, a former colonel in the Czarist army who has been fighting the Soviet government and who was to be an important character in *August 1914*, has the last word.

In a debate with Rubylov, a colonel in counter-intelligence, he argues that the revolution was a disaster that could have been averted, while Rubylov argues that the revolution was historically inevitable and progressive. Rubylov, knowing that he is shortly to die from an unspecified illness which causes him great pain—the play was composed shortly after Solzhenitsyn's cancer operation—commits suicide. No doubt his illness is meant to suggest merited retribution and his suicide is meant to foreshadow the demise of the regime he represents.[20]

Possibly Solzhenitsyn, an inveterate reviser of his work, "touched up" *Prisoners* before its publication although artistically it is far poorer than his mature work, just as he "touched up" his novels to seek to gain publication in the Soviet Union and "removed a number of passages disparaging Western democracy and Western institutions" from *Letter to the Leaders* before publishing it in the West (Scammell, p. 848). But whatever were his thoughts and feelings when he composed *Prisoners*, it seems clear that when he was writing *The First Circle* and *Cancer Ward* he suppressed in large degree his prison-camp doubts. Kostoglotov, the autobiographical protagonist of *Cancer Ward* (like Solzhenitsyn, he was sent from the war-time army to a labor camp for critical remarks about Stalin, contracted cancer there, almost died of neglect, and finally survived as a rare case of the remission of the illness), says in response to Shulubin's question as to whether he lost faith in socialism, "I don't know. Things got so tough out there, you sometimes went further than you wanted to, out of sheer fury."[21] Something like Kostoglotov's feeling that his bitterness in the past had perhaps carried him too far must have been Solzhenitsyn's when he wrote *Cancer Ward* itself.

*The First Circle* and *Cancer Ward* were started when Solzhenitsyn was in exile at a time when millions of prisoners were being released, and he continued to work on them after *One Day in the Life of Ivan Denisovich* had been sponsored by Khrushchev himself. The dream of authorship and recognition, to the achievement of which he had devoted himself from an early age with a remarkable dedication and self-discipline,[22] unrealizable as they had seemed to the prisoner at camp, had been realized. Although Solzhenitsyn tried to maintain the skepticism and the stoicism in the face of good or bad fortune of his prison-camp days, he could not but be affected by his new circumstances.

"Among other omens that encouraged Solzhenitsyn's optimism at this time," says Scammell (pp. 472–73),

> were some unexpected encounters with the establishment. In February 1963 he had been invited to address seventy members of the Soviet Union's supreme Military Tribunal, that same tribunal under whose auspices the Special Board had sentenced him in 1945 to eight years' imprisonment and perpetual exile. ". . . I looked about me," Solzhenitsyn later wrote, "and was amazed: they were human beings! Completely human! Now they were smiling, and frankly explaining how they had only wanted to do good." Solzhenitsyn realized that there was an element of show in this, but the very fact of their meeting him spoke volumes about the change. The deputy chief military prosecutor, Colonel D.T. Terekhov, had also received him in his office . . . Solzhenitsyn recognized in him a man of exceptional forcefulness, honesty, and talent, of the kind who might cleanse the land of injustice, and felt that there might really be on the way a new order that was ready to reform society.

All the greater was the shock of the neo-Stalinist reaction that toppled Khrushchev and struck out against the literary rebels. The biggest blow of all, which had a profoundly traumatic effect on him, was the KGB's capture of a cache of his manuscripts in a raid on the house of one of his friends. Among the manuscripts was *Victory Celebrations*, whose sympathetic depiction of Vlasovites and questionings of the October Revolution the bureaucracy made use of to brand Solzhenitsyn with subversion. In vain did he repudiate the play as the product of a transient fit of prison-camp bitterness. Every day he expected to be seized and imprisoned again in camp, and in any event it seemed as if his literary career were over.

"The catastrophe of September 1965," he says, "was the greatest misfortune in all my forty-seven years"[23]—greater than his arrest, greater than his transportation to the prison camp, greater than his cancer. The will power and determination that had always sustained him even in his worst days in the past collapsed so that he could scarcely "put one foot in front of the other." "I was convinced throughout my life," he says elsewhere, "that never in any circumstance would I contemplate suicide,"[24] but at this time he did think of suicide.

For the sense of his destiny that he had gained from his religious belief and his return to ordinary life as if from death, surviving both prison camp and cancer, now seemed in question. "I had long ago come to understand the meaning of my arrest, my deathly illness, and many personal misfortunes, but this disaster I could make no sense of. It rendered meaningless everything that had gone before."[25]

Solzhenitsyn was able to pull himself out of his depression and conduct a heroic battle with the Soviet bureaucracy that stirred people's imaginations everywhere, but it was at the price of a return to his prison-camp psychology. "His state of mind," says Natalia Reshetovskaya of this period, "came close to that which he had once experienced in the canps and which he ought to have got over but which returned in the end in much the same form as before" (Scammell, p. 835). "[T]he KGB raid that had reminded Solzhenitsyn so forcefully of his convict past," says Scammell (p. 657), "hastened" in him a "complete reorientation . . . in his mood and his thinking." The ideas about the destructiveness and the iniquity of communism adumbrated in *Prisoners* became the guiding ideas of his life. He, who had avowed that the purpose of his life was to write a novel about the October Revolution that would serve Leninism, now set out to work on the project he had harbored in his mind for thirty years with the idea of sweeping away misconceptions about Leninism and exposing it in all its evil.[26]

The depth of Solzhenitsyn's trauma that resulted in his political reorientation is indicated by its effects on his personal relationships.

He had found in Natalia Svetlova, who later became his second wife, a woman not only younger and more attractive than Natalia Reshetovskaya but one who was a strong co-worker in his struggle against the bureaucracy, as Reshetovskaya, despite her loyalty, faithfulness, and many sacrifices for him through the years, could not be. He had sought to keep his affair with Svetlova secret from Reshetovskaya and to continue his marriage with her, but now the rift between husband and wife became irrevocable. "It was the KGB raid that had reminded Solzhenitsyn so forcefully of his convict past and that hastened a reversion to his old way of thinking—to a period and frame of mind that was outside his relationship with Natalia [Reshetovskaya]. . . . [N]ow he was diving down to the depths again, depths to which she could not follow" (Scammell, p. 657).

The consequence was that Solzhenitsyn came to believe, when Reshetovskaya sought to meet with him after their estrangement, that she, to whom he had said he owed his life and, even more important than his life, the preservation of his youthful notebooks and manuscripts, was acting as an agent of the KGB. Scammell, after reviewing the evidence, finds this belief to be preposterous. "[T]he very fact that Solzhenitsyn treated her as an emissary [of the KGB] and was convinced (or convinced himself) that they were being photographed and taped on the open platform testified to a highly coloured vision of reality, if not symptoms of genuine paranoia" (Scammell, p. 825).

Similarly, Solzhenitsyn's relations with his old labor camp comrades, Panin and Kopelev, deteriorated. In camp they had been so trustful of each other that they had engaged in bitter political arguments even though each of them knew that the reporting to the camp authorities of Panin's anti-Soviet sentiments or of Solzhenitsyn's anti-Soviet doubts would mean in each case ten years added to the sentence of the one betrayed—and that the discovery of the failure to report these sentiments and doubts would also mean ten years more for the loyal confidant. But things were different now even though Solzhenitsyn had come over to Panin's political position (to be sure, Panin had been converted from Russian Orthodoxy to Roman Catholicism) and though Kopelev, who had first abandoned Stalinism and then, after the Soviet suppression of the Czech dissident regime, had given up Marxism altogether, had moved toward Solzhenitsyn's previous position.

With Panin Solzhenitsyn, charging him with "exploiting" Solzhenitsyn's "name in the West,"[27] completely broke relations. Richard Hallett in his study of the two versions of *The First Circle* finds that "practically all the revisions" in the second version, which was published after the quarrel, "cast shadows over Panin's personality."[28]

As for Kopelev, although he is reticent in his memoir about the cooling of his friendship with Solzhenitsyn, he does hint at it unmistakably: "In those [prison] years and for a long time afterward, I trusted him implicitly. I trusted him despite fleeting doubts, despite angry squabbles, despite the warnings of evil-tongued acquaintances."[29] The "for a long time afterward" indicates clearly that he no longer trusts him.

The reason for the alienation of Solzhenitsyn from those closest to him and the connection between his dealings with people and his politics is given by Lakshin:

> Solzhenitsyn's attitude toward other people as mere means to gaining his ends . . . has become second nature to him. He only believes and trusts those who follow him unquestioningly. The truth has been revealed to him; he is leading us toward the light and no one is supposed to ask questions. . . . That is why, I think, with all his tremendous gifts of artistic insight, he is doomed to be perpetually disappointed in other people, to live in a world of illusions and phantoms and to be hopelessly prone to error in his judgment of broader political perspectives, because his criteria derive only from himself and his immediate circumstances.[30]

Kopelev suggests that ambition, egocentrism, devious secretiveness and manipulativeness were present in Solzhenitsyn even in his labor camp days, telling us of how he learned that Solzhenitsyn had informed a camp official that he wanted to report to him on his work rather than to Kopelev, his sharashka superior. "The desire for independence is naturally inseparable from the youthful ambition I had noted long ago. But why hadn't he spoken of it openly to me and had instead, in violation of the unwritten laws of friendship—and even more so of prison brotherhood—gone to the authorities?"[31]

But these traits of Solzhenitsyn hardened under pressure. As Scammell says, "the crisis seems to have accentuated certain elements in Solzhenitsyn's character." His "inner self-confidence and driving ambition" were transformed into "intolerance and ruthlessness. At the same time his faith in his own instincts and intuition was intensified to the point where he no longer wished to listen to the voices of others" (Scammell, p. 538).

The repudiation of a friend that best exhibits the personal and political changes in Solzhenitsyn is that of Zhores Medvedev. The friendship had been initiated by Solzhenitsyn when he sent Medvedev a warm letter of praise for the "love of the truth and of science in our country" manifested in his samizdat book on Lysenko, Stalin's biologist protegé (Scammell, p. 513). In the course of their friendship Medvedev had performed many services for Solzhenitsyn. He had been deprived of an exchange visit to the United States as a result of supporting Natalia Reshetovskaya's application for a scientific position. He had sought to obtain medication from the United States for a painful physical condition from which Solzhenitsyn was suffering. He had surreptitiously arranged for an interview with Solzhenitsyn by reporters of *The New York Times* and *Washington Post*. He had written samizdat articles defending Solzhenitsyn against the Kremlin-inspired attacks on his work and had published a book in the West on the subject, *Ten Years after Ivan Denisovich*, with Solzhenitsyn's knowledge and approval.

When Medvedev was confined to a Soviet psychiatric institution, Solzhenitsyn issued a statement in his behalf in which he spoke of him as "a man of subtle, precise, and brilliant intellect and of warm heart (I know personally of his disinterested help to ordinary citizens in sickness or near death). . . . It is precisely his sensitivity to injustice, to stupidity, that is presented as a sick deviation: 'poor adaptation to the social environment!' "[32] In a footnote added in 1979, however, Solzhenitsyn expressed regret at having spoken up in defense of a Marxist even though he was a dissident being tortured by the regime:

> In our besieged circumstances it was difficult to avoid some missteps. At one point I, too, allowed my name to be exploited by a person alien to my world view. This was the other Medvedev brother, Zhores[33] . . . In the course of his years in the West, Zhores Medvedev has exhibited his true worth clearly enough in the diverse support he has given to Soviet policy. He has even made excuses for the compul-

sory psychiatric treatment to which he himself had been subjected.[34]

Medvedev in the West had exposed a grave atomic accident in the Soviet Union that the bureaucracy had sought to conceal. Nevertheless for Solzhenitsyn the fact that he was a Marxist now meant that he must be giving support to the bureaucracy. No longer did he regard him as inspired by the love of truth and justice. In Medvedev's account of his mistreatment in Soviet psychiatric institutions, he strangely found that Medvedev was excusing this mistreatment. Trying as best one can to find the basis for this bizarre statement, one can only surmise that what Solzhenitsyn is referring to is Medvedev's statement at the conclusion: "My purpose in writing the present work was certainly not to prove that there is *absolutely* nothing wrong with me. My aim is not so egocentric. It is rather to call attention to the dangerous tendency of using psychiatry for political purposes."[35] Solzhenitsyn extols the virtue of humility, but when Medvedev modestly refused to claim that he was in perfect mental health, this was for Solzhenitsyn an unnecessary concession to the bureaucracy, indeed an excuse for its actions. This made him feel justified in regretting his support for a man who, in accordance not only with the demands of friendship but with the dissidents' practice of supporting each other despite their political differences, a continuation of the practice of radical parties in Czarist times, had been so zealous in his support of Solzhenitsyn himself.

This is the Solzhenitsyn who is the author of *August 1914* and the polemical works against communism. "Solzhenitsyn's is a personality," says Scammell (p. 18), "that is writ uncommonly large. It would be idle to deny that he is a man with substantial faults, as well as with towering virtues." It should be added, however, that the virtues he displayed in his heroic fight for the publication of *The First Circle* and *Cancer Ward* have been overshadowed by the faults that have come to dominate him. He, who has written eloquently on the need not to participate in the official lies, has himself shown a careless disregard for the truth. He, who has written witheringly about Stalinist dogmatism, has succumbed to a dogmatism of his own. He, who has denounced the Stalinist hate campaigns, is himself possessed of a blinding hatred. If, however, these qualities have had a corrosive effect on his work since his two great novels, *The First Circle* and *Cancer*

*Ward*, these novels, together with the lesser *One Day in the Life of Ivan Denisovich* that won him world-wide fame, will endure.

## NOTES

1. Michael Scammell, *Solzhenitsyn: A Biography* (New York: W.W. Norton, 1984), p. 17. Future references to this book are incorporated into the text.
2. Vladimir Lakshin, *Solzhenitsyn, Tvardovsky, and Novy Mir* (Cambridge, Mass.: MIT Press, 1980), pp. 46–47. So too Zhores Medvedev, who had been close to Solzhenitsyn, said in an interview in exile ("Russia and Brezhnev," *New Left Review*, No. 117 [Sept.–Oct. 1979], p. 25), "It is inconceivable that Solzhenitsyn had the views he now expresses in the late 50's, when he was an absolutely different person. He is rewriting his own history."
3. *The New York Times*, Dec. 4, 1974. Quoted by Gary Kern, "Solzhenitsyn's Self-Censorship: The Canonical Text of *Odin den' Ivana Denisovicha*," *Slavic and East European Journal*, 20 (1976), 432.
4. Aleksandr Solzhenitsyn, *The Oak and the Calf: Sketches of Literary Life in the Soviet Union* (New York: Harper & Row, 1980), p. 10.
5. Olga Carlisle, *Solzhenitsyn and the Secret Circle* (New York: Holt, Rinehart and Winston, 1978), p. 19.
6. Cf. *The Oak and the Calf*, p. 320n. and *Solzhenitsyn and the Secret Circle*, pp. 201, 202.
7. *Times Literary Supplement* (London), Oct. 4, 1974. Thus Solzhenitsyn is scornful of Sholokhov for allegedly doing what he says he himself did. It is characteristic of him selfrighteously to condemn others for what he himself has done or states that he has done. He refused to sign a statement of protest against the sending of Soviet troops into Czechoslovakia but was contemptuous of Tvardovsky for having kept quiet about it (Scammell, p. 638); he welcomed the prospect of some day escaping to the West or being deported there (Scammell, p. 671) but bitterly attacked dissidents who left the Soviet Union on their own accord (Scammell, p. 845); he said of the Soviet government's abandonment of its soldiers captured by the

Germans by refusing to recognize the Hague Convention on war prisoners, "If a wife has become a whore, are we really still bound to her in fidelity? A Motherland that betrays its soldiers— is that really a Motherland?" (*The Gulag Archipelago* [New York: Harper & Row, 1974], I, 220), but he sharply criticized the critic Sinyavsky for having used the expression "Russia, you bitch," calling it "a blasphemous and impermissible slur on 'Mother Russia' " (Scammell, p. 897); he made much of the need for humility but, in the words of Scammell, was in the very same book "so bitter and shrill" in his "contempt for others' opinions" that his tone was "ridiculously at odds" with the humility that he preached (Scammell, p. 898).

8. Vladislav Krasnov, *Solzhenitsyn and Dostoevsky* (Univ. of Georgia Press, 1980), p. 214, n. 2.

9. However, three Marxist critics—Georg Lukacs, *Solzhenitsyn* (Cambridge, Mass.: MIT Press, 1969); Alan Swingewood, *The Novel and Revolution* (New York: Barnes & Noble, 1975), pp. 201–61; Daniel Singer, *The Road to Gdansk* (New York: Monthly Review Press, 1981), pp. 19–61—perceived *The First Circle* and *Cancer Ward* to be written from the point of view of a socialist opponent of Stalinism. Another Marxist critic, Francis Barker, including *August 1914* in his analysis, traced in Solzhenitsyn's writing (*Solzhenitsyn: Politics and Form* [New York: Barnes & Noble, 1977], p. 1) "the degeneration of a radical opposition into an authoritarian moralizing." Each of these critics contributed to the understanding of Solzhenitsyn, but each failed to see the Tolstoyan element in Solzhenitsyn's early thinking.

10. Lakshin, p. 68.

11. Scammell, p. 926 and Lakshin, p. 68.

12. My chapter on Solzhenitsyn's novels as a reflection of his political evolution is almost entirely the same as when it was published in *Clio*, 12 (1983), 211–32 before the appearance of Scammell's book. What I found in Scammell has corroborated most of what I had to say.

13. Scammell, p. 245.

14. Scammell, p. 302. Solzhenitsyn wrote "god" with a small *g* until his return to his childhood Christianity.

15. Lev Kopelev, *Ease My Sorrows* (New York: Random House, 1983), p. 13.

16. Kopelev, p. 15.

17. *Victory Celebrations: A Comedy in Four Acts* (London: The Bodley Head, 1983), p. 27. The title is given as *The Feast of the Victors* in *The Oak and the Calf* and as *The Feast of the Conquerors* in Scammell.

18. *Victory Celebrations*, p. 29.

19. Referred to in *The Oak and the Calf* as *Decembrists without December*, its original title. Scammell translates the revised title as *The Captives*.

20. Solzhenitsyn in prison hospital was deeply impressed by a Jewish doctor who, converted to Christianity, spoke with a convert's zeal and argued that "there was no punishment in this life that had not been preceded by a crime" (Scammell, p. 302). In commenting on Tvardovsky's cancer, which he attributed to his bitterness and depression at being deprived of *Novy Mir*, in contrast to Solzhenitsyn's own frame of mind ("I was . . . no weaker without the magazine, . . . only more independent and stronger"), he said: "Cancer is the fate of all who give themselves up to bilious, corrosive resentment and depression" (*The Oak and the Calf*, pp. 284, 285). In *Cancer Ward*, as we shall see, each of the patients except for the exemplary Kostoglotov and Dyomka has a form of cancer appropriate to his misguided view of life, and the remaining cancer cells in the bureaucrat Rusanov, unknown to him on his discharge from the hospital, will sooner or later cause his death, just as the political system he represents is doomed.

21. *Cancer Ward*, tr. Nicholas Bethell and David Burg (New York: Bantam, 1969), p. 440.

22. In 1944 he wrote to Natalia Reshetovskaya from the army rejecting her urging that they have children because fatherhood would interfere with his authorial ambition: "Practically anyone is capable of producing a child and bringing it up. But to write a history of the post-October years as a work of art is something perhaps I alone can do . . . You and almost everyone else think of the future in terms of your personal life and happiness. But the only terms in which I can think are: What can I do for

Leninism? How can I arrange my life for that?" (Scammell, p. 130).

23. *The Oak and the Calf*, pp. 103–04.

24. *The Gulag Archipelago*, tr. Thomas P. Whitney (New York: Harper & Row, 1975), II, 601.

25. *The Oak and the Calf*, pp. 111–12.

26. Solzhenitsyn states in *The Oak and the Calf* (p. 327) that "the appearance of *August 1914*," because in it he was no longer "concealing his features" and was now displaying his opposition to the Revolution, resulted in "the steady loss of supporters." He forgets that he had thirteen pages earlier stated it was fairly much politically innocuous (p. 314): "With the Lenin chapter removed, there was hardly anything in the novel that could have prevented our leaders from publishing it in its homeland." Neither of these two contradictory statements is accurate: *August 1914* is not politically innocuous—not, of course, that this justifies the bureaucracy's ban on its publication—and Solzhenitsyn was not concealing anti-Leninist sentiments when he wrote *The First Circle* and *Cancer Ward*.

27. Panin had discussed his plan to publish his reminiscences with Solzhenitsyn and had allowed Solzhenitsyn to dictate "the limits within which he would describe their friendship in the *sharashka* and Ekibastuz, and had promised not to deal with events after the date of their release" (Scammell, p. 895). Panin kept to the agreement but Solzhenitsyn, not content with setting limits on the content of Panin's book, objected to the title *The Notebooks of Sologdin* under which it had been published although Panin was the acknowledged model for Sologdin in *The First Circle*.

28. Richard Hallett, "Beneath a Closed Visor: Dimitry Panin and the Two Faces of Sologdin in Solzhenitsyn's *The First Circle*," *Modern Language Review*, 78 (1983), 374.

29. Kopelev, p. 62.

30. Lakshin, p. 58.

31. Kopelev, p. 60.

32. *The Oak and the Calf*, p. 494.

33. Scammell suggests (p. 896) that one reason for Solzhenitsyn's attack upon Zhores Medvedev was the critical articles on *Letter to the Leaders* and on Volume II of *The Gulag Archipelago* by

his twin brother, Roy Medvedev, the dissident Marxist historian, who remained in the Soviet Union while Zhores was exiled.

34. *The Oak and the Calf*, p. 369n.
35. Zhores Medvedev, *A Question of Madness* (New York: Knopf, 1971), p. 202.

# 2. Solzhenitsyn's Political Evolution Reflected in his Novels

How can we infer the political implications of a work of literature, which after all is not the same as a manifesto? Solzhenitsyn's novels are "polyphonic," that is, they have a multiplicity of characters, with things being seen from the point of view of each character as he or she becomes the center of attention. Who is to say which character, if any, speaks for the author and to what extent? Solzhenitsyn himself, as we have seen, has said that Shulubin's exposition of ethical socialism, contrary to the opinion of some early critics, is not an expression of his own belief.

Here it is useful to remember D.H. Lawrence's dictum, "Trust the tale, not the teller." We must endeavor to trace the subtle and complex design of a work of art to see what it has to tell us. The significance of Shulubin's statements is to be perceived by an examination of his character, the circumstances in which he makes the statements, the character and response of the person to whom he is speaking, the light they cast on the events in the novel. A novelist's comments about his novel may help to illuminate it but they can also be consciously or unconsciously misleading. He is a witness to the meaning of his work, but his testimony must be scrutinized in the light of other evidence and above all in the light of the work itself.

Thus in the light of Solzhenitsyn's subsequent novels and of what *The Gulag Archipelago* has to say about religion and the doctrine of salvation through suffering,[1] it is clear that Alyoshka the Baptist in *One Day in the Life of Ivan Denisovich* is not merely one of a gallery of characters present only to illustrate how all-inclusive the prison camp is. His final words to Ivan Denisovich near the end of the novel are a commentary on all that has gone before. "Things that people set store by are base in the sight of the Lord. You must pray for the things of the spirit so the Lord will take evil things from our hearts," he tells him, adding, "Rejoice that you are in prison. Here you can think of your soul."[2]

20

Ivan Denisovich Shukhov, a resourceful and resilient peasant experienced in the unremitting camp struggle for existence, if of limited vision, has learned to live one day at a time. Each day he is intent on getting as much food as he can, savoring the soggy black bread and thin gruel ("this was what the prisoner lived for, this little moment" [p. 175]), performing small services to get some tobacco, searching about to acquire the means to fix his boots or mend his clothes. Although he ranks high on the camp's moral scale (he refused packages of food from his wife in order not to deprive her and the children of food, is contemptuous of the camp beggars and squealers, and has self-respect and pride in his work), he has been reduced to this level of existence.

But, it is suggested, camp life is only an extreme, heightened form of life in the Soviet Union, to which Alyoshka's words also apply. Ivan has lost interest in the semi-annual letters from his wife, which tell of new bosses in the collective farm and of who has had his private plot reduced or taken away because he hasn't completed his work quota. At the same time he doesn't see any point in writing her about the gang in which he works or about the gang boss. He does not perceive the similarity between the role of the collective farm boss and that of the gang boss or between the loss of privileges on the collective farm and the penalties in the labor camp. Nor does he perceive the similarity between the fact that "the real work" in the collective farm "was done by the same women who'd been there since the start, in 1930" and the fact that the construction work in the labor camp is done by the veteran camp prisoners, who have survived and know their way around.

His wife tells him of how young people do their best to get away from the collective farm. Half of those who were in the army have not come back and the other half live there but earn their livelihood by such entrepreneurial activities as painting carpets with stencils and selling them. "They didn't have any regular jobs and they helped in the kolkhoz for only a month in the year getting the hay in and harvesting" (p. 48). Again, we, if not Shukhov, perceive the similarity between them and the "free" workers in the construction projects, generally former prisoners who after completing their sentences were not allowed to return to their previous places of residence.

In the "gangs 'outside,' where every fellow got paid separately" (p. 69), the whip of poverty forces each one, working at piece rates, to turn out as much as he can. In the prison gangs, where there is collective punishment and reward, each prisoner keeps the others on their toes so he will not go hungry. And both outside and inside the camps corruption and bribery are rampant.

"The people who ran the camps" make plenty through the deals they are able to engineer and receive bonuses on top of that, but all the prisoners get is six ounces of bread a day. So Fetyukov, now the camp beggar who is always trying to scrounge things from others, "used to ride around in a car" when he was "a big shot in an office" before he was imprisoned (pp. 71, 70). Of the authoritarian industrial and political structure of the Soviet Union the same comment can be made by the shepherded population as is made by Shukhov concerning the way things are done at camp, "The fellows at the top thought about everything for him, and it was kind of easier like that" (p. 49).

Thinking only of getting by from day to day, Shukhov has no time to think of the meaning of his life. When he goes to sleep after his conversation with Alyoshka, he thinks contentedly of what a good day it has been. "We'd had a lot of luck today. . . . Nothing had spoiled the day and it had been almost happy" (pp. 209–10). Among the good things that had happened was that "he'd finagled an extra bowl of mush at noon." Alyoshka might have said that he had given up his birthright as a human being for a mess of pottage.

Alyoshka's statements about the supreme importance of finding one's soul, about prison's affording the possibility of achieving this through suffering and contemplation, and about the pursuit of happiness being a chase after an illusion are echoed by Gleb Nerzhin's statements in *The First Circle* that "people waste themselves in senseless thrashing around for the sake of a handful of goods and die without realizing their spiritual wealth," that "the happiness of success and of total satiety . . . is . . . spiritual death," and that "for those who understand human happiness is suffering."[3] So too are they echoed by the statements of Shulubin in *Cancer Ward* that "happiness is a mirage," that "a beast gnawing at its prey can be happy too, but only human beings can feel affection for each other, and this is the highest achievement they can aspire to," and that "if we care only about 'happiness' and about reproducing our species, we shall merely crowd the earth senselessly and create a terrifying society."[4] Although, as Nerzhin states, there are many sources for these ideas, his reference to Tolstoy is significant: "When Lev Tolstoi dreamed of being imprisoned, he was reasoning like a truly perceptive person with a healthy spiritual life" (p. 40).

The ideas expressed by Alyoshka, Nerzhin, and Shulubin became part of a political philosophy in *The First Circle* and, most clearly, in *Cancer Ward*. Nerzhin, although he echoes Alyoshka, is not a Christian of simple faith. A character based on Solzhenitsyn himself (like Solzhenitsyn, he was born in 1918, was a student of mathematics, was drafted into the army in World War II and became a captain of artillery, was arrested for his critical turn of mind, and was placed in a special camp for scientists because of his mathematical training), he is a seeker of truth. Like two other autobiographical seekers of truth, Oleg Kostoglotov in *Cancer Ward* and Sanya Lazhenitsyn in *August 1914*, he receives enlightenment from other characters of the novel.

One of the two characters from whom he learns most is the mystical painter Kondrashev-Ivanov, whose paintings suggest the strength of the human spirit and the need to reach toward that "image of perfection" (p. 297) which everyone bears within himself, the moral perfection which Tolstoy said we must strive for. The other is the peasant Spiridon who, when Nerzhin is wondering if one can really distinguish between right and wrong, replies in a tone of "harsh conviction" with the folk-saying, "The wolfhound is right and the cannibal is wrong" (p. 466). The "simplicity and force" of this statement of the existence of absolute good, typified by the hunter of wolves, and of absolute evil, typified by the eater of men, strike Nerzhin deeply. It reinforces his belief that evil must be opposed.

Nerzhin is charged by his Stalinist friend Rubin with "rotten skepticism" (p. 41), but he tells his young disciple Ruska Doronin that, while skepticism is needed to "choke fanatical voices," it "can never provide firm ground under a man's feet" (p. 78). When his wife asks him if he has become a believer in God, he answers that Pascal, Newton, and Einstein were believers. This is a reminiscence of his old teacher who, immune from punishment as a result of protection from high up in the government, would tell his students, "Newton believed in God, like every other great scientist" (p. 48). The suggestion is that Nerzhin is a religious believer, but there is nothing that indicates he is of Orthodox faith. Mixing Eastern religions and Tolstoy, he is rather, like the Baptist Alyoshka, a religious dissenter from the Orthodox Church.

Rubin calls Nerzhin an eclectic who draws at random from different philosophies, but Nerzhin replies that he has formulated his own philosophy from what he has learned in prison, only to find it confirmed by his reading. Significantly, Lenin is among the thinkers he admires. To Kondrashev-Ivanov he enthusiastically cites Lenin as an illustration of the indominitability of the human spirit, and elsewhere he tells of how he was repelled by Stalin's writing after having read Lenin: "After a style that was direct, ardent, precise, suddenly there was a sort of mush" (p. 41). The study of society which he is secretly writing is on "the post-Lenin period" (p. 68), the implication being that this is when things in the Soviet Union really started to go bad.

Indeed the Lenin period is shown to be one of revolutionary idealism. Rubin, the Stalinist imprisoned in his own dogma, whose heart is at war with his head, had as a boy been one of Stalin's early prisoners, having been caught covering up for his worshipped cousin, a revolutionary opponent of Stalin's. In prison he heard prisoners being beaten while they screamed "Down with the Stalinist executioners!" Three hundred of their comrades listening in their solitary cells roared "Long live Leninism!" and then burst into "The Internationale," as "the jailers huddled together on the stairs, terrified by the deathless hymn of the proletariat" (p. 477). With the crushing of the revolutionary opposition Rubin had come to terms with Stalinism, even forcing himself to love Stalin, thinking that this was the way to serve the Revolution. In coming to terms with Stalinism, he came to terms with evil, participating, as he now remembers with burning shame and guilt, in the forcible collectivization of the peasants, with all of the atrocities attendant upon it.

Adamson, an old lone survivor of the early revolutionary opposition, has accommodated himself to prison, as Rubin accommodated himself to Stalinism. He "had trained himself to be totally indifferent to everything around him" so that he "now loved not those books which burned with truth but those which amused him and helped shorten his endless prison terms" (p. 358). But he had been of a generation of heroic idealists. Instead of "holding onto comfort and prosperity," they had "not accepted the perverting and disgracing of the Revolution but were ready to sacrifice themselves for its purification" (p. 357). In exile they met together when the temperature was 58 degrees below zero to discuss the political situation and "took an oath that no one present would ever sign a renunciation or capitulation."

To be sure, the portrait of Adamson and his comrades is not devoid of irony. Adamson is contemptuous of the subsequent generations of prisoners and does not deign to talk politics with them. They are "not to be compared with those giants" of the past "like himself" (p. 357). His arrogance recalls the cocksureness of his comrades, each of whom thought he knew all the answers with the result that they could not agree on a resolution at their conference. But, if they lacked the humility of the truth-seeker Nerzhin, they were animated by a noble ideal, and many of them were shot for standing firm against an evil system, as Nerzhin is sent to a labor camp for refusing to collaborate with evil.

Those who do cooperate with the system suffer a worse fate than these men: they degenerate in character. This is what happened, among others, to Makarygin, the prosecutor for political crimes. Makarygin had fought in the Civil War, and his wife, a machine-gunner attired in a leather coat who lived for the Communist party, had gone through it with him. Fortunately, she had died, for his present wife knew how to help him ingratiate himself with the higher-ups and to maneuver for social position as his first wife could not have done. After thirty years as a prosecutor, Makarygin receives the Order of Lenin and to celebrate gives a dinner party at which the guests discuss the difficulty of getting servants as a consequence of farm people having been "educated so rapidly that no one wanted to help cook, wash dishes or clothes" (p. 403).

Although the relationship is wearing thin, Makarygin has an old Civil War comrade, Radovich, a Serb who is a secret Tito sympathizer and who has been preserved from purges during the years as a result of his having been forgotten while he was confined to hospitals for chronic illnesses and of his having subsequently maintained a discreet silence. Radovich reproaches Makarygin for his eight thousand ruble salary while a cleaning woman gets 250, telling him, "What we need is to purge ourselves of this bourgeois rot. ... Look at what you've become!" He urges a return to "Leninist purity," and Makarygin exclaims, "You are a dried-up fanatic! A mummy! A prehistoric Communist!" (p. 428).

Obviously, Radovich's reproach is to be seen as justified, and Makarygin's Order of Lenin blazing amid the brilliance of the fine crystal on the dinner table is invested with ironic significance. Radovich's comment about Makarygin's attempted defense of inequality, "Anyone who hasn't suffered in twenty years shouldn't be allowed to dabble in philosophy," which recalls Nerzhin's statements about suffering as a way to knowledge, is another telling point against Makarygin's rationalizations. Yet Makarygin's retort has merit. The "parchment-faced" Radovich (p. 424) is indeed like a mummy. He is described as "a Marxist, flesh of their flesh, blood of their blood," who "held orthodox views about everything" (p. 420). As if nothing has changed in forty years, he affirms his agreement with the Comintern predictions of the early 1920s that "we will soon witness an armed conflict between America and England for world markets" (p. 429).

While political positions of the past stated as immutable dogma are evidently no guide for contemporary Soviet society, the spirit of Leninism is another matter. When the new rebels of the younger generation search for a criterion, it is to the basic principles of the Revolution that they turn. Clara, the daughter of Makarygin, whose first wife died in giving birth to her, is a continuation of her mother. As she observes the society about her, she gathers up in herself a store of critical questions that make her ready to be instructed by young Ruska, Nerzhin's disciple: "What was the Revolution against? Against *privileges*. What were the Russian people sick of? Privileges." And now "privileges . . . surround people like the plague" (pp. 268–69).

Agniya, the one person in the novel shown as a supporter of the Church, had paradoxically become a church member because she was trained to sympathize with the underdog by her mother and aunt, who hid fugitive Social Revolutionaries and Social Democrats before the Revolution. When the Church is persecuted under Stalin, she turns to it with the same feeling she had had as a child for a flogged horse and gives up her fiancé, who has an eye for the main chance and goes on to become the chief of operations at the Mavrino special camp for scientists.

Innokenty Volodin, the diplomat who ends up in a labor camp because his humaneness causes him to risk his career, is influenced to break with hedonistic selfishness not by his experience in the capitalist society of Paris and Rome, but by reading his mother's idealistic letters and diaries. A humanistic intellectual, she had married a Bolshevik hero of the Civil War. The marriage had not been a great success, the man of action and the woman of sensibility lacking rapport in many ways and yet there was an affinity between her idealism and his. The heritage of Bolshevism and more broadly the heritage of the entire radical milieu of Czarist Russia are thus a source of inspiration for the rebels against Stalinism.

Stalin himself is shown not as the continuator of Leninism but as its betrayer. The defeated old order through him takes its revenge against the Revolution, Czarist practices and Orthodox observances which the Bolsheviks had done away with returning under his regime. After having persecuted it, he has made the Church his creature, as the czars of old had done, and finds it gratifying to be acclaimed as "the Leader Elected of God." He makes use of chauvinistic patriotism, resurrecting the forgotten word "homeland," and when he speaks to the nation at war he addresses his listeners as "brethren," the old Russian form of address with religious overtones. "Neither Lenin nor any other leader would have thought of saying it" (p. 132).

> In general Stalin noticed in himself a predisposition not only toward Orthodoxy but toward other elements and words associated with the old world—that world from which he had come and which, as a matter of duty, he had been destroying for forty years ... Officers had to have "orderlies." High school girls were to study separately from boys. ... The Soviet people would have a day of rest, like all Christians, on Sunday and not on impersonal numbered days. Only legal marriage should be recognized, as had been the case under the czar. ... It was right here in his night office that for the first time he had tried on in front of the mirror the old Russian shoulder boards [worn by Czarist army officers and revived by Stalin]—and felt real satisfaction. In the final analysis, there was nothing shameful even in a crown, the highest sign of distinction.

We remember how Stalin's revolutionary opponents who had cried out "Long live Leninism!" had also cried out "We've another czar on our backs!"

But, if there is thus a reaction under Stalin against Leninism, there is also in at least one respect a continuity between the two regimes. Through the passage between the notorious Lubyanka prison and the building in which interrogations were carried on "for a third of a century all prisoners of the central prison had been led: Cadets, Social Revolutionaries, anarchists, Octobrists, Mensheviks, Bolsheviks ... " (p. 187). The parties of the political prisoners have changed, but the state investigative agency, although its name has changed many times, has remained. To be sure, in Spiridon's description of his adventures in the Civil War it is indicated that the Red Terror was a response to a White Terror, first the Whites shooting peasants they suspected of sympathizing with the other side and then the Reds doing so. Nevertheless, there is the suggestion that terror, once begun, cannot easily be discontinued.

If, therefore, Solzhenitsyn presents the Bolsheviks as praiseworthy for their dedication to fighting against the evils of injustice and inequality, their strength of character, and their sacrificing personal happiness for an ideal—qualities which Nerzhin regards as making life meaningful—he also suggests that their mistakenly thinking that they have all the answers and their readiness to use violence stand in the way of the construction of the good society. These ideas are brought more sharply into focus in *Cancer Ward* by the use of Shulubin as raisonneur.

Shulubin is the enlightener of Kostoglotov, as Kondrashev-Ivanov and Spiridon are of Nerzhin. Like Spiridon, who among other things participated in the campaign of forcible collectivization of peasants even though his moral revulsion against it caused him to take to drink, Shulubin has not led an exemplary life. Although he realized that the charges were false, he joined in the Stalinist witch-hunts to protect his wife, his children, and himself. But his wife died, and his children grew up to be unconcerned about him—and he was left with his guilt and shame. However, the suffering he has undergone has, as Nerzhin and Radovich said suffering could do, enabled him to learn, to understand better how to lead the good life and to build the good society. "Haven't I earned the right to a few thoughts through my suffering . . . ?" he asks (p. 444).

He reaffirms one of his ideas on the very verge of death immediately after his operation. Clutching Kostoglotov's hand, he assures him that he remains convinced of what he has said earlier about the immortality of man's soul. Just as the near-blind Spiridon speaks as if with the insight of Sophocles' blind Tiresias, so Shulubin seems to be invested with the knowledge, exemplified by the prophecy of Shakespeare's John of Gaunt, that folk-belief has assigned to dying men.

Shulubin combines religion with socialism. Like Nerzhin, he finds confirmation of his thoughts in writers of different philosophies, referring to Dostoyevsky, Tolstoy, Kropotkin, the religious thinker

Soloviev, and the populist Mikhaylovski as among the sources of his concept of "ethical socialism." He expounds his doctrine while grasping Kostoglotov by the shoulder, rejecting capitalism with the same kind of emphasis with which Spiridon rejected the idea of moral relativism. "Don't ever blame socialism," he tells him, "for the sufferings and the cruel years you've lived through. . . . If private enterprise isn't held in an iron grip it gives birth to people who are no better than beasts, those stock-exchange people with greedy appetites completely beyond restraint" (p. 440). Ethical living is impossible under capitalism. Thus, when Tolstoy "decided to spread practical Christianity through society," "his ideals turned out to be impossible for his contemporaries to live with," as in Czarist Russia, "his preaching had no link with reality."

On the other hand, Shulubin, who had been a Bolshevik in 1917, remembers how he and his comrades had been ready to give their lives for the world revolution and wonders how there had been such a decline from this high ideal. Although he expresses bewilderment at the Stalinist reaction to Leninist idealism, what he has to say a moment later suggests an answer: Tolstoy's asceticism and gospel of love have to be inculcated with the change in the social system.

> You can't build socialism on an abundance of material goods, because people sometimes behave like buffaloes, they stampede and trample the goods into the ground. Nor can you have socialism that's always drumming on about hatred, because social life cannot be built on hatred. . . . One should never direct people toward happiness. . . . One should direct them toward mutual affection.

Bolshevik egalitarianism enters into the melange of Shulubin's "ethical socialism." Shulubin had intervened in an argument between Kostoglotov and the bureaucrat Rusanov about the lack of equality in Soviet society to say that one of the points in Lenin's famous April theses, the program for the Revolution, was that no official should receive more than the average wage of a competent worker. Everyone in the ward, including a learned professor, was astonished by this piece of information, the orthodox histories having suppressed it in their distortion of Leninism. Now, in his exposition of his doctrine, Shulubin mixes Tolstoy's asceticism with Lenin's egalitarianism: "When we have enough loaves of white bread to crush them under our heels, when we have enough milk to choke us, we still won't be in the least happy. But if we share things we don't have enough of, we can be happy today!" (p. 433).

Rusanov finds Tolstoy's doctrine of the need to seek moral perfection to be "religious rubbish," but Kostoglotov tells him (p. 136) that "Lenin only attacked Leo Tolstoy for seeking moral perfection when it led society away from the struggle with arbitrary rule and from the approaching revolution."[5] Indeed early in the novel it is indicated that the Marxism of Lenin is closer in some respects to Tolstoyism than Rusanov realizes. Yefrem Podduyev, a man who has never thought about life until now he faces death, is struck by Tolstoy's short story "What Men Live By," which comes to him as a revelation. He goes about asking the various patients what do men live by. Rusanov, busily eating chicken, doesn't have to think about the answer. "He barely looked up from the chicken. 'There's no difficulty about that,' he said. 'Remember: people live by their ideological principles and by the interest of their society.' And he bit off the sweetest piece of gristle in the joint" (p. 103).

Yefrem, who despises Rusanov, is "furious that the bald man had almost guessed the answer. It is said in the book that people live not by worrying only about their own problems but by the love of others. And the pipsqueak had said it was by 'the interests of society.' Somehow they both tied up." The implication is that Marxism is linked with Tolstoyism by its altruism but that this has little meaning for Rusanov. Marxism is for him a series of memorized formulas which he repeats while finding the "sweetest piece" of everything for himself.

So, when he echoes Lenin's criticism of Tolstoy's doctrine of non-resistance to evil, he is totally unaware that it is he, who has sent so many to labor camps, who represents the evil which must be fought against. Significantly, the sixteen-year-old Dyomka, who, with his earnest "passion for social problems" (p. 22), represents the hope of the future, concludes the discussion by saying that he agrees on the need for fighting against evil.[6]

Rusanov recalls vaguely the regime's canned quotations from the writings of its designated heroes, but he is profoundly ignorant of genuine Marxism. Looking with pride upon his daughter Aviette, he reflects: "Was it Gorky who had said, 'If your children are no better than you are, you have fathered them in vain, indeed you have lived in vain'? Pavel Nikolayevich [Rusanov] had not lived in vain" (p. 276).

He does not see the relation between this quotation and Tolstoy's statement of the need to strive for moral perfection. And he is proud of his daughter because she is inveighing against the "injustice" of the de-Stalinization campaign, which is causing bureaucrats who sent innocent men to labor camps to tremble!

Talking about the appliances of his luxurious bathroom, he thinks to himself: "These weren't mere trifles, they were part of one's daily life and being, and 'Being determines consciousness.' A man's life had to be good and pleasant to give him the right kind of consciousness. To quote the words of Gorky, 'A healthy mind in a healthy body' " (p. 373). Thus Marx's statement, "Being determines consciousness," a commentary on the history of philosophy and religion, is used to justify luxurious bathrooms. According to this reasoning, the luxurious bathrooms of wealthy capitalists must give them "the right kind of consciousness," and the classical precept, "A healthy mind in a healthy body"—ignorantly attributed to Gorky—becomes not a matter of exercising the mind and body but of pampering the body.

The grossness of Rusanov's concept of socialism, which is the diametric opposite of Shulubin's "ethical socialism," serves to suggest the validity of Shulubin's doctrine. This doctrine, moreover, is corroborated by the events of the novel. Kostoglotov on being discharged from the hospital is in a state of bliss, but before the day is over he comes to feel lost and depressed in the humming complexity of the town, which is strange and alien to him after his years in labor camp and exile: happiness is indeed an ephemeral will o' the wisp which it is a mistake to set up as a social goal. The crowd surging into the department store, by which Kostoglotov is carried along, is indeed, as Shulubin said, like a herd of buffalo in its frenzy to obtain the newly available goods.

Above all, Shulubin's forceful rejection of capitalism is validated by the depiction of Chaly, the energetic and cheerful black-market entrepreneur. Willfully convincing himself in his breezy optimism that he will be speedily cured by a simple operation, Chaly tells Rusanov: "Let the others croak if they want to. You and I'll have a good time!" (p. 317). His ordinarily amiable face assumes an expression of "ferocity" as he says this. The depressed Rusanov is attracted by the cheeriness of Chaly and his philosophy of "To hell with you! I'm going to get mine." Despite the superficial differences between them and despite Rusanov's habitual denunciations of illegal profiteering outside the system, the bureaucrat and the businessman are spiritually kin.

In *August 1914*, however, it is socialism, not capitalism, which is rejected, and with it Tolstoyism.[7] The truth-seeker in this novel, Isaaki (Sanya) Lazhenitsyn, is a Tolstoyan whose quest for truth takes him away from Tolstoy. Gleb Struve calls the name Isaaki Lazhenitsyn "a more than transparent pseudonym for the author's father, Isai Solzhenitsyn,"[8] who, like Sanya, was a university student volunteer in World War I. Patricia Blake adds that "Sanya is not a diminutive for Isaaki (or Isai), but for Alexander" and that consequently there is suggested "the interchangeable identities of father and son."[9] Indeed, Solzhenitsyn was an artillery officer in World War II, as his father was in World War I. Both fought in East Prussia, a region that Solzhenitsyn in his autobiographical sketch stated "has been strangely linked to my fate,"[10] it having aroused his interest when, as a first-year university student, he wrote a research paper on the "Samsonov Debacle," the precursor of *August 1914*. Solzhenitsyn's father died on the battlefield before Alexander was born, and son and father, merged in the character of Sanya Lazhenitsyn, are therefore to be regarded like Clara Makarygin and her mother, who died at Clara's birth, of whom Clara was a kind of spiritual reincarnation.

Sanya is an earnest young man in whose eyes "you could see that his mind was working all the time."[11] A secondary school admirer of Tolstoy, he actually goes to meet the grand old man just before he enters the university. He speaks to Tolstoy as a youthful worshipper and yet one who has doubts. Since so few seem to be animated by good will, he asks, is not Tolstoy exaggerating the power of love? "If so, ought we not envisage some intermediate stage, ask less of people to start with and then try to awaken them to universal benevolence?" (p. 17).

Tolstoy "had, of course, seen more than his share of visitors, schoolboys included. He knew the sort of thing they were likely to ask and had his answers ready" (p. 16). He replies: "Love is the only way! The only way. No one will ever find a better" (p. 17). It is a ritualistic formula, not an attempt to cope with Sanya's perplexities, uttered by a prophet who seems "saddened or offended by the doubt cast on the truth he had discovered." Sanya is not disappointed, only "grieved" that "he had upset one whom he worshipped." However, Tolstoy's obvious desire "to resume his walk around the rectangle and think his own thoughts"—he had already twice "walked around all four sides of the rectangle" formed by the avenue of trees surrounding the glade—suggests to the reader the closed confines of his thought (pp. 17, 15).[12]

At the university Sanya's hesitant doubts about Tolstoyism grow although he never quite gives it up. "He was confused by the multiplicity of truths, and exhausted by the struggle to find one more convincing than another" (p. 18). He reads in succession the populist Mikhailovsky, the father of Russian Marxism Plekhanov, and the anarchist Kropotkin—representatives of currents of thought which, we may remember, were sources of Shulubin's "ethical socialism"—and finds each in turn to be utterly convincing, only finally to question all of them. "Then he opened *Vekhi* and realized with a shock that here was something completely contrary to what he had read before. The truth of it pierced him to the quick!" (p. 18).

*Vekhi* [*Landmarks*] was a book published in 1909 consisting of essays by seven intellectuals, some of them ex-Marxists, each of which deplored the radicalism of the Russian intelligentsia, with its trust in science and the scientific method, its confidence in political prescriptions, and its talk of a revolution that would sweep away Russian social and intellectual backwardness. These are the ideas opposed by Varsonofiev, the character in *August 1914* who plays the role of the enlightener of the autobiographical truth-seeker. In the course of enlightening Sanya, Varsonofiev. although he does not discuss Tolstoyism directly, suggests that it is one element of a fashionable radicalism that is fundamentally mistaken.

Varsonofiev, a scholar at the great Rumyantsev Museum Library, is the antithesis of Tolstoy. He is equally impressive in his physical appearance, which, like Tolstoy's, proclaims him to be a philosopher, but he is much less remote from ordinary humanity than Tolstoy. Whereas Tolstoy walks looking at the ground, Varsonofiev walks with his head slightly forward, "as though he were straining to hear or see something" (p. 340). Whereas the sunlight shining on the visor of Tolstoy's cap seems "to surround his head with a bright halo" (p. 15), Varsonofiev is entirely at home in the beerhouse to which he has invited Sanya and his friend Kotya. Whereas Tolstoy gives a brief, oracular reply, Varsonofiev engages in a discursive conversation. Although, knowing the young men of his day, he assumes that Sanya and Kotya are either socialists or anarchists, he is neither condescending nor dismissive but treats them as equals even though he wonders to himself if they can take in everything he is saying.

To the populist idea of sacrificing one's self for "the people," Varsonofiev replies: "What if they [the people] are not ready for change themselves? In that case neither a full belly, nor education, nor institutional reform will help" (p. 344). It is the very question that Sanya had asked Tolstoy, which had so vexed the Sage. Moreover, Varsonofiev questions whether the populist (and the Tolstoyan) identification of "the people" with the peasantry is accurate: "How long will you go on saying that only the peasant counts? Yes, we all like to look scientific, but nobody has ever defined what, precisely, is meant by 'the people.' In any case, 'the people' don't just comprise the peasant mass" (p. 344).

When Varsonofiev says, "[N]othing is more precious to a man than the order in his own soul," Sanya immediately thinks: "But wasn't that just what Tolstoy said?" (p. 346). But Varsonofiev's concern for the soul is quite different from Tolstoy's. He says nothing of love and self-sacrifice. Instead, he upholds against the populists devoted to the problematic future generations of "the people" "any one . . . who practices one of the arts, or inquires into the ultimate meaning of life, or . . . turns to religion and the salvation of his own soul" (p. 344). For Tolstoy, on the other hand, art for its own sake, abstract speculation that does not eventuate in ethical living, and religion divorced from life are equally worthless.

When Varsonofiev says, "History is not governed by reason," Sanya asks: "What is history governed by then?" To himself he thinks, grasping for the Tolstoyan catchword "love": "By goodness? By love? If only Pavel Ivanovich [Varsonofiev] would say something like that, thoughts heard from different people in different places could all be tied together. It was nice when things fitted so neatly" (pp. 346–47). But Varsonofiev does not give simple Tolstoyan answers. "The most important questions," he says, "always get circular answers" (p. 348). The course of history is not to be fathomed by simplistic logic; it "has its own organic fabric which may be beyond our understanding."[13]

History, Varsonofiev continues, flows like a river, and any attempt to change its course will only stop its flow. "The bonds between generations, institutions, traditions, customs, are what keep the stream flowing uninterruptedly" (p. 347). Talk of ideal schemes for humanity is the arrogant impatience of "wiseacres." In what is to be seen as prophecy, he warns: "Don't get carried away by the idea that you can invent a model society and then twist your beloved people into the right shape to fit it" (p. 346).

Finally, with regard to the question of the rightness of Sanya's and Kotya's volunteering to fight, Varsonofiev justifies Sanya's feeling that he must do so even though it violates his Tolstoyan pacifist and anti-state principles: "When the bugle sounds, a man must be a man—if only for his own sake. That's another thing you can't put into words. I don't know why, but Russia's back mustn't be broken" (p. 348).

The correctness of Varsonofiev's observations is confirmed by all of *August 1914*. The hope for Russia, we see, lies not in its radical young intellectuals, who are presented as uniformly immature and irresponsible. It lies in such people as the capitalist farmer Zakhar Tomchak, the industrialist Arkhangorodsky, the engineer Obodovsky, and the junior officer Colonel Vorontyntsev. They represent the modernization which is going on without the carping intellectuals even being aware of it. It is a modernization that is growing organically within the old Russia, not one that is foisted upon it. "Give us ten years of peaceful development," says the dynamic Obodovsky, "and you won't recognize Russian industry—or the Russian countryside" (p. 807). But, of course, the devastation of the war, which gave the Bolsheviks their opportunity, will strike down the shoots of industry and agriculture.

Each of these men, speaking from the knowledge acquired through his experience, repeats in different ways what Varsonofiev has to say. Although Tomchak, Vorontyntsev, Obodovsky, and Arkhangorodsky view the war as an unmitigated disaster entered into by an incompetent government which, like the radical intelligentsia, is irresponsible and lacking in understanding of the new growing up in the midst of the old, Arkhangorodsky says that it is necessary nevertheless to come to the defense of one's country, and Vorontyntsev acts upon this premise. To serve one's country, says Arkhangorodsky, it is necessary to adapt oneself to "the laborious process of history." "The paths of history," he tells his radical daughter Sonya and her friend Naum, "are more complicated than you would like them to be" (p. 815).

Just as Varsonofiev finds all governments to be evil, although some are more evil than others, so Obodovsky states: "Clever, practical people don't exercise power, they create, they transform. Power is a dead toad" (p. 807). Just as Varsonofiev says that democracy is not the highest form of government, so Arkhangorodsky states in a prophetic anticipation of Kerensky's regime that a republic would merely mean "a hundred lawyers will get together and try to outtalk each other." "The people will never govern themselves whatever happens" (p. 815). So too, just as Varsonofiev discourages the idea of combatting special privilege with his talk of the importance of adhering to tradition and custom, so Obodovsky states, in opposition to the Tolstoyan asceticism and the Bolshevik egalitarianism of Shulubin, that creation is more important than distribution: "When enough has been created, nobody will be left without a share even if distribution is erratic" (p. 812).

When Sonya says that "the whole intelligentsia is for revolution!" her father replies, "We engineers who make and build everything of importance—don't we count as intellectuals?" (p. 814). So likewise Varsonofiev had said with good-natured sarcasm that of course members of the clergy and philosophers who are accounted reactionary are not to be regarded as members of the intelligentsia while students, including those unable to pass their exams without trots, are to be so regarded. Indeed Sonya and Naum, whether or not they have to use trots, come off as the "immature" young people Obodovsky inwardly regards them as being. Ill-mannered and only able to hurl revolutionary phrases, they are easily vanquished in the dinner-table political argument they have provoked. Arkhangorodsky has the last words that close the discussion (and the chapter), and they are once more prophetic: "On this side you have the Black Hundreds, and on this side the Red Hundreds, and in between a handful of practical people are trying to make their way through. They aren't allowed to! They will be crushed! They will be squashed flat!" (p. 816).

Tomchak's children are likewise spoiled pseudo-intellectuals. Roman, who is seeking to evade the draft through bribery, is cowardly and conceited. He tells his wife that she is "incapable of appreciating how short their barbarian country was of bright and enterprising minds like that of her husband" (p. 20). He decorates the house with a number of paintings of Tolstoy, snobbishly telling his father that "this was something all educated people went in for, and that Tolstoy was one of Russia's great men, and a count into the bargain" (p. 24). His fashionable radicalism also prompts him to display a photograph of Gorky.

His sister Ksenia is infatuated with the culture of Moscow—its ballet, theater, university, public lectures—which makes her ashamed of her native Ukraine. But, although she has the cultural interests of the mother of *The First Circle*'s Innokenty Volodin, these interests are quite superficial and she herself is shallow and devoid of idealism. Looking at herself in a mirror, she is pleased that "her expression had become more refined, *much* more refined, *and* more intellectual, *and* more thoughtful. An abnormally healthy look, though, not a hint of pallor (must work on being pale!)" (p. 30). She objects to the religious fasts at home as stupid tradition. "Fasting was no additional hardship to a poor man, but when you had as much money as the Tomchaks and could take your pick of the most delicious dishes in the world, why waste half your life fasting? It was barbarous."[14] It is these two "progressives" who take it on themselves to denounce their country as "barbaric."

Solzhenitsyn's scorn is even greater for the revolutionary-minded Sasha Lenartovich. Drafted into the army, Sasha hopes for the defeat of his own country, believing that this will bring the revolution. Arguing with a medical officer, he goes so far as to say, "Let the sufferings of the wounded be added to the sufferings of the workers and peasants. The scandalous lack of facilities for treating them is a good thing because it brings the end much nearer" (p. 122). But when the medical officer replies that Lenartovich may be brought to see him tomorrow with a smashed shoulder, Lenartovich hastily reverses his position: "Nobody's against humanitarianism. Heal as many as you like! Let's look upon it as a form of mutual aid" (p. 124). It is a different matter when it comes to getting his own wounds treated. So he reveals himself throughout as selfish and cowardly, using his principles to rationalize his running away from battle but being ready to violate these same principles if it serves his purpose.

But of course the portrait that is most etched in acid is that of Lenin in the twenty-second chapter, which Solzhenitsyn removed from *August 1914* and published in *Lenin in Zurich*. Like Roman Tomchak, he is bitterly scornful of his own country. Like Sasha Lenartovich, he is utterly indifferent to others' suffering. Only concerned with gaining power for himself, he has no sympathy for anyone else. This is not the Lenin admired by Nerzhin. But then the political implications of *August 1914* are at utter variance with those of *The First Circle* and *Cancer Ward*.

In *Lenin in Zurich*, which consists of chapters drawn from three volumes of Solzhenitsyn's work in progress on the Russian Revolution, he goes beyond *August 1914* to suggest that behind Lenin, plotting and using German money to bring about the Revolution, was the figure of the Jewish financier-revolutionist Alexander Parvus. Parvus was a Russian Jew, born Israel Lazarevich Helphand (Solzhenitsyn refers to him throughout as Israel Lazarevich, emphasizing his Jewishness), who left Russia at the age of nineteen, knocked about Europe, and finally settled in Germany. He became a prominent theoretician and journalist in the Social Democratic Party and acquired great wealth through an export-import business. For Solzhenitsyn he is the behind-the-scenes guiding genius of the Revolution, just as for the Nazis he was the very incarnation of the Jewish international capitalists who were the secret leaders of both "stock exchange capitalism" and Marxism.[15] Whereas for the Nazis, however, Parvus was the destroyer of imperial Germany, for Solzhenitsyn he is the destroyer of Czarist Russia.[16]

Solzhenitsyn's picture of Parvus conforms to many features of traditional anti-Semitic stereotypes. Solzhenitsyn had from very early on regarded Jews and Russians as opposed to each other. In their sharashka discussions, says Kopelev, Solzhenitsyn could not believe that there were Jews in the pre-revolutionary Socialist Revolutionary Party since "the SRs were a Russian peasant party" and was firmly convinced that "all Trotskyites were Jewish and all the Bukharinites, on the contrary, were Russian."[17] Nevertheless, although he argued that Kopelev could never truly become a Russian, he was his friend and admirer. In *The First Circle* the three Jews—the stockroom head Kagan, the bureaucrat Roitman, and the intellectual Rubin—are not stereotypes but complex characters possessing varying degrees of decency, this in spite of the fact that Kagan is a prison camp informer and has "an almost fiery passion for gain."[18] Parvus, however, is in some respects a reversion to the chief clerk Solomon, a clever, unscrupulous, self-seeking Jew who by manipulating the camp commandant is in effect the real boss of the labor camp in Solzhenitsyn's play *The Love-Girl and the Innocent*, one of the early works in which he gave vent to feelings that were subsequently expressed also in works that followed *The First Circle* and *Cancer Ward*. He also resembles the Jewish fat, dirty, revolting old stock clerk Isaak Bershader in *The Gulag Archipelago*, another prisoner who really runs the camp, directing trustees and jailers to engage in harassment of a young woman prisoner to force her to give herself to him.

Parvus "had knocked around Europe for twenty-five years like the Wandering Jew,"[19] who in the centuries-old legend had struck Christ on his way to the cross and was condemned to roam the earth until the second coming without finding rest. Like the Wandering Jew, he has no root in any national soil, as is indicated in his letter to Lenin, which alternates between Russian and German from sentence to sentence and is full of spelling mistakes in the Russian.

But, although he has no attachment to any country, it is Russia that he hates, for he had early "come to the conclusion that the liberation of the Jews in Russia was impossible unless Tsardom was overthrown" (p. 120). "From the shadows" in which "he always tried to operate," he fathered in 1905 "what looked like a set of rough-hewn, primitive demands from the illiterate masses," but was "really the program of a clever and experienced financier striking at the foundations of the hated Russian state, to bring it down in ruins in a single blow." The "inventor" of the Petersburg Soviet, which he "directed . . . from behind the scenes" (pp. 126, 124), Parvus was the arch-manipulator of the masses, whom he deceived and incited.

After the defeat of the 1905 revolution Parvus went into business and in 1915 "he decided, with as little conscious thought as he gave to breathing, that he and his collaborators would make commerce their first and chief occupation, and that revolution would be run in tandem with business." He did not have to think about it, as commerce, his "natural occupation," and the insidious undermining of the social order were instinctual with him. He was, oddly, both a "desperate revolutionary whose hand would not tremble in the act of overthrowing an empire" and "a passionate trader whose hand trembled as it counted out money" (p. 120).

In appearance Parvus is grotesquely repellant. He has an "exquisite ugliness" (p. 162), is "the size of a large boar," with an "unhealthily enlarged head" and "an enormous belly," and has a "marshy breath." In his vagabond youth he had gone about with "torn shoes and shiny trousers," but now, when he lives like an "Oriental pasha," surrounded by "bosomy blondes," he has an expensive suit "with diamond studs in his dazzlingly displayed cuffs" (pp. 120–27). These snow-white cuffs, however, become soiled on the dirty oilcloth of Lenin's table.

All of these characteristics are reminiscent of anti-Semitic depictions of Jews in print and in cartoons as shabby pawnbrokers, fences, and itinerant peddlars, dirty and emitting a foul odor; repulsively or comically ugly gargoyles; grasping merchants trembling with cupidity; vulgarly ostentatious, bloated speculators and commercial magnates, gross in their manners and corpulence; Orientals possessing the sinister quality and mystery of the exotic East; degenerate voluptuaries; lascivious defilers of blonde Christian maidens; devious and ruthless financial manipulators secretly gathering immense power into their hands; and (especially in the post-revolution literature and cartoons of the Czarist emigrés) the stage managers of the Russian revolution.[20]

Just as anti-Semitic stereotypes were formed through exaggerating the social traits of a commercial people and depriving this people of diversity and complexity, dehumanizing them, so Solzhenitsyn heightens some of the traits of Parvus he found in his source, Zeman and Scharlau's *The Merchant of Revolution*, omits traits that do not answer to his purpose, and adds others that do.

Zeman and Scharlau's book can be faulted on its historical accuracy in important respects[21] and it is not sympathetic toward Parvus and his revolutionary objectives, but it gives facts about him that do not conform to the anti-Semitic stereotypes of the Jew, and these Solzhenitsyn discards. Such is the case with the statements that "in comparison with most business magnates of his time, Helphand was by no means as unscrupulous and grasping as he was later described," that his "laziness prevented him from developing his talent" and that "he found time to take enthusiastic pleasure in the cultural life" of St. Petersburg during the 1905 revolution,[22] for these conflict with Solzhenitsyn's picture of Parvus as singleminded, unremitting, and ruthless in his pursuit of money and revolution.

*The Merchant of Revolution* states, moreover, that the members of the executive committee of the 1905 St. Petersburg Soviet came to regard Parvus as "an ineffectual intellectual," one who was "unable to convince and inspire."[23] It was this experience and his stay in Constantinople, where he built his fortune, which brought about a great change in him. "[H]e had failed dismally as a leader of men," and in Constantinople he "was able to cut off the ties that bound him to past failures and disappointments," becoming "interested in political influence rather than in the exercise of direct political power."[24] In Solzhenitsyn's depiction of him, however, there was no change in Parvus: he had been the adept behind-the-scenes operator in 1905 and he was the adept behind-the-scenes operator in 1917 (although, to be sure, Solzhenitsyn contradicts himself in having Lenin envy Parvus's exploit in blowing up a battleship with his own hands). Always he is the machinating Jew who, crafty and contriving, is in control of events.

In his physical description of Parvus, Solzhenitsyn follows his source closely (although Zeman and Scharlau do not characterize Parvus as ugly[25] and record no complaints about his bad breath), but with a significant difference. "His massive, gigantic figure," say Zeman and Scharlau, "was more puffed out than ever. The broad, bull-like face with its high forehead, tiny nose, and carefully trimmed beard, had developed a flabby double-chin . . . "[26] Solzhenitsyn describes him as follows (p. 128): "There he stood, life-sized, in the flesh, with his ungovernable belly, the elongated dome of his head, the fleshy bulldog features, the little imperial . . . " In view of the many ways in which Solzhenitsyn's Parvus conforms to anti-Semitic stereotypes, it would seem appropriate to ask whether Solzhenitsyn consciously or subconsciously omitted the "tiny nose" of Zeman and Scharlau's description because it did not conform with the exaggeratedly prominent nose of anti-Semitic cartoons.

The character of Bogrov in that portion of the expanded *August 1914* taken from previous "knots" or segments of Solzhenitsyn's saga, that is, that portion which is not, properly speaking, part of *August 1914* at all, is drawn in accordance with still another anti-Semitic stereotype, the sickly, neurasthenic Jewish intellectual represented by Du Maurier's Svengali, "self-indulgent and highly-strung . . . —a very bundle of nerves—especially sensitive to pain and rough usage, and by no means physically brave."[27] So too Bogrov is "always either pale or unhealthily flushed" and is "weak and sickly in appearance," "with puny arms, and a stoop." "His pampered body was used to luxuries" and "had a physical dread of prison," whose "absence of comforts seemed unbearable." Because "he felt himself that his penchant for the comforts of life was a form of corruption," without abandoning these comforts, he embarked on a "secret and meaningful life," "the life of the revolutionary," to which "his own instincts and the mood of society alike impelled" him (pp. 486, 491, 499, 635).

Even among revolutionists, he is aloof and self-centered, suspicious of everyone, armed with a mordant, destructive wit that spares no one. "It cost him an effort not to express himself caustically" (p. 486). Stolypin, seeing Bogrov advance upon him and realizing that he has murder in mind, immediately recognizes the type: "He had a long face, and looked both suspicious and witty (such people often are witty). A young Jew" (p. 605). "They had all been perverted in this way," he thinks later (p. 647), lying wounded, as he recalls the "wry smile" on Bogrov's "intellectual face" at the thought of his having outwitted the Czarist secret police.

However, Lev Navrozov, a Russian emigré literary critic, using *Dmitri Bogrov and the Assassination of Stolypin*, the book by Dmitry's older brother, Vladimir Bogrov, points out that Stolypin's assassin was different from what Solzhenitsyn represents him as having been. "The real Dmitry Bogrov had gone in for all imaginable sports since childhood."[28] Although he was of Jewish origin, his grandfather had adopted Russian Orthodoxy and the family had become culturally Russian. But Solzhenitsyn, making Bogrov the very incarnation of Jewishness, does not use the Russian name Dmitry and uses instead the Jewish name Mordko, a fictitious name invented by anti-Semites of the time in order the better to incite pogroms. He also makes all of the associates of Bogrov bear Jewish names whereas in actuality most of Bogrov's fellow-adherents of the Russian anarchist Bakunin were Russian.

The motive for the assassination is made to be Jewish hatred of the Russian state. The Social Revolutionary Lazarev tells Bogrov: "But you are a Jew. Have you considered carefully what the consequences could be?" Bogrov replies: "Precisely because I'm a Jew I cannot bear the knowledge that we are still living . . . under the heavy hand of the Black Hundred leaders. The Jews will never forget . . . " (p. 499). The historical Lazarev, however, relates in his memoirs that Bogrov referred to the pogroms as signs of continuing Czarist reaction only after having stated that the reform decree of 1905 was followed by "punitive expeditions" that "flooded the country with proletarian and peasant blood."[29] Solzhenitsyn thus converts an anarchist speech into a Jewish declaration of hatred.

Solzhenitsyn has Bogrov say to a rabbi before his execution, "Tell the Jews that I didn't want to harm them. On the contrary, I was fighting for the benefit of the Jewish people" (p. 665). It was necessary to risk a pogrom in order to protest. Later he asks to be allowed to speak to the rabbi in private, suggesting that he has some deep, dark Jewish secret to communicate. "Actually," says Navrozov, "Bogrov said he wanted no 'spiritual mentor.' He lived as an atheist, and as an atheist he wanted to die."[30]

It might be added that Bogrov, like Parvus, is not only a revolutionist by reason of his "instincts" but is also instinctively a businessman, intellectual though he is. "He wrote detailed business letters to his father (he would have been perfectly capable of running a successful business!)," suggesting a bribe to get an order from the city council (p. 502). Thus both Bogrov and Parvus combine in themselves the classic attributes of shrewd, scheming businessman and insidious revolutionist assigned to Jews by Russian anti-Semites. And in drawing Bogrov, as in drawing Parvus, Solzhenitsyn suppresses features in his sources that are not in conformance with anti-Semitic stereotypes.

## NOTES

1. *The Gulag Archipelago*, tr. Thomas P. Whitney (New York: Harper & Row, 1975), II, 597–617.

2. *One Day in the Life of Ivan Denisovich*, tr. Max Hayward and Ronald Hingley (New York: Praeger, 1963) pp. 204–05.

3. *The First Circle*, tr. Thomas P. Whitney (New York: Bantam, 1969), pp. 40, 39.

4. *Cancer Ward*, tr. Nicholas Bethell and David Burg (New York: Bantam, 1969), p. 443.

5. Kostoglotov continues: "Or perhaps you think Tolstoy should have been burned at the stake? Perhaps the Government Synod didn't finish its work?" Solzhenitsyn explains that Kostoglotov, who hasn't had the opportunity to further his education, is confusing the Holy Synod which excommunicated Tolstoy with a governmental body. Rusanov in his turn makes an error: "This was a direct attack on a governmental institution (true, he had not quite heard *which* institution)." What is suggested in this little comedy of errors is that the Orthodox Church, the Czarist government, and the Stalinist regime can be equated as repressive institutions. It is the same suggestion as emerges in *The First Circle* from Stalin's "predisposition" toward "Orthodoxy" and "other elements" of "the old world."

6. So too Nerzhin rejects Tolstoy's adjuration that we be guided by Christ's "Judge not, and ye shall not be judged." We have to judge evil in order to oppose it.

7. It should be noted that Solzhenitsyn has most emphatically denied that he was ever influenced by Tolstoyism ("An Interview on Literary Themes with Nikita Struve, March, 1976," *Solzhenitsyn in Exile: Critical Essays and Documentary Materials*, ed. John B. Dunlop, Richard S. Haugh, and Michael Nicholson [Stanford, Calif.: Hoover Institution Press, 1985], pp. 325–26). In an answer to the question "But at one time Tolstoi was a moral authority for you?" he replied, "Rather to the contrary." To the follow-up question "You did not go through the experience of Tolstoianism?" he responded, "Never . . . In the novel [*August 1914*] I talk about it because it was fashionable at that time. I try to show how it eventually led to the revolution."

8. Gleb Struve, "Behind the Front Lines: On Some Neglected Chapters in *August 1914*," *Aleksandr Solzhenitsyn: Critical Essays and Documentary Materials*, ed. John B. Dunlop, Richard Haugh, and Alexis Klimoff (Belmont, Mass.: Nordland Publishing Co., 1973), p. 431n.

9. Patricia Blake, "Solzhenitsyn and the Theme of War," *Solzhenitsyn: A Collection of Critical Essays*, ed. Kathryn Feuer (Englewood Cliffs, N.J.: Prentice Hall, 1976), p. 87n.

10. Dunlop *et al.*, p. 460.

11. *August 1914*, tr. H.T. Willetts (New York: Farrar, Straus and Giroux, 1989), p. 343. The first English translation was by Michael Glenny and was published by Farrar, Straus and Giroux in 1972. I quote from the revised and expanded 1989 edition throughout.

12. Oddly, just as Solzhenitsyn's Lenin, as we shall see, bears points of resemblance to himself, so Solzhenitsyn also has the habit, acquired during his stay at the sharashka, of walking back and forth within a confined area. He would spend time, says a friend at whose dacha he was staying, "pacing the path that ran from fence to fence" so that she asked him if "he did not get bored walking up and down" (Scammell, p. 824). It might be added that Solzhenitsyn's house in Cavendish, Vermont, as described by Scammell, has features—extensive grounds (fifty acres), adjacent woods, winding lanes through a dense thicket, a wooden foot-bridge over a stream, a pond, a summer-house in addition to the main house—that are the same as those of

Tolstoy's estate described in *August 1914*. Here he, a bearded prophet like Tolstoy, lives, as Tolstoy did, in seclusion except for receiving his disciples.

13. Although Varsonofiev is clearly a spokesman for Solzhenitsyn, this statement would seem to be in contradiction to Solzhenitsyn's authorial assertion (p. 324) that Tolstoy was wrong in finding in *War and Peace* that individuals can have no effect on the inevitable course of events. If history is incomprehensible, if one cannot analyze cause and effect, then individuals cannot make meaningful choices and are merely carried along by the stream of history.

14. P. 28. So too Roman's "private reason for revering and promoting Tolstoy was the great man's rejection of confession and Holy Communion, both of which Roman detested" (p. 24). But if the self-indulgent brother and sister consider themselves too "advanced" for Orthodox ritual, Vorontyntsev perceives in the men under his command, simple peasants who do not question the Church, the spiritual strength of the Russian people. This spiritual strength is typified by the loyal, devoted, courageous Arsenii Blagodaryov, the orderly of Vorontyntsev, who impressively leads the funeral services of a dead officer, having sung in a church choir.

15. For Parvus's role in Nazi propaganda, see Z.A.B. Zeman and W.B. Scharlau, *The Merchant of Revolution: The Life of Alexander Israel Helphand (Parvus) 1867–1924* (New York: Oxford University Press, 1965), pp. 2–3.

16. For the actual role of Parvus, see below, pp. 95–96.

17. Kopelev, p. 18.

18. For the characters of Kagan, Rubin, and Roitman, see below, pp. 133–34, 140–41, 146–47. Significantly, Roitman's bad conscience about having as a child unjustly accused a classmate of anti-Semitism is based on an incident in Solzhenitsyn's own childhood in which, he alleges, as a cross-wearing ten-year-old he was unfairly attacked as an anti-Semite. Significantly also, Kagan was the name of another boy, who in a different childhood incident had a scuffle with him that resulted in the scar on his forehead that he has until this day.

19. *Lenin in Zurich*, tr. H.T. Willetts (New York: Farrar, Straus and Giroux, 1976), p. 118.

20. For these images of the Jew, see Edgar Rosenberg, *From Shylock to Svengali: Jewish Stereotypes in English Fiction* (Stanford, Calif.: Stanford Univ. Press, 1960), a study of the use in English literature of anti-Semitic stereotypes that were also prevalent in Europe, and "Anti-Semitism," *Encyclopedia Judaica* (New York: Macmillan, 1971), particularly its reproductions of anti-Semitic cartoons. Anti-Semitism was above all to be found in pre-revolutionary Russia. There "the classic grievances and accusations of the ultraconservatives and anti-Semites against the Jews"—grievances and accusations that affected Solzhenitsyn's master, Dostoyevsky—were alleged Jewish "financial hegemony, enslavement and exploitation of the masses, fomenting social unrest and revolutionary activity."— David I. Goldstein, *Dostoyevsky and the Jews* (Univ. of Texas Press, 1980), p. 95.

21. See below, p. 96.

22. Zeman and Scharlau, pp. 204, 67, 86.

23. Zeman and Scharlau, p. 92.

24. Zeman and Scharlau, p. 279.

25. In the two photographs of Parvus in *The Merchant of Revolution* he is not at all ugly, and his massive head is impressive.

26. Zeman and Scharlau, p. 157.

27. Rosenberg, p. 257.

28. Lev Navrozov, "Solzhenitsyn's World History: *August 1914* as a New *Protocols of the Elders of Zion*," *Midstream*, June–July 1985, p. 48.

29. Navrozov, p. 51.

30. Navrozov, p. 51.

# 3. Truth and Distortion in *The Gulag Archipelago*

*The Gulag Archipelago* was begun in the winter of 1964–65 after Solzhenitsyn had lost the Lenin Prize and was caught up in the struggle against the recrudescence of Stalinism following the downfall of Khrushchev. It was completed in 1968. Most of it, that is, was written after the crucial turning point of the KGB capture of his manuscripts in September 1965. The circumstances in which it was written help to explain the many contradictions in the book. To be sure, Solzhenitsyn has always been prone to contradict himself. But it should be noted that, as is explained in the "Afterword," in the conditions in which he wrote it in the Soviet Union, secreting portions of it in the process of completion, he never saw the manuscript in its entirety. Moreover, bitterly anti-communist as it is, it was written before the further development of his political position manifested in his later polemics. Facts that he here seeks to gloss over or to explain away he did not admit in his subsequent works.

*The Gulag Archipelago* is at once a mighty achievement that has contributed to our knowledge and understanding of the horror of the Stalinist prison camps as no other writing has done and a shoddy account of their origin and history that has ministered greatly to the false concept current in the West that Stalinism is merely the logical development of Leninism. Just as Solzhenitsyn, as we shall see, projected the personal traits of Stalin back upon Lenin, so did he project the characteristics of the Stalinist labor camps upon the early camps of the Bolsheviks.

Making use of his own experience and the testimony of 227 former prisoners, who communicated with him after the publication of *Ivan Denisovich*, Solzhenitsyn through his artistry was able to show how it feels to be arrested and to live in the inhuman conditions of the camps, how the prisoners' will was beaten down and broken, how the camps were able to function by establishing a hierarchy of prisoners that divided them from each other, how guards acquired the psychology to

47

do their jobs, how ordinary Soviet citizens willfully remained ignorant concerning the extent and nature of the archipelago in their midst by averting their eyes. Of the general authenticity of Solzhenitsyn's exhaustive account there can be no doubt.

As Roy Medvedev, who has read many dozens of samizdat memoirs by former prisoners and listened to hundreds of first-hand accounts, has said, although Solzhenitsyn was unable to verify much of what he was told, his personal experience and his artistic insight allowed him by and large to distinguish between truth and camp folklore. However, especially when he deals with the distant past or relates stories about people at the top (Medvedev singles out as an example a story of how a fourteen-year-old boy at the price of his life told Gorky in 1929 the truth about the Solovetsky camp, which Gorky failed to reveal), such folklore does enter the book. On the other hand, it contains an enormous amount of detail, nine-tenths of which was previously unknown.

Moreover, for the reflective reader *The Gulag Archipelago* reveals much not only about the camps but about life in our terrible century. The description of how prisoners played an essential part in the construction and functioning of the camps and of how good Russians blinded themselves to what was happening in them recalls the extermination camps of the Nazis. The camps, however, not only have analogies with the Nazi camps; they represent a carrying to a monstrous extreme not only of Stalinist society, as suggested in *Ivan Denisovich*, but of capitalist society. In the struggle for existence in the United States different strata of the working class are played off against each other, the well-paid against the poorly paid, whites against blacks, employed against unemployed, men against women, as the camp administrators played off the prisoners against each other. So also comfortable citizens turn their eyes away from the homeless in the streets of American cities, a shameful archipelago of degradation, as did the Russians from the camp transports.

But the truth of *The Gulag Archipelago* and the power of its revelations are accompanied by a very one-sided and tendentious presentation of the archipelago's history that is, unfortunately, the more readily accepted because of its authenticity in other respects. Reading this book is like being buffeted by the surges of the tide. Just as the crash of the waves after a while dulls the senses, so the overwhelming effect of the book dulls the critical faculty so that the reader is all too liable to fail to distinguish the false from the true.

The word "gulag," which, thanks to Solzhenitsyn, has become international, has come to carry the message, "Don't strive for socialism. What you believe will bring you a better social order will only bring you regimentation and concentration camps." So the Loyalists at the time of the American Revolution, invoking the history of the Greek democracies and the authority of Aristotle, argued that democracy, despite its deceptive promises, must lead finally to tyranny.[1]

This kind of deterministic reading of history—it happened that way; therefore it had to happen that way and can only happen that way in the future—of which Marxists are falsely accused is not employed, however, when it comes to Germany, where capitalism, operating under the Weimar constitution, hailed as the most liberal constitution in the world, gave birth to fascism. Socialism is blamed for Stalin, but capitalism is not blamed for Hitler. What Solzhenitsyn and those who follow him fail to see is that both Stalin and Hitler, the products of our time, an epoch of transition, came at a moment of most intense social crisis when violent social struggles led to a disregard for moral restraints. Stalinism in the last analysis is the result of the failure of socialist revolution in the advanced capitalist countries to bring an end to the prolonged death agony of capitalism that has brought Auschwitz, Hiroshima, and the carpet-bombing and pulverization of Vietnam.

Since the virtues of *The Gulag Archipelago* have been sufficiently recognized and its distortions have passed almost unnoted, I shall devote the rest of this chapter to the latter. They are the consequence of Solzhenitsyn's anti-Bolshevik squint.

Solzhenitsyn sees the Gulag as having been established by the Bolsheviks in 1918 and as operating since then essentially in the same way, ready to receive the great waves of prisoners that came with the collectivization of the farms in 1929 and 1930, the purges in 1937 and 1938, and the imprisonment in 1944 to 1946 of the Volga Germans, the Crimean Tartars, and other nationalities and of the Russians captured by the Germans early in the war and "liberated" by the Red Army later in the war. In the grip of their fanatical ideology, the Bolsheviks engaged in executions on an enormous scale. The concentration camps of the Gulag were only one aspect of the wholesale violence. The

Cheka, the revolutionary supra-legal power, operated arbitrarily and cruelly, but then so did the courts.

All of this was part of a consciously planned sinister design that gradually unfolded, as the Bolsheviks consolidated their power. Although the Soviet government began as a coalition between the Bolsheviks and the Left Social Revolutionaries, the purpose of the Bolsheviks from the beginning was to get rid of all members of any party other than theirs and to fasten a one-party dictatorship on the people.

> This whole operation was stretched out over many years because it was of primary importance that it be stealthy and unnoticed. . . . This was a grandiose silent game of soli-taire. . . . Someone's far-seeing mind, someone's neat hand, planned it all, without letting one wasted minute go by. They picked up a card which had spent three years in one pile and softly placed it on another pile. . . . Patience, overwhelming patience, was the trait of the person playing out the solitaire. . . . [A]nd thus—imperceptibly and merci-lessly—was prepared the annihilation of those who had once raged against tyranny . . . .[2]

Solzhenitsyn's thesis of a secret plan put into effect by the Bolsheviks over the years, for which he offers no proof, goes against all the evidence. Bertram D. Wolfe, a strong anti-Bolshevik who served as Chief of the Ideological Advisory Staff of the Voice of America, states flatly, "Lenin had no idea of outlawing all other parties and creating a one-party system."[3] Marcel Liebman in his heavily documented *Leninism under Lenin* states that in the writings before the Revolution in which Lenin educated the members of his party on how socialism in Russia was to be attained he "never suggested anything remotely resembling a single-Party system."[4] Even when, with the Revolution in gravest peril, the government outlawed other parties, he "never depicted what he considered to be a necessity as being either a virtue or as a really lasting system."[5]

That this was not mere pose is shown, as is acknowledged by American historians not at all sympathetic to the Bolsheviks, by the conduct of the Bolsheviks in their negotiations for a coalition government with the Mensheviks and Social Revolutionaries, the minority parties in the soviets. R.V. Daniels "points out" that "at the time of the October insurrection the Bolsheviks as a whole had no notion of ruling the country alone." Radkey says of the S.R.'s, who had retreated from an even more intransigent position to the position that such a coalition government could include Bolsheviks only as individuals and must exclude Lenin and Trotsky, that they demanded that the Bolsheviks "come round by the back way to share in power the plenitude of which they already possessed." Yet one-third of the members of the Bolshevik Central Committee resigned because they felt that the Bolsheviks should accede. But Lenin and the majority, who were equally desirous of a coalition government, declared, in the words of Lenin's motion, that "to yield to the ultimatums and threats of the minority in the soviets means finally rejecting not only Soviet power but democracy itself, for such concessions signify fear by the majority to make use of its majority."[6]

How much opposed to a one-party monopoly Lenin was is indicated by his "Greetings to Hungarian Workers" at the time of the socialist revolution in Hungary in 1919. "Hungarian workers! Comrades!" he wrote, "You have set the world an even better example than Soviet Russia by your ability to unite all socialists at one stroke on the platform of genuine proletarian dictatorship."[7]

But what is most noteworthy in Solzhenitsyn's account of the early years of the Bolshevik regime is a complete disregard for the historical circumstances. There is not a word about the intervention of the armies of fourteen nations, led by England and the United States, on seven different fronts. Bolshevik repressive measures are related without reference to the desperate fight they were leading against the merciless White Armies backed by the Allies. The White terror gets only one passing mention, when Solzhenitsyn contrasts (I, 266) "the exceptional few" among the White Guards "who hung every tenth worker without trial and whipped the peasants" with "the soldierly majority." In *The First Circle* Solzhenitsyn had Spiridon, to whom Nerzhin gives absolute credence, describe the systematic terror of the Whites, who killed peasant leaders and coerced the others to fight for them, but here he speaks only of the excesses of an "exceptional few."

The reality was far different than the picture given in *The Gulag Archipelago*. Here it will be necessary to quote at some length from Liebman. The Revolution, says Liebman, toppled the old regime with very little bloodshed, mostly confined to Moscow. In the provinces Czarism fell like rotten fruit. During this period, before counter-revolution gathered its latent forces and acquired foreign assistance, there was a euphoria such as occurred immediately after the fall of the Bastille and in the early days of the Paris Commune that expressed itself in a remarkable generosity for the vanquished.

"When the Red Guards captured the Winter Palace in Petrograd, the seat of the Provisional Government," says Liebman,

> they released the officer-cadets who had fought against them, requiring only that they give their word not to take up arms against the revolution any more. A few days later this same body of cadets organized an armed uprising in the capital. The Bolsheviks easily overcame them—and then once again released their prisoners. General Krasnov, commanding the counter-revolutionary forces that were brought up to reconquer Petrograd, also obtained his freedom in return for a promise not to fight against the soviets again—and almost immediately joined the anti-Bolshevik forces gathering in the south. . . . Moreover, the members of the Provisional Government who had been arrested on October 26—or at least those of them who belonged to the socialist parties[8]—were released, *at Martov's request.*"[9]

This generous behavior on the part of the Bolsheviks by no means stemmed from a desire to hide their nefarious purposes from the people. On the contrary, it was they who restrained the enraged masses.

> During the first months of their rule, the Bolsheviks, far from inflaming the anger and vindictiveness of the masses, sought to set bounds to the manifestation of such feelings. . . . Indeed, one of the first decrees of the new Government abolished the death penalty, which Kerensky's Government had restored in September 1917. . . . In July 1918, after suppressing the armed revolt of the Left S.R.s, the Bolsheviks showed such moderation in their measures of reprisal that the German Government, whose ambassador had been killed by the rebels,[10] protested to the Soviet authorities. The moderation of the Bolsheviks is all the more remarkable in that it contrasted in this period with the first outbursts of "White" terror, both on a small scale, like the massacre of their "Red" prisoners by the officer-cadets during the Moscow insurrection of 1917, and on a grand

scale, as in Finland, where between ten and twenty thousand workers were slaughtered by the counter-revolution, not including the more than two thousand prisoners who died in internment camps.[11]

It was only in the face of such an enemy and when the Revolution was in the direst danger that the Bolsheviks in turn took up the weapon of terror.

> With the beginning of the civil war and foreign intervention the Bolshevik Government, yielding to the spirit of the time, itself resorted to terror. Undoubtedly it was the numerous attempts on the lives of some of their leaders that helped to overcome their last hesitations in this matter: the attempt to kill Lenin on January 1st, 1918, the murder of Volodarsky in June, the unsuccessful attempt on Trotsky's life at the beginning of August, and, at the end of that month, the murder of Uritsky and the attack on Lenin that nearly killed him, immobilizing the head of the Government for several weeks.[12]

Unlike the White Guards, who practiced terror without discussing it, the Bolsheviks defended their use of terror, scornfully rejecting the accusations of the European social democrats who had supported the governments engaged in the enormous slaughter of World War I but who criticized the revolutionary use of violence. It is this frank acknowledgement of the use of terror that Solzhenitsyn quotes as evidence of cold-blooded fanaticism, but he quotes selectively, omitting the justification advanced[13] and barely mentioning the terror on the other side, only to minimize it.

In a description of the spiritual experience he had in prison camp, Solzhenitsyn gives the basis for his own objection to revolutionary violence. He does not realize the contradictions and fallacies it contains. "In the intoxication of youthful successes," he says (II, 615–16),

> I had felt myself to be infallible, and I was therefore cruel. . . . Gradually it was disclosed to me that the line separating good and evil passes not through states, nor between classes, nor between political parties either—but right through every human heart. . . . Inside us, it oscillates with the years. . . . And since that time I have come to understand the falsehood of all revolutions in history: They

destroy only *those carriers* of evil contemporary with them (and also fail out of haste, to discriminate the carriers of good as well). And they then take to themselves as their heritage the actual evil itself, magnified still more.

What Solzhenitsyn is saying is that as a youthful Marxist certain of his dogma he was ready to commit any crime in its name. But then he came to realize that not all evil was concentrated in the Czarist state and the states opposed to the Soviet Union or in the capitalist and land-owning classes or in non-Communist parties: there is both good and evil in all states, classes and parties, for there is both good and evil in each of us. But if there is both good and evil in all parties, what becomes of his description of the Bolshevik party as the epitome of evil?

The recognition expressed in this passage of the complexity of human nature and of the fact that people can degenerate in character or rise above their previous selves is one of the great strengths of *The First Circle* and *Cancer Ward*, but it is a ludicrous distortion for Solzhenitsyn to imply that revolutionists regard all those on their side as incorruptible saints[14] and all their opponents as "carriers of evil" whom they must "destroy." It is, of course, not a matter of destroying individuals but of destroying a social system that crushes people and does not allow them to realize their potential as human beings. The destruction of the old order does not produce a lightning transformation in humanity, for the heritage of the past is not so easily gotten rid of, but the new order enables humanity to progress.

The amazing thing is that Solzhenitsyn, without realizing it, completely reverses himself about the morality of revolutions at the very end of *The Gulag Archipelago*. In some of the most moving of his more than 1,800 pages, he tells of the uprisings in the camps in the last years of Stalin. A vital part in the preliminary phase of these uprisings was the killing of the stool pigeons on whom the camp administrators depended to prevent any possibility of common action. In the morning a stool pigeon would be found dead, stabbed to the heart by an improvised knife. This would terrify other stool pigeons and give confidence to the other prisoners. Solzhenitsyn gives the arguments of moralists that such actions can only bring further violence so that "there will be no end to it." He replies, "If you ever get twenty-five years for nothing" and "are trodden deeper and deeper into the ground," "the fine words of the great humanists will sound like the chatter of the well-fed and the free." "There will be no end to it!" it is said—but without such action "will there be a beginning?"[15]

When the prisoners broke out of their isolation, united, men and women together, defied the camp authorities, and fashioned weapons for their defense, the authorities told the inhabitants of the adjoining settlement that the prisoners were mutinying in order to engage in sexual orgies. But, says Solzhenitsyn, using the language of revolution, although he had stated that revolution had brought only evil throughout history, "in the puritanical air of that revolutionary springtime, men and women behaved with proper dignity . . ." (III, 306).

In fact, there was an immense moral transformation. "[I]n the new revolutionary atmosphere" the prisoners in the kitchen did not steal food and the trustees did not get anything extra. Even the criminals, who had preyed upon the political prisoners with the support of the authorities, were affected by "the stern and cleansing wind of rebellion." They participated in the uprising as comrades and ceased demanding a special cut of everything for themselves. "So long suppressed, the brotherhood of man had broken through at last! We loved the thieves! And the thieves loved us!" (III, 307, 306, 297).

The leader of one mutiny rejected the secret promise of the camp bosses that his life would be spared if he caused the mutiny to break up by provoking a pogrom against the Jews and other racial minorities. Instead, he announced, "Anybody who doesn't turn out to defend the camp will get the knife." This was "the inevitable logic of any military authority and any war situation," comments Solzhenitsyn approvingly (III, 314), forgetting his moral objections to the punitive measures taken by the Bolsheviks against waverers and slackers.

In a footnote, to be sure, Solzhenitsyn adds some darker colors to his generally glowing picture of the uprisings:

> It was not all as clean and smooth as it looks from this description of the main trend. There were rival groups—the "moderates" and the "ultras." Personal predilections and dislikes and the clash of ambitions among men eager to be "leaders" also crept in. The "hit men" . . . were far from being men of broad political vision; some were apt to demand extra rations for their "work" . . . In a word, corruption and decay—old, invariable features of revolu-

tionary movements throughout history—were already bur-
rowing into the healthy core.

"But," he concludes, "in spite of these lapses, the movement as a
whole kept going strictly on course. We knew where we were going.
The required social effect was achieved" (III, 240n.).

Parallels to Solzhenitsyn's description of the uprisings can be found
in the descriptions of the October Revolution by John Reed, Albert
Rhys Williams, and other eye witnesses. There is the same sense of
exhilaration, the same moral elevation, the same comradeship, the
same self-restraint for the sake of revolution, the same tremendous
release of energies, and the same heroism. Thus Larissa Reisner, a
commissar and journalist in the revolution at the age of twenty-one, a
remarkable woman in whose honor Boris Pasternak wrote a poem at
her death of typhus in 1926, wrote of the legendary stand at Svyazhsk,
in which she had participated:

> Brotherhood! Few words have been so abused and ren-
> dered pitiful. But brotherhood does come sometimes, in
> moments of direst need and peril, so selfless, so sacred, so
> unrepeatable in a single lifetime. And they have not lived
> and know nothing of life who have never lain at night on a
> floor in tattered and lice-infected clothes, thinking all the
> while how wonderful is the world, infinitely wonderful!
> That here the old has been overthrown and that life is
> fighting with bare hands for her irrefutable truth, . . . for
> the future of all mankind. . . . Everybody, including the
> cowardly and the nervous and the simple mediocre workers
> and Red Army men—everybody, without a single excep-
> tion, performed unbelievable, heroic deeds; they outdid
> themselves, like spring streams overflowing their banks they
> joyfully flooded their own normal levels.[16]

But Solzhenitsyn omits all light colors in his picture of the October
Revolution and paints only dark colors, made blacker than in reality.
A nation no longer able to endure war, landlord oppression, and
hunger was roused against the old order by the Bolshevik slogan
"Peace, land, and bread." Many excesses were undoubtedly committed in this revolt, and the Bolshevik leaders in many instances made
seriously wrong political decisions. It could not have been otherwise.
As Lenin was fond of quoting Napoleon, the only way not to make
mistakes is not to take any action—but the failure to take action can

itself be the worst mistake. In Ernest Mandel's words, "the thousands of victims of Horthy's white terror in Hungary . . . would have been nothing compared to the hundreds of thousands of workers and peasants who would have been massacred in Russia had the White terror been victorious."[17] Solzhenitsyn, however, who is able to see that despite the "lapses" of the prisoner uprisings "the required social effect was achieved," is unable to see the same for the October Revolution.

The justice executed during the Civil War, often summary and sometimes not well considered, was, Mandel points out, "a thousand miles removed from the caricatures of justice staged by Stalin. Two trials cited by Solzhenitsyn himself perfectly illustrate the basic difference between the Bolshevik revolution and the Stalinist counter-revolution." The first trial involved V.V. Oldenborger, the chief engineer of the Moscow water-supply system, and the second trial a Tolstoyan conscientious objector during the Civil War.

Although his fellow engineers went out on strike against the October Revolution, Oldenborger, who was highly devoted to his work, did not do so. He did, however, agree to disburse money to the strikers from the strike committee. Despite his faithful service and his popularity among the workers at the plant, he was attacked continually as a saboteur by the local party committee, and when he was finally denounced by it to the Cheka he committed suicide. Solzhenitsyn, comments Mandel, cannot contain his indignation about Bolsehvik repressiveness and injustice, but

> It's not until you read the end of Solzhenitsyn's account that you find out that the trial he is talking about was organized by the Soviet state *to defend Oldenborger*, a trial organized *against* the communist cell that had persecuted him, a trial that ended by *sentencing* his persecutors,[18] a trial that proved that the workers in the plant had been able freely to elect Oldenborger to a soviet *against* the unanimous pressure of the communist cell.

In the trial of the Tolstoyan conscientious objector, he was sentenced to death. However, the soldiers assigned to guard him sent a petition to Moscow, and the verdict was overturned. "So," concludes Mandel,

> we have workers who can *elect* an apolitical technician to the soviet, despite the opposition of a communist cell

composed of members who were at best ultra-sectarians and at worst totally corrupted careerists. We have soldiers who revolt against the verdict of a court, organize a general assembly, interfere in the "great affairs of state," and save the life of their prisoner. Solzhenitsyn—without realizing it—is describing the real difference between an era of revolution and an era of counter-revolution. Let him cite similar examples from the Stalin era to prove that basically it was all the same under Lenin and under Stalin![19]

After the Civil War the need for the swift-striking Cheka disappeared. On February 7, 1922, it was changed to the GPU, whose name ("Main Political Administration") indicated that it was now concerned only with counter-revolutionary activity and espionage, and not also with crimes such as theft and black marketeering, as before. It could only investigate and refer to court, not punish.

The limitations on the GPU were accompanied by the development of a body of laws in the first half of the 1920's. However, "after the deaths of Lenin and Dzerzinsky, . . . [u]nder pressure from Stalin, a punitive organization reappeared, with the right to put people in jail and camps, to exile them to remote places, and later even to shoot them without any juridical procedure, simply as an administrative act."[20]

The Stalinist jurists themselves, unlike Solzhenitsyn, recognized the difference in jurisprudence between the two eras. Vyshinsky, the ex-Menshevik lawyer who was Stalin's chief legal theorist and the prosecutor of the Moscow trials, attacked the work of earlier Soviet jurists as "in essence aimed at suggesting the 'thought' that . . . the army, navy, counter-intelligence, NKVD, courts, procuracy . . . had . . . exhausted their historic role."[21] This earlier generation of jurists was influenced, of course, by Lenin's idea of the withering away of the proletarian state. As Moshe Lewin says of Vyshinsky's attack, "One couldn't have expressed more clearly this defense of the police state, as a principle, against the Old Bolshevik ideas . . . ."

Just as justice differed in the two periods, so did the prisons and labor camps. "Soviet penitentiary reforms of earlier years, inspired by humanitarian motives," wrote Isaac Deutscher in 1949, "viewed the imprisonment of criminals as a means to their re-education, not punishment." During the forcible collectivization under Stalin, which brought with it famine, the peasants who resisted it were "treated like criminals." "As the number of rebellious peasants grew, they were organized in mammoth labor camps . . . Amid the famine and misery of the early thirties the provisions for their protection were completely disregarded. 'Re-education' degenerated into slave labor . . . ."[22]

After the assassination of Kirov, when the purges filled the labor camps with oppositionists and those who in the witch-hunt hysteria were falsely charged with being oppositionists,

> the treatment of the political prisoners underwent a radical change. Hitherto it had not been different from that accorded to them in Tsarist days. Political offenders had enjoyed certain privileges and been allowed to engage in self-education and even in political propaganda. Oppositional memoranda, pamphlets, and periodicals had circulated half freely between prisons and had occasionally been smuggled abroad. . . . From now on all political discussion and activity in the prisons and places of exile was to be mercilessly suppressed; and the men of the opposition were by privation and hard labour to be reduced to such a miserable, animal-like existence that they should be incapable of the normal processes of thinking and of formulating their views.[23]

Solzhenitsyn himself implicitly acknowledges that there was a tremendous difference between the prisons and labor camps in the early years of the regime and the prisons and labor camps of the Stalin era, but he seeks to reconcile the existence of this difference with his idea of a diabolical Bolshevik master-plan. Political prisoners, he says, had a tradition of struggle against the Czarist prison system, from which they had won various rights, to which the Bolsheviks initially had to accede. Prisoners of the new system therefore "accepted as their legal due a special *political ration* (conceded by the Tsar and confirmed by the Revolution), which included half a pack of cigarettes a day" and "purchases from the market (cottage cheese, milk)." In addition to this, they inherited many other rights from Czarist times, some of them being the right to the free election of spokesmen for themselves, the right to be addressed politely by prison personnel, and the right "to have newspapers, magazines, books, writing materials, and personal articles, even including razors and scissors" (I, 460).

However, Solzhenitsyn himself indicates, although mentioning it only in passing and speaking with heavy irony, that the Bolsheviks not only retained the rights that prisoners had won through struggle in Czarist times but greatly extended them.

> [T]he new rulers ... proclaimed immediately that the horrors of the Tsarist prisons would not be repeated; that *fatiguing correction* would not be permitted; that there would be no compulsory silence in prison, no solitary confinement, no separating the prisoners from one another during outdoor walks, no marching in step and single file, not even any locked cells. Go ahead, dear guests, get together, and talk as much as you like and complain about the Bolsheviks (I, 459).

"The horrors of the Tsarist prisons" is ironic, for Solzhenitsyn throughout *The Gulag Archipelago* contrasts the lax Czarist prisons with the Stalinist prisons and just before this sentence has been discussing the concessions granted to the prisoners by the weakening system.[24] The irony implies that these are the words of demagogues who exaggerate the evils of the present, which are as nothing compared to what they will perpetrate once they are able to put their plan into effect. This evidently is the point also of the sarcastic "Go ahead, dear guests, get together and talk as much as you like and complain about the Bolsheviks." The spider is gloating over the ignorance and naiveté of the fly, who does not know that this web is far stronger than those he has known in the past.

The Bolshevik promises themselves, however, indicate that, no matter what the concessions political prisoners wrested from Czardom, hard labor and isolation remained an integral part of the Czarist system. Moreover, they indicate that what Solzhenitsyn a page later suggests were traditional rights—"unrestricted visits from cell to cell" and "freedom to choose companions for outdoor walks"—were in reality Bolshevik innovations. The traditional rights of political prisoners, it may also be observed, were not adhered to in "the numerous concentration camps set up in territory held by the White armies and foreign interventionist forces," which, Roy Medvedev states, "were usually far more savage than those in the RSFSR [Russian Soviet Federated Socialist Republics]."[25]

When Solzhenitsyn later outlines the prison labor system inaugurated by the Bolsheviks, its provisions, far more progressive than those governing American prisons today, make his sarcasm pointless, a knife without a blade.

Because of the novelty of it all, the hasty decision was made to pay the prisoners for all their work, other than camp maintenance, at 100 percent of the rates of the corresponding trade unions. (Oh, what a monstrous thing! The pen can barely bear to write it!) . . . For "conscientious prisoners" there was a special benefit: to be allowed to live in a private apartment and to come to camp for work only. And release ahead of term was promised as a reward for "special labor enthusiasm" (II, 15–16).

Solzhenitsyn is also sarcastic about the whole Bolshevik idea of work as being an essential part of a humanitarian prison program ("After all, Marx himself had pointed out in his 'Critique of the Gotha Program' that productive labor was the only method of prisoner correction"), asking "Why is it that our prisoner must not chew the rag or read nice little books in a cell, but must labor instead?" (II, 13). He forgets that he has told us that the prison system provided for an eight-hour day, that reading matter was allowed in the cells, and that prisoners were allowed to visit each other and to walk together on the grounds. He forgets also that he showed Ivan Denisovich as deriving deep satisfaction, despite Stalinist camp conditions, from having lain a row of bricks straight and that he showed the sharashka prisoners in *The First Circle* as being, despite their dissatisfaction with their impossibly long hours, often carried away by their scientific work.

Despite the Bolsheviks' humanitarian intentions, there were undoubtedly many brutal jailers, as there are everywhere, the very nature of the work having a brutalizing effect. Brutality is, for instance, customary in the jails of the United States, as is testified by the constantly erupting riots and complaints of mistreatment, from Attica to Rykers Island. The Bolsheviks were forced, furthermore, to rely for many of their guards on former Czarist jailers, as they were forced to rely in large part upon the lower ranks of the bureaucracy to run the government.

Nevertheless, the Bolshevik leaders sought to fight against brutality.[26] Solzhenitsyn quotes with his usual satirical comment the words of Dzerzhinsky (II, 537), the head of the Cheka, who had spent a large part of his life in Czarist prisons: "Whoever among you has become hardened, whose heart cannot respond sensitively and attentively to those who suffer imprisonment—get out of this institution!" "Who was this meant for?" he asks scoffingly "And how seriously? . . . (And maybe a different kind of advice was given on another occasion, but we simply don't have the quotations.)" Solzhenitsyn does not consider the possibility that he can't find the quotations with a contrary tenor because they do not exist, these words expressing Dzerzhinsky's undeviating idealism. It is impossible to imagine Stalin's NKVD chief Beria ever having uttered them.

Solzhenitsyn does not claim that any of the prisoners' rights in the Bolshevik reform program were rescinded before 1925. At the Solovetsky Camp[27] in December 1923 it was announced that new rules were to be instituted. "They wouldn't, of course, take everything away, not by any means" is Solzhenitsyn's sarcastic comment. "They would cut down on correspondence, and then on something else, too, and, as the most keenly felt measure of the lot, from that day on, December 20, 1923, the right to go in and out of prison buildings twenty-four hours a day would be curtailed—limited to the daylight hours up to 6 P.M." (I, 463). As a protest, he goes on to relate, the prisoners decided to go outside at exactly 6 P.M., and the guards fired upon them (Solzhenitsyn claims that it was actually some minutes before the hour), killing six. The next day the camp commander apologized to the prisoners, and the chief of the guards was deprived of his position. A solemn funeral having been conducted for the victims, their names were inscribed on a great stone. "[T]he prisoners had defended the regimen successfully! And for a whole year no one spoke of changing it" (I, 463–64).

The "They wouldn't, of course, take everything away, not by any means" and the "and then on something else, too," imply that the Bolsheviks were practicing "salami tactics," planning to take away a bit at a time until nothing was left. After having, in their thoughtless haste, set up a prison system with features superior to those in other countries, they were determined to take it all back and to set up the Gulag of their original intentions. They began by limiting the right to enter and leave prison buildings to daylight hours, a limitation that goes beyond what prisoners in the United States have at present—and then desisted from enforcing the order or making any other changes for an entire year.

A more plausible explanation of what took place would seem to lie in Isaac Deutscher's description of the changes within the Bolshevik party at this time, the period of the triumvirate, in which Stalin became the dominant figure. These internal changes were the result of adverse social conditions and in turn affected life in the Soviet Union.

After the proscription of other parties, a violation of the Soviet democracy of which the Bolsheviks were the proponents, and after the banning of factions within the ruling party, a violation of its traditions, the party, "at loggerheads with its own nature," more and more

> ceased to be a free association of independent, critically minded and courageous revolutionaries. The bulk of it submitted to the ever more powerful party machine. . . . The administrator began to elbow out the ideologue, the bureaucrat and committee-man eliminated the idealist. . . . This trend of events did not very rapidly become apparent. It developed gradually, in contradictory zigzags, always at odds with the inertia of earlier habits.[28]

These "contradictory zigzags" in the development of the party were reflected in the zigzags of prison administration.

The culmination of the changes in the Bolshevik Party was the purge of 1937, which set its seal upon them. Here the facts are so glaring and widely known that Solzhenitsyn perfunctorily acknowledges them but without realizing the significance of this acknowledgement for his thesis that Stalinism is basically the same as Leninism. "There is hardly any need," he says (I, 68–69),

> to repeat here what has already been widely written . . . about 1937: that a crushing blow was dealt the upper ranks of the Party,[29] the government, the military command, and the GPU-NKVD itself. . . . In the arrest of rank-and-file members of the Party there was evidently a hidden theme not directly stated anywhere in the indictments and verdicts: that arrests should be carried out predominantly among Party members who had joined *before* 1924.

But why did Stalin deliver this "crushing blow" against so much of the leadership of Soviet society and why were those who had been party members before 1924 singled out for arrest?[30] Solzhenitsyn does not explain, but he makes an inadvertent admission: "Stalin picked more suitable people for his purposes." If, however, these people were not suitable for Stalin's purposes, how can it be claimed that Stalinism is merely the continuation of Bolshevism?

The explanation for Stalinism is not to be found in the unchanging nature of Bolshevism but in the historical conditions that acted upon

Bolshevism. Basic to them is the victory of a socialist revolution in a backward country without revolutions in advanced capitalist countries coming to its help. Revolutionary Russia was left isolated after the German revolution, to which the Bolsheviks had looked hopefully, was crushed. The cumulative effects of the war, the Allied blockade, the civil war, famine, and typhus were devastating. Production fell, and the working class was decimated and almost ceased to exist as a class. Many of its most politically conscious and self-sacrificing members were killed in the civil war; others were demoralized. Workers' economic and political democracy receded, as a bureaucracy, many members of which were demobilized Red Army commanders accustomed to military methods, at first served the working class but then assumed increasing independence and power. It was on this bureaucracy, whose privileges and power he extended, that Stalin based himself.

This process received a brilliant analysis by none other than one of the two outstanding leaders of the Russian Revolution, Leon Trotsky, of which the above paragraph is all too compressed a summary. Solzhenitsyn himself had once had some understanding of the changes that took place. "The revolutionary vanguard of the proletariat," says Trotsky, "was in part devoured by the administrative apparatus and gradually demoralized, in part annihilated in the civil war, and in part thrown out and crushed. The tired and disappointed masses were indifferent to what was happening on the summits."[31] Makarygin in *The First Circle* is an example of those who had been absorbed in the administrative apparatus and had lost their revolutionary zeal as the rewards of their positions increased. His first wife, who had fought with him in the Civil War and who could never have accommodated herself to his present position, and Volodin's father, who died heroically in the Civil War, are examples of those lost to the revolutionary vanguard in the struggle with the Whites. Rubin's cousin and Adamson are examples of those in the revolutionary vanguard thrown out and crushed by the triumphant bureaucracy.

And how did the masses of people come to accept the betrayal of the socialist ideals for which they had fought? How was it that, in the words of Shulubin, "a whole people" lost "its social drive and courageous impulse"? How did it accept the outrageous lie that "the whole of Lenin's old guard" were "enemies of the people"? Shulubin's answer is that "the people are intelligent enough, it's simply that they wanted to live" (*Cancer Ward*, pp. 439, 434). They had, as Trotsky said, become indifferent to what was happening at the top and had learned not to question what they were told.

But this was written when Solzhenitsyn had had an entirely different outlook. In *The Gulag Archipelago* Bolshevism is for him an ugly monster that sprang fully formed from the brow of Lenin and has remained unchanged ever since.

He cannot give up this view even in describing the heroism of that portion of the revolutionary vanguard thrown into the camps. He seeks to hurry over this portion of the historical record, saying, "I am writing for mute Russia and therefore I have but little to say about the Trotskyites; they are all people who write." While acknowledging that they were "heroic people," he adds without attempting to substantiate his statement, "I fear, however, that if they had come to power, they would have brought us a madness no better than Stalin's." In telling of how they planned to celebrate the anniversary of the October Revolution by hanging out black mourning flags, singing the "Internationale," refusing to work for the day, and shouting "Hail Leninism!" his comment on this courageous protest is "In this plan we find a sort of hysterical enthusiasm mixed with futility, bordering on the ridiculous."

He does give the facts of the Vorkuta hunger strike, which was famous in camp lore: "The greatest achievement of the Trotskyites was their hunger strike and work stoppage throughout the entire Vorkuta system of camps. . . . It began on October 27, 1936, and it continued for 136 days. [They were fed artificially, but did not lift the hunger strike.] Several died of starvation." But, again, his comment emphasizes the futility of the strike and says nothing of the valor of the strikers or of the inspirational effect of the memory of the strike.

> [T]he security officer of Vorkutlag, Uzkov, taunted the "hunger-strike leadership" of hostile prisoners by saying: "Do you think that Europe knows about your strike? We don't give a damn about Europe!" And he was right. . . . Their hunger strike had provided . . . the list of those executed (II, 317–21).

Far different is the tone of his description of the hunger strike in which he participated: "[T]here was a sort of satisfaction in this feeling of hopelessness. We had taken a futile, a desperate step, it could only end badly—and that was good. . . . [S]ome higher need was being served" (III, 259).

Solzhenitsyn is equally ungenerous in speaking of the Communist prisoners who were not oppositionists. Although he concedes that some of them maintained solidarity with the other prisoners, he dwells at length on the "loyalists" who considered every one other than themselves to have been justly imprisoned. They sought, he says, to curry favor with the camp bosses as fellow Communists and did indeed get preferential treatment. "[W]ere there not perhaps," he asks (as usual, without any proof), "some written or at least oral directives: to make things easier for the Communists?" (II, 345).

Roy Medvedev, however, found from his study of the testimony of former prisoners that there were not many of the kind of Communists ridiculed by Solzhenitsyn. After some months of "interrogation" few continued to extol the regime and the NKVD. Solzhenitsyn, he says, drew general conclusions from the behavior of a limited number. The Communist Buinovsky, who was punished for standing up to the authorities in *Ivan Denisovich*—and, one may add, Kopelev, to whom Solzhenitsyn trustingly confided his doubts—were more typical. As for special protection going to Communists, "In many respects their circumstances were even worse than those of the prisoners in other categories and . . . it is likely they died in greater numbers than other prisoners. . . . [T]hroughout the USSR, out of a million party members arrested in the latter half of the 1930s, not more than 60,000–80,000 returned after 15 to 18 years of imprisonment."[32]

Solzhenitsyn is especially vitriolic in discussing the famous purge trials. "If you study in detail the whole history of the arrests and trials of 1936 to 1938, the principal revulsion you feel is not against Stalin and his accomplices, but against the humiliatingly repulsive defendants . . ." (I, 130). The victims being more disgusting than their executioners, compassion would be wasted upon them. "[T]he powerful leaders of the fearless Communist Party, who had turned the entire world upside down and terrified it," he says with savage sarcasm, "now marched forth like doleful, obedient goats and bleated out everything they had been ordered to, vomited all over themselves, cringingly abased themselves and their convictions, and confessed to crimes they could not in any wise have committed." "[T]he 'Leninist guard,' " he adds, not content with having them vomit over themselves, "came before the judges drenched in their own urine" (I, 408–09).

Earlier in the book, after describing in excruciating detail how prisoners were broken, Solzhenitsyn exclaimed, "Brother mine! Do not condemn those who, finding themselves in such a situation, turned out to be weak and confessed to more than they should have. . . . Do not be the first to cast a stone at them" (I, 117). Later he described his spiritual ascent to Christian forgiveness: "Once upon a time you were sharply intolerant. . . . [Y]ou never forgave anyone. You judged people without mercy. . . . And now . . . [y]ou have come to realize your own weakness—and you can therefore understand the weakness of others" (II, 611). But Solzhenitsyn in discussing the Bolshevik defendants did not heed his own adjuration to the reader or stay on the spiritual heights to which he had ascended.

He is, however, it must be said, more forgiving toward himself than toward the Bolshevik leaders. He describes how after an interrogation that was comparatively lenient—"[m]y interrogator had used no methods on me other than sleeplessness, lies, and threats"—he was brought to sign a statement attesting to the truth of an entirely distorted summary of his testimony. "Looking back upon my interrogation from my long subsequent imprisonment," he says, "I had no reason to be proud of it. I might have borne myself more firmly; and in all probability I could have manuevered more skillfully. But my first weeks were characterized by a mental blackout and a slump into depression." He makes no such excuses for the purge trial defendants of mental incapacity brought on by emotional shock and depression.

Although Solzhenitsyn presents his conduct under interrogation as typical, he does not choose to judge the conduct of the defendants in the purge trials by it. "I repented just as much as I had to," he says, without seeing the resemblance between his behavior and the defendants' "confessions," "and pretended to see the light and reject my political mistakes." When his qualifying statements and equivocations were omitted from the summary of his testimony, which was written up in the tendentious manner of a Stalinist prosecutor's brief, Solzhenitsyn, exhausted, fearful of the consequences if he didn't sign, hopeful that he could make the best of the situation, and conforming to "our [national] habit of obedience," signed after a weak remonstrance. He, like the Old Bolsheviks, was playing the part assigned to him (I, 134–42).[33]

What was once called the mystery of the confessions at the show trials is no longer a mystery. The defendants were made to confess as thousands were made to confess centuries earlier in witchcraft trials before religious tribunals that they had made pacts with the devil: their will broken through physical and psychological torture, they were made to do the behest of those who had them in their power. Solzhenitsyn has a fifty-page chapter, "The Interrogation," devoted to the fearsome means of torture used by the NKVD. These were obviously used to the maximum extent for the trials on which the attention of the whole world was focused. The experienced torturers also manipulated most skillfully the kinds of fears and hopes that brought Solzhenitsyn to the signing of the self-incriminating statement, threatening death for those dearest to the defendants if they did not comply and promising them rehabilitation after prison terms if they did comply.[34]

Moreover, as Solzhenitsyn states, many prominent persons were executed without trials, evidently because they could not be brought to participate in the sham trials.[35] Finally, those who had confessed had been broken earlier by the ritualistic self-castigation and recantation in which they engaged in order to keep functioning politically in an increasingly totalitarian society. Solzhenitsyn also points this out, but he does not say that this was an accommodation to Stalinism, entirely foreign to the traditions of the Bolshevik party.

These explanations are, however, not enough for him. He finds the "talented inquiry of Arthur Koestler" to have had "particular success" in solving the "riddle" of the trials (I, 412, 409). Rubashov, the protagonist of Koestler's *Darkness at Noon*, confesses to crimes he did not commit because he suffers a suppressed guilt for the real crimes he did commit for the party, and his false confession is simultaneously, he feels, the last service he can render the party and an expiation for his genuine crimes.

It is easy to see why Rubashov's behavior appeals to Solzhenitsyn as an explanation of the confessions, although in some moods he would deny that Communists are capable of feeling guilt at all, but the psychology of Rubashov is internally inconsistent. Koestler represents him as finally at peace with himself, but how can he be at peace in lying once more for what he has come to realize is a party based on twisted ethics and twisted logic?[36] Moreover, this psychological theory does not explain the confessions of the Menshevik leaders in a 1931 trial that anticipated the purge trials. The French Socialist leader Leon Blum said of these astonishing confessions, which resembled those that were to be made by the Bolsheviks but cannot be explained by postulating a peculiar Bolshevik psychology, "They have confessed volubly, ostentatiously, with a kind of relish for public confession and contrition."[37] The Koestler theory is both unnecessary and dubious as an explanation of the "confessions" at the purge trials. A survivor of the purges told Stephen F. Cohen that for most of the victims at least the theory "would have been the subject of gay mockery."[38]

The Bolshevik defendant against whom Solzhenitsyn levels most of his fire is Bukharin, whom Lenin in his "Testament" had called "the rightful darling of the party." In *The First Circle* Solzhenitsyn suggested (p. 121) a fundamental difference between Stalin and Bukharin: "Most of all, Stalin was wary of people committed to staying poor, like Bukharin. He did not understand their motives." In *The Gulag Archipelago* he finds Bukharin to have been little different from Stalin in his outlook, wanting only to be accepted as an accomplice in Stalin's crimes, as is revealed by his final political statement.

Bukharin just before he was arrested had his twenty-two-year-old wife memorize his statement to posterity, "Letter to a Future Generation of Party Leaders." In 1961, after having spent twenty years in prison camps and exile, she felt that the time was ripe to make this letter public. "[W]hat," Solzhenitsyn asks, "were the last words this brilliant theoretician decided to hand down to future generations? Just one more cry of anguish and a plea to be restored to the Party. . . . And that is how he himself certified that he, too, deserved to plunge into those waves" (I, 417). Bukharin deserved what he got—let us not be moved by his anguish—because he wanted to be restored to the party.

What Solzhenitsyn neglects to say is that Bukharin asked to be reinstated in a party of the future, when it will have been cleansed of monstrous crimes foreign to the tradition of Bolshevism, not in the party of the present. "I feel my helplessness," wrote Bukharin,

> before a hellish machine, which, probably by the use of medieval methods [i.e., torture such as practiced by the medieval czars and the Orthodox Church], has acquired gigantic power, fabricates organized slander. . . . [T]he remarkable traditions of the Cheka have gradually faded into the past, when the revolutionary idea guided all its actions. . . . At present most of the so-called organs of the

NKVD are a degenerate organization of bureaucrats, without ideas, rotten, well-paid, who use the Cheka's bygone authority to cater to Stalin's morbid suspiciousness. . . . I appeal to you, a future generation of Party leaders, whose historical mission will include the obligation to take apart the monstrous cloud of crimes that is growing ever huger in these frightful times . . . I ask a new young and honest generation of Party leaders to read my letter at a Party Plenum, to exonerate me, and to reinstate me in the Party.[39]

Solzhenitsyn attributes Bukharin's false confession to his having been a weakling, to his having "grown used to his ordained role" through repeated capitulations, to his willingness, like Rubashov, to perform any service, no matter how shameful, for the party, to his fear of death, to the promise of a secluded academic life if he complied and to the threat of torture and death if he did not. "And so perhaps there isn't any insoluble riddle?" he asks triumphantly after having presented these conjectures as certainties. Bukharin, caught in the web of Stalinism, was undoubtedly weakened by his ineffectual struggles against it and by his accommodations to it; nevertheless scholars who have studied the matter paint a markedly different picture than does Solzhenitsyn.

While Bukharin was in Paris in 1936, he confided to Boris Nicolaevsky, an emigré Menshevik historian with whom he was friendly, that he expected to be killed on his return. Nevertheless he decided to conduct the struggle as best he could within the Soviet Union and went back. A major reason for his having done so—undoubtedly taken into account by Stalin in sending him abroad—was that he had left behind a father, a brother, a daughter, and other persons close to him, who were in effect hostages for him.[40]

Bukharin's perception of the danger of German fascism as well as the difficulty of political struggle in the Soviet Union must have affected his conduct. In writing of fascism, he counterposed "terrorist dictatorships" using "permanent coercion" to "the principle of socialist humanism," "the freedom of maximum development of the maximum number of people." This counterposition was, both Stephen F. Cohen and the Oxford historian George Katkov declare, in its historical context not only a warning against fascism but a veiled warning against Stalinism.[41]

After having been imprisoned and under the duress of the NKVD for a year, Bukharin finally agreed to make his "confession" when, according to Alexander Orlov, a former high-ranking member of the NKVD, he was told that, if he did not, his wife and infant son would be killed.[42] However, says Cohen, he sought to "turn his trial into a counter-trial."

His strategy was "to make sweeping confessions that he was 'politically responsible' for everything, thereby at once saving his family and underlining his symbolic role [as the representative of 'pre-Stalinist Bolshevism'], while at the same time flatly denying or subtly disproving his complicity in any actual crime." A seemingly casual statement in his closing speech, "The confession of the accused is a medieval principle of jurisprudence," undercut the testimony of the entire trial, which was based solely on such confessions. This view of Bukharin's behavior at the trial was the opinion of the British attaché, Brigadier Fitzroy Maclean, who attended it, and is borne out by the transcript of the proceedings.[43] In carrying through his strategy, Bukharin's conduct was not that of a man terrified by death and desperately trying to escape it. Harold Denny, the correspondent of *The New York Times*, wrote that, although he showed "in his last words" that he "fully expected to die," he was "manly, proud, and almost defiant," turning on his accusers "with flashes of logic and scorn, which held the Court spellbound."[44]

Solzhenitsyn, then, is deficient in his understanding of the purges, which sent millions of people into the camps, and wrong about many of the facts about them. In his discussion of the next great wave of camp prisoners, those who were imprisoned during World War II and immediately after it, he presents two conflicting interpretations of the reasons for it.

Speaking of the former prisoners who in the latter stages of the war fought in Hitler's army, Solzhenitsyn says in Volume III: "The time has come for us to give our views on the Vlasov movement once again. In the first part of this book the reader was not yet prepared for the whole truth . . . There at the beginning, before the reader had traveled the highroad and byroads of the camp world with me, he was merely alerted, invited to think" (III, 27).

What Solzhenitsyn presents as being to all intents and purposes "the whole truth" is that the Vlasovites were representative of the entire Soviet population, which thirsted to take action against a regime that it rightly regarded as the worst in history, worse even than "the regime of its pupil Hitler." Given the opportunity of the war, "the natural impulse of the people was to take a deep breath and liberate itself, its natural feeling one of loathing for its rulers." This explains the stupendous losses of the beginning of the war. Never in history was an army rolled back so rapidly and so much territory, resources, and people lost in such a short time. It was "the instant paralysis of a paltry regime whose subjects recoiled from it as from a hanging corpse." The Vlasov movement was a part of this recoil and indeed redeemed the honor of Russia: "[O]ur folk would have been worth nothing at all, a nation of abject slaves, if it had gone through that war without brandishing a rifle at Stalin's government . . ." (III, 28, 29, 31).

What stymied this elemental movement of the people against the regime was the stupid brutality of the Nazis, whose regime seems not to have been inferior in viciousness to Stalin's regime, after all. Moreover, the Russians innocently trusted the words about democracy of the Allies and thought that they would not abandon them to Stalin after the war.

It would seem, then, that there was good reason from the government's point of view for imprisoning not only the Vlasovites but those who had been in the territories occupied by the Nazis or who had been prisoners of war. With the entire population so seething with revolt, these must have collaborated with the enemy and therefore had to be suppressed lest they continue their overt activity against the regime.

In Volume I, however, the explanation for the imprisonment of these people is said to be found in Stalin's paranoia: "Spy mania was one of the fundamental aspects of Stalin's insanity. It seemed to Stalin that the country was swarming with spies." The many Russian POWs who agreed to act as spies for the German army, however, were "still, in fact, acting very patriotically. . . . Almost to a man, they decided that as soon as the Germans sent them across to the Soviet side, they would turn themselves in to the authorities, turn in their equipment and instructions, and join their own benign command in laughing at the stupid Germans. They would then . . . return to fight bravely in their units." Whereas in the other interpretation of events the entire people knew from experience that their regime was the worst in the world and were eager to fight against it, in this interpretation, the spies, "almost to a man," regarded their army commanders as "benign," little knowing the depths of the government's perfidy, and were eager to resume their brave, patriotic fight against the enemy.

Nor were the Vlasovites animated by a burning need for "brandishing a rifle" against the Russian government.

> The recruiters had explained to them jeeringly—or rather, it would have been jeering if it hadn't been the truth: "Stalin has renounced you! Stalin doesn't give a damn about you!" . . . So they signed up—some of them simply to get out of a death camp, others with the hope of going over to the partisans. . . . Some . . . wanted the chance to speak out about themselves and their awful experience (I, 247, 246, 261).

Even those whose primary reason for joining the Vlasovites was neither to survive nor to find the opportunity to fight once more against the German army did not so much want to take up arms against the Motherland as to "speak out" to their fellow countrymen. Their imprisonment, let alone the imprisonment of the POWs who had not become Vlasovites or of the inhabitants of the occupied territories, was entirely unjustified.

For a far more balanced account of the actual feelings of the Russian people during the war than either of these two contradictory hyperbolic interpretations, we must turn to Alexander Werth's *Russia at War 1941–45*. Werth, the Russian correspondent of the *Sunday Times* of London and the writer of the war-time commentary from the Soviet Union of the BBC, kept a day-to-day record of his observations. Raised in St. Petersburg as a child, he spoke Russian like a native and traveled about freely at a time when foreign correspondents had more access to the people than they ever had under Stalin. He talked to thousands of soldiers and civilians, whom he found utterly uninhibited in what they had to say. His book, enriched by scholarship in addition to his personal experience, is generally acknowledged to be the definitive history of the Soviet Union in the war.

"In the fearful days of 1941–42 and in the next two-and-a-half years of hard and costly victories," writes Werth,

> I never lost the feeling that this was a genuine People's War. . . . It may seem strange today to think that this immense People's War was successfully fought under the barbarous Stalin regime. But the people fought, and fought, above all, for "themselves," that is, for Russia; and Stalin

... succeeded in getting himself almost universally accepted as Russia's *nationalist* leader. . . . Later, he even deliberately singled out the Russians for special praise, rather at the expense of the other nationalities of the Soviet Union, . . . for never having lost faith in the Soviet regime—and, by implication, in Stalin himself. This was one way of saying that, in fighting for Russia, the Russian people also fought for the Soviet system, which is at least partly true. . . .[45]

It was at least partly true because, despite the terror in which Stalin engaged, the Soviet system had given the Russian people a good deal. Even though a parasitic bureaucracy exacted a tremendous toll, there had been an unheard-of advance in production, education, and science, made possible by the nationalization of the means of production and economic planning. As Deutscher says, although Stalin's words extolling labor as heroic and glorious "sounded like mockery to the inmates of the labour camps," they

did not sound so to those more fortunate workers to whom industrialization spelt social advance. Industrial labour and technical efficiency were surrounded by unusual glamour, which made them attractive to the young generation. . . . The doors of technical schools of all grades opened to workers from the bench; and such schools multiplied with extraordinary rapidity. . . . Throughout the thirties the ranks of that new intelligentsia swelled. . . .[46]

Indeed Solzhenitsyn himself, just a few pages before he wrote of "the natural impulse of the people" to "liberate itself" from its loathed rulers, in discussing his own experiences at the front and for the moment freeing himself in this recollection of actual events of his distorting ideological spectacles, spoke of the new working class and the new intelligentsia as supportive of the Soviet system.

Idolization of Stalin, boundless and unquestioning faith, were not characteristic of the whole people, but only of the Party and the Komsomol; of urban youth in schools and universities; of ersatz intellectuals . . . ; and to some extent of the urban petty bourgeoisie (the working class)[47]. . . . All the same, there was an urban minority, and not such a small one, . . . who . . . saw merely a spreading stain of lies . . . (III, 22–23).

Thus in the cities it is only a minority which is now declared to have been opposed to the system.

At the same time it should be said that support of the system did not necessarily mean support of its distortions. As Solzhenitsyn went on to say in explaining his "to some extent" qualification about the working class, workers could not very well have supported the draconian labor laws. Nor did support of the system, although undoubtedly Stalin was widely regarded as a father figure whose sternness was necessary, invariably mean the idolization of Stalin. One university youth, Captain Solzhenitsyn, we may remember, detested Stalin but wrote from the front to his wife that his only thought was what he could do for Leninism.

Moreover, by the late 1930's the social structure of the countryside had acquired a stability it did not have during the period of forced collectivization or immediately after. After that near disaster reforms had been granted which altered the character of the collective farms and caused peasant opposition to die down.[48] The enormous losses at the beginning of the war are, therefore, not to be explained by the opposition to the regime by the population but by the lack of preparedness, the disorganization of the army attendant upon the decapitation of its leadership in the purges, and by the effect of the purges on Soviet society generally.

This is what is indicated by Werth.

> [A]ccording to the current German version, partly supported by certain Americans, it was only afterward, because of German "mistakes," that an anti-German partisan movement developed. . . . The truth is that in the grim months of 1941, following the invasion, everything in the vast newly-occupied territories was in a state of flux and chaos, and very little, if anything, had been done to organize a partisan movement in these parts of the country *in advance.* . . . The lack of arms, much more than any goodwill towards the Germans, explains why there was no major partisan movement in 1941.[49]

The Vlasov forces, says Werth, were formed at the end of 1942, when the German high command adopted the policy "either go into the Vlasov Army or starve." Prior to that, in 1941 and a good part of 1942, the German army made no effort to use Russian manpower. The Vlasov forces were, therefore, an opportunity to survive. Many of their soldiers became "broken in mind and spirit" and degenerated into "cynics and bandits."[50] Many POWs, however, refused to serve Vlasov and were found as corpses or only half-alive at Dachau and Mauthausen.[51]

There was strong opposition to the regime, but it was mostly concentrated in the areas incorporated into the Soviet Union after 1939. In Lithuania, Latvia, Estonia, and the Western Ukraine, "pro-Nazi and other anti-Soviet influences were strong. In these areas the German invasion was either welcomed or suffered with relative indifference."[52] The great majority of Ukrainians and Byelorussians outside of the recently incorporated areas were, however, despite the existence of nationalist opposition, pro-Soviet.

On invading the Caucasus, the Germans sought to woo the various nationalities there, which included peoples who historically were opposed to the Russians. The Soviet bureaucracy itself had misgivings concerning their loyalty. Werth tells of a conversation he had in July 1942 with Konstantin Oumansky, the Soviet ambassador to the United States, in which Oumansky, not without some racist remarks, expressed his concern about how these nationalities would respond to the German presence. "This anxiety, however," Werth comments, "as it turned out, was largely unjustified, all the more so as the Germans stayed only a short time in both the Kuban and the Northern Caucasus, and their policy was, to say the least, a confused and contradictory one. Nevertheless the anxiety was not entirely groundless."[53]

Finally, it should be added, that the Nazis were able to recruit a corps of collaborators to serve in the government of occupation, "people picked from what they considered 'reliable' elements, ex-bourgeois, or ex-kulaks," in all of the occupied territories.[54] Werth says it is uncertain how many of them acted willingly and how many under duress. We know, however, that in the Ukraine and Byelorussia many of the collaborators were guilty of participating in and indeed directing mass murders in the Nazi exterminations.[55]

The picture, then, is not at all so simple as Solzhenitsyn paints it in either of his two interpretations of events. The losses the Soviet Union suffered at the beginning of the war were unprecedented, but so were the victories it gained afterwards. Solzhenitsyn does not explain why the Czarist empire foundered as the result of Russian losses in World War I while the Soviet Union went on to win after its far greater losses in World War II. Russian patriotism alone is not the answer, for the Czar as well as Stalin called on the nation to fight in its name.[56] The difference was that, as Werth says, in World War II the Russian people felt that in fighting for Russia they were fighting for themselves, that is, for all that they had received from the revolution, much as had been taken away by an arbitrary, capricious, and cruel regime.

Nor was it only a matter of morale. The victory over Nazi Germany was made possible by the industrialization of the country, especially in the eastern section, which survived the initial onslaught. Soviet factories produced the military supplies for which the Czar's army was dependent on its allies. Mechanized agriculture had trained the masses of peasants, unlike the Czar's army of muzhiks, for mechanized warfare. From the products of the Soviet educational system were developed in the course of the war a capable cadre of officers. The result was an army that, in Churchill's 1944 words, "tore the guts out of the German Army,"[57] the Eastern front being responsible for eighty percent of the German casualties.

Yet, as we have seen, there were areas of disaffection. Czarist Russia, said Lenin, was "a prison-house of nations." The oppressed nationalities gained from Soviet industrialization and the extension of education but felt aggrieved about being dominated by a centralized Russian bureaucracy. It was recognition of these grievances, not merely paranoia, which caused Stalin to deport whole nations—the Chechens, Ingushi, Karachais, Balkars, Kalmuks, Crimean Tartars, and Volga Germans—to the prison camps. He was proceeding on his ruthless principle of throwing out bushels of apples because one or two apples in each of them were bad—but these "apples" were people, including women, children, and the aged, who suffered because of the disaffection of some.

The same ruthlessness was manifested towards the millions of soldiers who had been captured early in the war and spent a long sojourn in Germany. The regime which in its lack of preparedness had caused millions of soldiers to be encircled took punitive action against them for having permitted themselves to be captured, fearing too that they had been subjected to the temptations of collaborating with the enemy, with it being difficult to tell how far they had in fact collaborated.

This ruthlessness also extended toward those who had been in other foreign countries and who were often likewise interrogated and imprisoned. "Stalin feared," says Solzhenitsyn (I, 238), that "those who had spent any time in Europe . . . might bring European freedom back from their European crusade. . . ." This statement contains a great deal of truth, but it should be added that those who came home from Europe were not in a blaze to change the Soviet Union into a capitalist country. Most of them found the idea that the factories could have private owners free to discard workers as if they were used machines or that people could not get necessary medical care because they did not have the money for it to be repellent.

This is the conclusion to be drawn from the report of two American social scientists writing for the Harvard Project on the Soviet Social System. In extensive interviews in the mid-1950's with 3,000 Soviet emigrés, who could be expected to be more strongly anti-Soviet than the average Russian citizen, they found that "the former Soviet citizen overwhelmingly supports government ownership and control of industry," that "refugees of all social groups respond to contact with American society with a renewed desire for the welfare provisions of Soviet society," and that, although the regime is bitterly hated, "alienation is from the regime rather than from the system."[58] If this is true of those who experienced American society in the 1950's, it must have been even more true of those who had experienced the society of war-torn Europe.

Nevertheless those who returned had their minds shaken up by what they had seen. The lies and exaggerations of the regime were more apparent than ever. They had been told that they were better off than the people of the capitalist countries. The fact that they were not was not the fault of socialism, the Soviet Union, in addition to having to sustain the incubus of its bureaucracy, having started from so far back and having suffered more than other countries in the war, but their standard of living had been represented to them as a triumph of socialist achievement. They saw too that Poles, Czechs, Hungarians, and Yugoslavs had a measure of freedom such as they themselves did not have. The awareness that this perception existed was enough to render suspicious a regime intent on maintaining totalitarian controls after a war that had aroused the dream of a new day in the population at large.

Solzhenitsyn does not provide an explanation of why the new wave of post-war prisoners was succeeded not by the continuing growth of the prison camp system but by the release of millions of prisoners under Khrushchev, but certainly the widespread feeling that the wartime sacrifices must bring a better life could not be disregarded by the new regime. As Pasternak said at the conclusion of *Doctor Zhivago*, "although victory had not brought the relief and freedom that were expected at the end of the war, nevertheless the portents of freedom filled the air throughout the postwar period."[59]

The sense of what had been accomplished and of what was possible was strong. This was already manifested in the last years of Stalin, when prison camp revolts were beginning to shake the system. These, says Solzhenitsyn, were led by young ex-soldiers, with "their war-time élan and belief in themselves" (III, 229) still intact. This is valuable and interesting information, but Solzhenitsyn does not note that similar feelings stirred in the nation outside the camps and had their influence on the decisions of the bureaucracy. "One question," recalled Khrushchev in his reminiscences, "was sure to come up at the [Twentieth] Congress: Why were so many people still in prison and what was to be done about them now? In short, we would have to answer both for what happened while Stalin was alive and for problems stemming from his policies, which were still with us after his death."[60]

The need to solve the problems stemming from Stalin's policies explains de-Stalinization. The Stalinist method of unrelieved terror and unabashed lying would no longer do. The modernization of society has made it necessary for the bureaucracy to institute Gorbachev's glasnost, but the problems inherited from Stalinism can only be solved by a working-class political revolution bringing socialist democracy. This is what Solzhenitsyn, who did not believe that Stalinism could crumble from within, does not understand.

**NOTES**

1. Bernard Bailyn, *The Ideological Origins of the American Revolution* (Cambridge, Mass: Harvard Univ. Press, 1967), p. 287.

2. *The Gulag Archipelago 1918–1956: An Experiment in Literary Investigation I–II*, tr. Thomas P. Whitney (New York: Harper & Row, 1974), I, 35–36.

3. Bertram D. Wolfe, *Lenin and the Twentieth Century* (Stanford, Calif.: Hoover Institution, 1984), p. 179.

4. Marcel Liebman, *Leninism Under Lenin* (London: Merlin Press, 1980), p. 258.

5. Liebman, p. 267.

6. Liebman, pp. 241, 242 and n.

7. Roy Medvedev, *The October Revolution*, tr. George Saunders (New York: Columbia Univ. Press, 1979), p. 43.

8. Liebman explains in a footnote that E.H. Carr states that all the ministers were set free but that Isaac Deutscher and Leonard Shapiro state that only the socialist ministers were released.

9. Liebman, p. 312.

10. The Left S.R.'s, strongly opposed to the Treaty of Brest-Litovsk, sought to set off a new war with Germany by assassinating the German ambassador.

11. Liebman, p. 313.

12. Liebman, p. 313.

13. He does not quote, for instance, Lenin's comment in his report to the All-Union Central Executive Committee on Feb. 2, 1920 on the abolition of the death penalty: "We were forced to use terror because of the terror practiced by the Entente, when strong world powers threw their hordes against us . . . We would not have lasted two days had we not answered these attempts of officers and White Guardists in a merciless fashion; . . . but this was forced upon us by the terrorist methods of the Entente. But as soon as we attained a decisive victory, even before the end of the war, immediately after taking Rostov, we gave up the use of the death penalty and thus proved that we intend to execute our program in the manner that we promised."—Quoted by Nikita Khrushchev, "Appendix 4: Khrushchev's Secret Speech."

14. Cf. Leon Trotsky, *The Revolution Betrayed: What Is the Soviet Union and Where Is It Going?* (Garden City, N.Y.: Doubleday, Doran, 1937), pp. 100–01: "At the 11th Congress of the party, in March 1922, Lenin gave warning of the danger of a degeneration of the ruling stratum. It has occurred more than once in history, he said, that the conqueror took over the culture of the conquered, when the latter stood on a higher level. The culture of the Russian bourgeoisie and the old bureaucracy was, to be sure, miserable, but alas the new ruling stratum must often take off its hat to that culture."

15. *The Gulag Archipelago*, tr. Harry Willetts (New York: Harper & Row, 1978), III, 235.
16. Larissa Reisner, "Svyazhsk," *Leon Trotsky: The Man and His Work* (New York: Merit Publishers, 1969), p. 114.
17. Ernest Mandel, "Solzhenitsyn, Stalinism and the October Revolution," *New Left Review*, No. 86 (July–Aug. 1974), 55.
18. The leader of the cell was sentenced to a year in prison. Without presenting any evidence, Solzhenitsyn expresses doubt that the sentence was carried out.
19. Mandel, pp. 54–55.
20. Roy A. Medvedev, *Let History Judge: The Origins and Consequences of Stalinism* (New York: Knopf, 1971), p. 391.
21. Quoted in Moshe Lewin, "The Social Background of Stalinism," *Stalinism: Essays in Historical Interpretation*, ed. Robert C. Tucker (New York: W.W. Norton, 1977), p. 133.
22. Isaac Deutscher, *Stalin: A Political Biography* (New York: Oxford University Press, 1949), p. 336.
23. Deutscher, p. 358.
24. On this point, what Deutscher has to say (p. 360) is relevant: "What was reasserting itself [under Stalin] was the ferocious spirit of the early, pioneering, empire-building Tsars rather than the later, milder, more 'liberal' spirit of Tsardom in decay."
25. Roy Medvedev, "Solzhenitsyn's *Gulag Archipelago: Part Two*," *Dissent*, 23 (1976), p. 158.
26. One way of doing so was to treat the jailers with dignity. For the only time in Russian history they were permitted to form a trade union and to elect the prison administrators. Cf. *The Gulag Archipelago*, II, 11.
27. This seems to have been one of the few labor camps left at the time. Cf. Medvedev, "Solzhenitsyn's *Gulag Archipelago: Part Two*," 158.
28. Deutscher, pp. 225–27.
29. Khrushchev in his secret speech before the Twentieth Congress revealed that in Stalin's great purge 70 percent of the Central Committee and the major part of those who participated in the party congress just before the purge were put to death. Of these 80 percent had joined the Bolsheviks before 1921.
30. By 1927 only one-quarter of the Communist party consisted of members who had joined the party before 1923. The rest were

new members untrained in its traditions and shaped by "the ever more powerful party machine," which impressed on them new ways of thinking. Moreover, those attracted to the party of the victorious revolution were all too frequently not the same kind of people as those attracted to the party before the revolution. Cf. Leon Trotsky, *Stalin: An Appraisal of the Man and His Influence* (New York: Stein and Day, 1970), p. 385.

31. Trotsky, *The Revolution Betrayed*, p. 105.

32. Medvedev, "Solzhenitsyn's *Gulag Archipelago: Part Two*," p. 161.

33. In Volume II Solzhenitsyn, speaking in the manner of a "born-again" Christian revelling in self-abasement about his former sinfulness in order that he may more triumphantly proclaim that he is now touched by the grace of God, tells of how in labor camp he was inveigled into signing a statement that he would act as an informer. Here too he began by seeking to hold back partly, saying that he would inform against the thieves but not the political prisoners, and ended by agreeing to inform against all the prisoners. He says that he would have undoubtedly had to observe the agreement but was just then fortunately transferred to the sharashka. Again, he is notably gentler on himself than on other informers, of whom he asks, in defending the prisoners' killing them (III, 235), "How can you say that stoolies are human beings?" "Oh, how difficult it is, how difficult it is," he exclaims of himself (II, 367), "to become a human being! Even if you have survived the front and bombing and been blown up by land mines, that's still only the very beginning of heroism." Despite his agreeing to become an informer, he reminds us, he had been a war hero and would in the future rise to greater heights of heroism.

34. Cf. Medvedev, *Let History Judge*, pp. 187–88.

35. Robert C. Tucker states that Boris Nicolaevsky pointed out to him that the three principal defendants in the 1938 trial, Bukharin, Rykov, and Krestinsky, "all had children with whom they were very close, whereas Yenukidze and Kharkhan, both of whom would have been in Stalin's eyes logical candidates for major roles as defendants in this trial, did not. These two men were executed in 1937 without public trial."—"Introduction,"

*The Great Purge Trial*, ed. Robert C. Tucker and Stephen F. Cohen (New York: Grosset & Dunlap, 1965), p. xiin.

36. For a fuller analysis of Koestler's thesis and of his novel generally, see my *Revolution and the 20th-Century Novel* (New York: Monad Press, 1979), pp. 110–30.

37. Leon Blum, *The Moscow Trial and the Labour & Socialist International* (London: 1931), p. 31.

38. Stephen F. Cohen, *Bukharin and the Bolshevik Revolution: A Political Biography 1888–1938* (New York: Oxford University Press, 1980), p. 375.

39. Medvedev, *Let History Judge*, pp. 183–84.

40. Cohen, p. 472, n. 144.

41. George Katkov, *The Trial of Bukharin* (New York: Stein and Day, 1969), p. 94.

42. Alexander Orlov, *The Secret History of Stalin's Crimes* (New York: Random House, 1953), pp. 280–81. Cf. Cohen, p. 375.

43. Cohen, pp. 375–77. Cf. the trial transcript and Tucker's acute analysis of it in his "Introduction" to *The Great Purge Trial*.

44. Cohen, p. 380.

45. Alexander Werth, *Russia at War 1941–45* (New York: Dutton, 1964), pp. xvi–xvii.

46. Deutscher, *Stalin*, pp. 336–37.

47. Like some American political analysts who regard skilled American workers as middle class, Solzhenitsyn says (22n.), "It was in the thirties that the working class merged completely with the petty bourgeoisie, and became its main constituent part."

48. Cf. Deutscher, *Stalin*, p. 331.

49. Werth, pp. 712–13.

50. Werth, p. 704.

51. Werth, pp. 707–08.

52. Werth, p. 145. But even in this region there were "strong pro-Soviet currents among the Latvian working class."—Werth, p. 95.

53. Werth, p. 576.

54. Werth, p. 376.

55. John Loftus, who had a high position in the U.S. Justice Department's Office of Special Investigations, has revealed that thousands of Nazi collaborators in Byelorussia, including war criminals of the worst sort, were recruited as spies and

prospective guerilla troops against the Soviet Union by United States intelligence, beginning in 1945 when World War II was drawing to a close. Cf. his *The Belarus Secret* (New York: Knopf, 1982).

56. Deutscher, *Stalin*, p. 490.
57. Werth, p. xiv.
58. Alex Inkeles and Raymond A. Bauer, *The Soviet Citizen: Daily Life in a Totalitarian Society* (Cambridge, Mass.: Harvard Univ. Press, 1959), pp. 237, 238, 253.
59. Boris Pasternak, *Doctor Zhivago* (New York: New American Library, 1958), pp. 431–32.
60. *Khrushchev Remembers*, p. 345.

# 4. *Lenin in Zurich*: Solzhenitsyn's Portrait of Lenin and the Real Lenin

In *Lenin in Zurich* Solzhenitsyn, while using the methods of the literary artist, which permit him to enter his characters' heads, emphasizes in an author's note that his fictional Lenin's "choice of words" and "way of thinking and acting" are drawn from a study of Lenin's works (p. 269). In a BBC interview he stated: "I gathered every grain of information I could, every detail, and my only aim was to re-create him alive, as he was."[1] Solzhenitsyn's portrait of Lenin is, therefore, to be judged for its historical authenticity as well as its artistry. It is with the former that this chapter will be concerned.

Despite Solzhenitsyn's avowed aim to re-create Lenin as he was, his hatred of Bolshevism caused him to draw a portrait that flies in the face of scholarly opinion, of the historical record, and of the testimony of those who knew him well, including his enemies. Leonard Schapiro's statement of the three character traits of Lenin "so generally accepted" by scholars who have gone through the literature on Lenin "that it is unlikely that they will ever be seriously challenged"[2] furnishes an excellent means of judging Solzhenitsyn's portrait, in which each of these traits is replaced by another opposed to it. Schapiro was a leading historian well-known for his hostility to Bolshevism; his essay appeared in a book published in association with the right-wing Hoover Institution on War, Revolution, and Peace; the publisher of the book was Praeger, which at that time was receiving secret subsidies from the CIA to publish scholarly anti-communist books.[3] His appraisal of Lenin is not, therefore, at all sympathetic, but, since Schapiro is a responsible scholar, in giving the irreducible minimum on Lenin on which scholars agree, he is accurate.

The first of these traits, says Schapiro, is "Lenin's complete dedication to revolution, and the consequent subordination by him of his personal life to the cause for which he was prepared to sacrifice everything or anyone. . . . The second generally accepted characteristic follows from the first: his kindliness on many occasions to individuals, coupled with ruthlessness on other occasions, to the same or different individuals. It simply depended on whether the 'cause' was involved or not. . . . The third characteristic of Lenin which all scholars would now accept was his complete lack of personal vanity or ambition."[4]

This utter lack of vanity or ambition—attested to among others by Arthur Ransome, the *Manchester Guardian* correspondent who had ready access to Lenin, by Pavel Axelrod and Angelica Balabanoff, close associates who became antagonists of his, and by Anatoly Lunacharsky, the Bolshevik leader whose *Revolutionary Silhouettes* objectively presented the strengths and weaknesses of the major figures of Bolshevism[5]—is at sharp variance with the constant preening of himself of Solzhenitsyn's Lenin on his ability and his constant looking down with scorn upon others. When, for instance, he is in despair, he ruminates:

> All his incomparable abilities (appreciated now by everyone in the party, but he set a truer and still higher value on them), all his quickwittedness, his penetration, his grasp, his uselessly clear understanding of world events, had failed to bring him not only political victory but even the position of a member of Parliament in toyland, like Grimm [a Swiss Social Democratic leader]. Or that of a successful lawyer (though he would hate to be a lawyer—he had lost every case in Samara). Or even that of a journalist. Just because he had been born in accursed Russia (p. 108).[6]

The self-satisfaction over the recognition he has achieved but the hunger for a still greater recognition, the loving elaboration of his self-proclaimed "incomparable abilities," the secret envy of the bourgeois careerists he outwardly despises, the blaming of his own failures upon his country—this does not bear any semblance to the Lenin who scholars agree was lacking in vanity and ambition.

When Parvus, whose superiority to himself as a theoretician and man of action Solzhenitsyn's Lenin enviously recognizes in the inner recesses of his being, proposes that they form an alliance to make a revolution with German money, Lenin rejects the idea because he does not want to be superseded. "Oh yes," he thinks, "I understand your Plan! You will emerge as the unifier of all the party groups. Add to that your financial power and your theoretical talent, and there you are—leader of a unified party and of the Second Revolution? Not again?!" (p. 166). Thus the Revolution to which Lenin has dedicated his life is seen to be really a projection of his own ego, something which he will not sacrifice his leadership role to attain. This is not the Lenin who scholars agree would have sacrificed everything for the Revolution.

Looking with scorn at those about him, not only at his opponents but at his associates, whom Solzhenitsyn portrays as rogues Lenin despises but cynically uses, Lenin gives loose in his speech and in his thoughts to a constant stream of vituperation. The historical Lenin, it is well known, did not adhere to the "my respected opponent" manner of parliamentary debate in his polemics and made use of invectives such as "philistine," "renegade," and "lackey of the bourgeoisie" in demolishing his opponents. Solzhenitsyn uses some of the epithets Lenin did and adds some choice ones of his own ("piss-poor slobbering pseudo-socialists," "little shit," "snot-nosed guttersnipes" [pp. 34, 94]). The unremitting flow of vituperation without a single kind word for anyone is indicative of both venomousness and coarseness. Although the correspondence of the real Lenin, as Schapiro observes, "shows his concern for the personal welfare of Bolsheviks and their families even at his busiest time,"[7] there is no hint of this in Solzhenitsyn.

Lenin, says Solzhenitsyn in an authorial comment, "never forgave a mistake. No matter who made it, he would remember as long as he lived" (p. 24). But Bukharin, in his last words to posterity, spoke of Lenin's magnanimity toward those who had been mistaken: "If, more than once, I was mistaken about the methods of building socialism, let posterity judge me no more harshly than Vladimir Il'ich."[8] Gorky, reminiscing on Lenin, exclaimed, "But how many times, in his judgment of people, whom he had yesterday criticized and 'pulled to bits,' did I clearly hear the note of genuine wonder before the talents and moral steadfastness of these people. . . ."[9]

The historical Lenin, moreover, continued to recognize and pay tribute to the past accomplishments of those who became and remained his greatest political enemies. He insisted that Plekhanov, toward whom Solzhenitsyn's Lenin is full of bitter hatred, and Kautsky, whose picture Solzhenitsyn states he cannot look at without retching as though he were swallowing a frog, be published in full and studied. He wrote an obituary for the Left Social Revolutionary P.P. Prosh'ian, who had participated in the S-R insurrection against the Soviet government, in which he said, "Comrade Prosh'ian did more before July, 1918, to strengthen the Soviet regime than he did in July, 1918, to damage it."[10] Lenin's wife Krupskaya tells of how, after he broke with his intimate associate Martov, he eagerly welcomed every position Martov took which he considered worthy of a revolutionist, and of how when he was struggling with his fatal illness he remarked sadly, "They say Martov is dying too."[11] None of this is compatible with the Lenin of Solzhenitsyn's portrait.

Solzhenitsyn's Lenin not only regards both his political enemies and his associates with hatred and contempt; he regards everyone with hatred and contempt: peasants ("as obtuse as peasants the world over" [p. 12]), workers ("the workers had swarmed like ants out of their holes and into legal bodies," disregarding the Bolsheviks [p. 21]), women ("silly bitches" [p. 66]), young people ("these little piglets . . . were . . . so very sure of themselves, so ready to take over the leadership at any moment" [p. 66]). Above all, he despises the Russian people. "Why was he born in that uncouth country?" he asks himself. "Just because a quarter of his blood was Russian [Solzhenitsyn refers to Lenin throughout as an 'Asiatic'], fate had hitched him to the ramshackle Russian rattletrap. A quarter of his blood, but nothing of his character, his will, his inclinations made him kin to that slovenly, slapdash, eternally drunken country" (p. 103).[12]

The real Lenin, however, was not at all contemptuous of ordinary people, talking easily with them and learning from what they had to say. This is attested to not only by Trotsky and Gorky,[13] but by Balabanoff, who writes, "The desire to learn from others was characteristic of him. . . . He would ask peasants about agricultural matters. . . . He did not do it to attract attention or cause sensation, but rather unobtrusively."[14] A number of accounts tell of Lenin visiting a Soviet art school, where he got into an animated exchange with two dozen students, who defended the futurist movement in art and literature against him. Lenin was delighted by the spirit of the youngsters and at the conclusion of the controversy good-naturedly joked that he would go home, read up on the subject, and then come back to defeat them in debate.[15]

The historical Lenin was opposed to the party leadership granting itself special favors. Solzhenitsyn, however, has him make cavalier use of party funds, disbursing them freely to his favorites and stingily to others. "Find somebody to look after the children, we'll pay the expenses out of party funds," he tells Inessa Armand,[16] urging her to attend an international congress, and in the next moment (pp. 25, 26) he thinks of how his associate Hanecki is not going because of his demand for expenses at a time when "party funds must be used carefully." But the real Lenin did not have such control of the money for functionaries' living expenses, and he himself was at times in dire need in his exile. "Lenin's personal finances were stretched," says Robert H. McNeal in his biography of Krupskaya, "and he implored the editors of *Pravda* to pay for Nadezhda's [Krupskaya's] operation. . . . [B]ut they must have let him down, for the request was repeated soon afterwards. . . . "[17]

Tamara Deutscher in her *Not by Politics Alone . . . The Other Lenin* has a letter from Lenin to the office manager of the Council of People's Commissars officially reprimanding him for having raised Lenin's salary from 500 rubles a month to 800 rubles a month contrary to the decision of the Council, of which Lenin was chairperson. In a letter to the Library of the Rumyantsev Museum requesting permission to borrow certain books, Lenin wrote in 1920: "If, according to the rules, reference publications are not issued for home use, could not one get them for an evening, for the night, when the library is closed? *I will return them by the morning* [Lenin's emphasis]."[18]

Lenin's unbending dedication to the Revolution and to revolutionary principles was a source of strength to him as a leader. Another source of strength, says Schapiro, was the combination of his lack of vanity and his "unwavering conviction" that "in any matter in dispute, he alone had the right answer."[19] Solzhenitsyn's Lenin, however, despite his overweening vanity, is haunted by inner doubts. "His self-confidence had failed him [in 1905], and Lenin had skulked through the revolution in a daze. . . . It took years for the ribs dented by Parvus to straighten out again, for Lenin to regain his assurance that he, too, was of some use to the world" (pp. 125–26). But the ribs dented by Parvus were not really straightened out. In 1916, when Parvus boasts to him of having sunk a battleship in 1905, Lenin thinks of himself that he can write, give lectures, influence young leftists, polemicize, but "there was only one thing he was incapable of— *action.*"

His very insecurity makes Solzhenitsyn's Lenin incapable of admitting any error in judgment. "Yes, I made a mistake," he thinks to himself (p. 22). "I was short-sighted, I wasn't bold enough. (But you must not talk like that even to your closest supporter, or you may rob him of his faith in his leader.)" The real Lenin, however, who believed that theory can never keep pace with changing reality, not infrequently admitted in retrospect to having erred. This was especially true at the end of his life when he saw the growth of bureaucracy and of indifference to the rights and needs of the national minorities, to which he felt he had not paid sufficient attention. "In his statements, speeches, and notes made in the last period of his activity expressions such as 'the fault is mine,' 'I must correct another mistake of mine,' 'I am to blame,' are repeated several times,"[20] says Deutscher, quoting from documents in her book.

Beset by secret doubts he cannot voice, made irritable by people, exhausting himself in feverish activity whose value he often questions to himself, Solzhenitsyn's Lenin is a jangle of nerves. Calmed for a moment as he walks along the bank of a Swiss lake, "he realized how hard-pressed and harassed he normally was" (p. 76). But Lunacharsky says of the Lenin he knew that, although at times he drove himself to exhaustion, he knew how to relax so that he emerged from his rest "freshened and ready for the fray again." "In the worst moments that he and I lived through together, Lenin was unshakeably calm and as ready as ever to break into cheerful laughter."[21] The aged Boris Souvarine, one of the founders of the French Communist Party, who knew Lenin well and came to be a strong anti-Bolshevik, is astounded at the feverishness of Solzhenitsyn's Lenin. "Day and night, even in response to the smallest thing, Lenin seems to be whirling. In all this we do not recognize the real Lenin and his habitual self-control."[22]

The readiness to break into cheerful laughter of which Lunacharsky speaks is alien to Solzhenitsyn's Lenin. "Lenin often wore a mocking look," says Solzhenitsyn, "but very rarely smiled" (p. 145). On the occasions he does smile it is a "crooked little grin—suspicious, shrewd, derisory" (p. 167). When it occurs to Hanecki that Lenin's appearance is such that he might readily be taken for a Russian spy, he "wanted to tease him about it, but he knew that Lenin couldn't take a joke, and refrained" (p. 17).

But one of the distinctive characteristics of the real-life Lenin was his gaiety of disposition, which did not permit him to stand on false dignity. Arthur Ransome said of him, "I tried to think of any other man of his caliber who had a similar joyous temperament. I could think of none."[23] Gorky said, "I have never met a man who could laugh as infectiously as Lenin."[24] Trotsky described Lenin as "always . . . even-tempered and gay" and spoke of his "famous laughter."[25] He told of how Lenin, in presiding over small committees, conducted the meetings in an efficient manner but sometimes, especially towards the end of a long, hard session, would be provoked to laughter by something that had amused him. "He tried to control himself as long as he could, but finally he would burst out with a peal of laughter which infected all the others."[26] Even during what Bertram D. Wolfe calls the "bleak years" of his exile, his laughter did not leave him. "Even now he could laugh heartily at times and stir others to hearty laughter. This is testified by all who came in contact with him."[27]

Far from being unduly sensitive, he was ready to laugh at himself. N. Valentinov, an associate of Lenin's early in the century who later broke with him politically, related how on a picnic he observed that Lenin, instead of making a sandwich for himself, rapidly cut off pieces of bread, egg, and sausage and, with the nimble dexterity characteristic of him, popped them successively into his mouth. Valentinov commented on this, comparing Lenin's dexterity with the dexterity with which a character in Tolstoy's *War and Peace* put on his leggings. Instead of taking offense, Lenin found the comparison amusing. "His laughter was so infectious that Krupskaya also started to laugh at the sight of him; then I joined in too."[28] There is no thin-skinned sensitivity here.

Solzhenitsyn's egocentric, dour Lenin, incapable of human warmth and hating everyone, is utterly indifferent to others' suffering. He gleefully reads the figures on Russia's enormous war casualties, seeing them as evidence of the doom of the Czarist regime. The climactic presentation of his indifference to suffering comes at the end of the first chapter of *Lenin in Zurich*, Chapter 22 in *August 1914*. Lenin is on a parapet in a railroad station when a hospital train comes in. The dying are fearfully regarded by a crowd of people come to see if their dear ones are on the train, and the wounded are joyfully embraced. As Lenin surveys the scene, he has no thought for the emotions of the crowd: in a kind of demonic frenzy, he has been seized by the inspiration for his slogan "Convert the war into a civil war!" A civil war "without quarter" that will "bring all the governments of Europe down in ruins!!!" "Daily, hourly, wherever you may be—*protest* angrily and uncompromisingly against this war! But . . . ! (The dialectical essence of the situation.) But . . . will it to continue! See that it does not stop short! That it drags on and is *transformed*! A war *like this one* must not be fumbled, must not be wasted. Such a war is a gift from history!" (p. 37).

Remarkably, Lenin is made responsible for the continuation of the war. He will "will it to continue." How can he, however great his willpower, achieve this extraordinary feat? Earlier he had thought to himself, "You must find channels for negotiations, covertly reassure yourself that if difficulties arise in Russia and she starts suing for peace, Germany will not agree to peace talks, will not abandon the Russian revolutionaries to the whim of fate" (p. 35). The unknown emigré will somehow influence the German government not to free itself from one front in a two-front war in order not to "abandon the Russian revolutionaries." This simply does not make sense.

Not only is the responsibility for the war foisted from the warring governments upon Lenin, but the bloodiness of the Russian Civil War is attributed to the bloodthirstiness of Lenin. The White forces and the allied governments that supported them are absolved of all responsibility. Lenin's denunciations of the war are dismissed as mere verbiage to mask his sinister design. He is incapable of genuine moral indignation.

Lenin undoubtedly was, as Schapiro says, ruthless in the defense of the revolution. The question is, however, whether Lenin was like a humane surgeon who cuts off a limb to save a life or like the Nazi doctors who engaged in cruel experimentation without any regard for their concentration-camp victims. How one judges his acts will depend in good part upon one's own politics. Many who condemn as the acts of a fanatic such measures as holding hostages subject to execution to break the opposing side's will do not feel the same way about the fire-bombing of Dresden or the atomic bombing of Hiroshima and Nagasaki in World War II, which killed innumerably more innocent people. But however one regards his actions, serious scholars do not find Lenin to have been the totally unfeeling person Solzhenitsyn makes him out to be.

Thus Peter Reddaway, co-editor with Leonard Schapiro of *Lenin: The Man, The Theorist, The Leader*, while speaking of the "fanaticism" of Lenin's "revolutionary morality," speaks also of

> the human side of Lenin, which he had to keep so rigidly under control. This is the Lenin of whom Lepeshinsky said: "He possesses a remarkably tender soul, not lacking, I would say, even a certain sentimentality"; who rebuked Bogdanov with the words: "Marxism does not deny, but, on the contrary, affirms the healthy enjoyment of life given by nature, love and so on"; who, as a youth, suddenly saw he must not become a farmer because "my relations with the peasants are becoming abnormal"; who could not shoot a fox because "really she was so beautiful"; who told Gorky: "It is high time for you to realize that politics are a dirty business"; and who said in E. Zozulya's presence: "O happy time, when there will be less politics."[29]

Indeed Gorky, whom Wolfe credited, as we have seen, with being artistically faithful in his depiction of Lenin, presented him as feeling most keenly the suffering of the oppressed. "In a country where the inevitability of suffering is recommended as the universal road to the 'salvation of the soul,'" wrote the author of *The Lower Depths*, himself so sensitive to human misery, "I never met, I do not know a man who hated, loathed and despised human unhappiness, grief, and suffering as strongly and deeply as Lenin did."[30]

The indifference to others' suffering as well as the other traits which Solzhenitsyn gives Lenin—vanity, ambition, coarseness, and unforgivingness, a sense of inferiority (at least, with regard to Parvus), readiness to use and dispense special privileges, readiness to take personal offense, unwillingness to admit mistakes—are, interestingly enough, those that he gives to Stalin in *The First Circle* and that were indeed part of Stalin's character. Solzhenitsyn regards Stalin as the legitimate political heir of Lenin, and this opinion is reflected in his projecting the personal traits of the heir upon his predecessor.

There is another person beside Stalin who, without Solzhenitsyn being aware of it, acted as a model for Solzhenitsyn's portrait of

Lenin—Solzhenitsyn himself. "The picture of a lonely and unheeded prophet," says Scammell (p. 943),

> self-centered, short-tempered, miserly with his time ("a single wasted hour made Lenin ill"), suspicious of others, virtually friendless, cut off from his homeland, and dreaming of leaving his wife for another woman seemed uncannily close to certain biographical details in the life of the author—breathtakingly so to those who knew him well—and there was much comment among Russian readers about Solzhenitsyn's psychological identification with his revolutionary predecessor and ideological opponent.

But, working in the very Zurich in which Lenin had worked, with the same object of undermining the Russian government, Solzhenitsyn unconsciously identified Lenin with himself not only in the personal realm but in the political realm.

Just as his Lenin believes himself (p. 19) to be "the infallible interpreter" of a "compelling power which manifests itself through him," so Solzhenitsyn in his self-revelatory *The Oak and the Calf* marvels at his own ability to "hold out single-handed, yes, and fork over mountains of work" and exclaims: "Where do I get the strength? From what miraculous source?" He answers himself some pages later: "How wise and powerful is thy guiding hand, O Lord!" (p. 297). Even the style of Lenin's interior monologues is similar to that of Solzhenitsyn's memoir, making free use of parenthetical interjections, italics, and exclamation points to convey febrile excitement. Lenin's confrontation with Parvus, in which each of them seeks to penetrate the mask of the other, resembles Solzhenitsyn's description of his confrontation with his wife, who he is convinced has become a KGB agent.

Solzhenitsyn regards himself as alone in knowing how to combat the present Russian regime. Of the efforts of the other dissidents he is scornful. He regards the "soft" Tvardovsky, the editor through whom he had been published, in much the same way that his Lenin regards the Mensheviks.

Just as Solzhenitsyn's Lenin is contemptuous of the Russian people, so the erratic Solzhenitsyn in one passage is contemptuous of them: "We spent ourselves in one unrestrained outburst in 1917, and then we *hurried* to submit. We submitted with *pleasure*! . . . We purely and simply *deserved* everything that happened afterward" (*The Gulag Archipelago*, I, 13n.). Just as Lenin rejoices in World War I as an opportunity for revolution, so Solzhenitsyn relates how he longed in prison camp for the United States to use its monopoly of the atomic bomb to start a new war against the Soviet Union: "World war might bring us a speedier death or it just might bring freedom. In either case, deliverance would be much nearer than the end of a twenty-five-year sentence" (*The Gulag Archipelago*, III, 47–48). Just as his Lenin was ready to serve the Kaiser against Russia, so Solzhenitsyn praises and justifies the Red Army soldiers who fought in the ranks of Hitler's army after having been captured, himself making the explicit comparison: "Came the time when weapons were put in the hands of these people, should they have . . . allowed Bolshevism to outlive itself . . . ? . . . No, the natural thing was to copy the methods of Bolshevism itself: it had eaten into the body of a Russia sapped by the First World War, and it must be defeated at a similar moment in the Second" (*The Gulag Archipelago*, III, 27–28).

The feverish energy, sectarianism, and fanaticism of Solzhenitsyn's Lenin is, then, a mirror image of Solzhenitsyn's feverish energy, sectarianism, and fanaticism. How does Solzhenitsyn explain the triumph of his "mad sectarian" (p. 165) Lenin? He gives more than one answer to this question in *Lenin in Zurich*, in *August 1914*, and in his political works. These answers I shall discuss in the next chapter. In this chapter I shall confine myself to one of the answers, that German money, channeled through Parvus, was of immense aid in making the Revolution, for it is relevant to Solzhenitsyn's mode of research concerning Lenin.

Lenin, as we have seen, fearful of Parvus superseding him and also of the deal being discovered and his reputation destroyed, refused Parvus's offer of German money. Subsequently, however, the Bolsheviks—despite the historical Lenin's bitter attacks on Parvus as a "social patriot" and "lackey of Hindenberg"—are said to have accepted vast sums from him, enabling them "quickly to reinforce their press and their membership, which were ineffectual and low in February 1917," and to pay "tavern scroungers" to start strikes and riots and to acquire "weapons" and "people capable of using these weapons to kill" (pp. 286, 174–75, 145).

In his article already cited, Boris Souvarine asks: "One can detest Lenin but is that a reason for violating the truth?"[31] Far from the alleged events Solzhenitsyn describes having been "carefully concealed from history," with "little attention" having been paid to them "because of the direction of development taken by the West,"[32] as he asserts, there has been a vast tendentious literature purporting to show that Lenin was a German agent. This literature, however, has been thoroughly exploded by two American professors, Alfred Erich Senn and Alexander Dallin. Senn proved that "an impartial analysis of both the pertinent 'documents' and related commentaries reveals the absence of any proofs [of German financing of the Bolsheviks]." His close examination of Parvus's Swiss bank records confirmed the analysis of Dallin, a Senior Fellow at the Hoover Institution, which showed that "Parvus duped his [German] money-lenders and that no serious evidence exists"[33] of the financing he claimed to have engaged in.

Parvus, says Souvarine, was "an original thinker" and "a talented Marxist writer,"[34] but he became more and more a charlatan and a megalomaniac. He did not play a major role in the 1905 revolution, and the biography of him by Z.A.B. Zeman and W.B. Scharlau, like the other works to which Solzhenitsyn expresses his indebtedness, is "tainted": it "is filled with errors, inaccuracies, false allegations, and insinuations; my article 'L'or et le wagon' points out a goodly number."[35]

"Any impulse to explain [the October Revolution] in terms of German money," Souvarine concludes, "will, on reflection, appear puerile and absurd to Solzhenitsyn, whose sincerity is beyond question."[36] The editors of *Dissent*, in which Souvarine's article on Solzhenitsyn appeared, stated that they were sending a copy to Solzhenitsyn with an invitation to comment. No comment by him appeared, probably one reason being that *Dissent* is a social demo-cratic journal, but three years later a reply to Souvarine by Solzhenitsyn appeared in a Parisian Russian-language periodical.

Souvarine had referred to "respectable but not infallible Lenin haters, whose judgment is clouded by passion" and to "short-sighted Leninophobes," but he had made clear his own strong opposition to Leninism, which was of long duration:

> To charge Lenin with inexpiable grievances is more than legitimate if one considers only his pseudodictatorship of the proletariat—or his creating and then entrusting to Stalin

a monstrous state apparatus for coercion that is without historical precedent. Solzhenitsyn has performed a distinguished service by proclaiming the truth about Lenin's liabilities. But this is no reason for thereafter relating stories that have nothing to do with history under the cover of writing a novel with historical pretensions.[37]

Solzhenitsyn's reply, however, takes the form of a fierce attack on Souvarine: "You can scarcely conceal your admiration for this great Villain. Several times you let slip such expressions as 'Lenin's denigrators,' 'Lenin-haters,' 'slanderers'—but only Virtue can be slandered or denigrated. And how can anyone blacken Lenin's name more than he himself did . . . ?"[38] His reasoning is that since nothing one can say about Lenin can be worse than what he was guilty of, one can say about him whatever one pleases, regardless of whether it can be substantiated.

Not content with making Souvarine a secret admirer of Lenin, he goes on to call him a defender of what Souvarine had described as "a monstrous state apparatus for coercion": "In 1921–23, when you occupied a leading position in the Comintern . . . it may be that your youth prevented you from grasping what was happening. But today, . . . it is morally inadmissible to go on sowing the same old seeds in new generations, and to regard Lenin's Terror as 'historically justified.' " In actuality, Souvarine did not use the words "historically justified," which Solzhenitsyn encloses in quotation marks as if they were Souvarine's, nor had he in any way suggested such a justification.

As for the substance of Solzhenitsyn's reply, Scammell fairly summarizes his argument (p. 945): "[I]n the end it came down to whom you believed, and he preferred his authorities to the ones Souvarine had cited." Souvarine responded with an article calmly listing the flaws in the points Solzhenitsyn cites from his sources and in his interpretation of them.

Again, Solzhenitsyn replied with vituperation: Lenin was "the greatest villain in Russian and world history," and how, then, could Souvarine "use the word 'exculpate' with reference to this murderer of millions . . . ?"[39] But in the only sentence to which Solzhenitsyn could have been referring—"Parvus's biography, upon which Solzhenitsyn draws extensively, completely exonerates Lenin and his supporters (p.

181)"—Souvarine was speaking only of the question of Lenin having been a German agent, not about any other of his alleged crimes.

In his second response Solzhenitsyn for the most part simply reiterates the integrity of his sources and the validity of his interpretation of the documentary materials. He does not attempt to rebut Souvarine's analysis of them. For instance, in answering Solzhenitsyn's statement that German money enabled the Bolsheviks to flood the country with anti-war propaganda that far exceeded what the pro-war parties were able to put out, Souvarine said:

> Leonard Schapiro, a reliable historian, has counted some forty newspapers (not hundreds, as Solzhenitsyn rashly asserts), and these were ephemeral little newssheets of between two and four pages, many of which only ran to a few issues. In this regard, the socialist patriots of all hues published a hundred times more. Contrary to what Solzhenitsyn tells us, Lenin's opponents had enormous sums of money at their disposal. I have already . . . referred to Oliver Radkey's book, which gives precise figures. . . . [40]

Disregarding Souvarine's refutation of his previous statement, Solzhenitsyn repeats it: "This money . . . enabled the Bolsheviks . . . to publish hundreds of newspapers and pamphlets in editions large enough to demoralize an army of ten million men in the space of three months. . . ."[41]

Instead of perceiving the ridiculousness of the idea that ten million mostly illiterate soldiers could be demoralized in three months because anti-war forces supposedly issued more printed propaganda than did pro-war forces, Solzhenitsyn sees the Russian soldiers turning against the perpetrators of the war they hated as evidence that the volume of Bolshevik propaganda must have been so huge that it can be explained only by German money. The exercise of critical intelligence in the evaluation of evidence offered by differing "authorities" is clearly unnecessary as far as Solzhenitsyn is concerned; one simply selects statements that assert what one believes. It is no wonder that his Lenin bears so little resemblance to the real Lenin.

# NOTES

1. Solzhenitsyn, *Warning to the West*, tr. H.T. Willetts (New York: Farrar, Straus and Giroux, 1976), p. 113.

2. Leonard Schapiro, "Lenin after Fifty Years," *Lenin: The Man, The Theorist, The Leader: A Reappraisal*, ed. Leonard Schapiro and Peter Reddaway (New York: Praeger, 1967), p. 6.

3. For CIA subsidies to Praeger, see David Wise, *The American Police State* (New York: Random House, 1976), p. 200.

4. Schapiro and Reddaway, pp. 6–7.

5. Arthur Ransome in Albert Rhys Williams, *Lenin: The Man and his Work* (New York: Scott and Seltzer, 1919), p. 173; Angelica Balabanoff, *Impressions of Lenin* (Ann Arbor: Univ. of Mich. Press, 1965), p. 121; Anatoly Vasilievich Lunacharsky, *Revolutionary Silhouettes* (New York: Hill and Wang, 1967), p. 67. Axelrod is quoted in Bertram D. Wolfe, *Three Who Made a Revolution* (Boston: Beacon Press, 1960), p. 122.

6. Solzhenitsyn here distorts by both omission and commission. In a year and a half, studying by himself, Lenin was able to pass the bar examination, which was normally taken after four years of law school study, coming in first among 134. In ten months he appeared as counsel for the defense ten times, seven of them by court appointment, in open-and-shut cases of petty crime in which the court routinely delivered verdicts of guilt. The one case which he undertook as a prosecutor he won. He gave up law not because he was a failure at it but because he had become a revolutionist. Cf. Leon Trotsky, *The Young Lenin* (Garden City, N.Y.: Doubleday, 1972), pp. 170, 178–79, and Wolfe, *Three Who Made a Revolution*, pp. 86–87. Although Wolfe wrote *Three Who Made a Revolution* as an opponent of Bolshevism, it is a work of rigorous and honest scholarship. He was not always so objective afterwards.

7. Schapiro and Reddaway, p. 7. Cf. Maxim Gorky, *Lenin* (Edinburgh: University Texts: 1, Oxford Univ. Press, 1967), p. 45. Gorky's book was used for hagiographical purposes by Stalin's regime, but it was not itself hagiographical. The consequence was that many passages such as Gorky's relating of a conversation in which Lenin praised Trotsky were censored. Bertram D. Wolfe said of Gorky's *Lenin* that it revealed its "faithfulness to himself as an artist and observer of his subject." Cf. his *The Bridge and the*

*Abyss: The Troubled Friendship of Maxim Gorky and V.I. Lenin* (New York: Praeger, 1967), p. 165.

8. Medvedev, *Let History Judge*, p. 183.
9. Gorky, p. 46.
10. Medvedev, *Let History Judge*, p. 344.
11. N.K. Krupskaya, *Reminiscences of Lenin* (Moscow: Foreign Language Publishing House, 1959), p. 99.
12. Wolfe says (*Three Who Made a Revolution*, p. 44) that Lenin's "family, Great-Russians, had some Tartar blood in their veins."
13. Trotsky, p. 195 and Gorky, p. 20.
14. Balabanoff, p. 121.
15. For one account of this incident by a participant, see Tamara Deutscher, *Not By Politics Alone . . . the Other Lenin* (London: Allen & Unwin, 1973), pp. 188–91.
16. Solzhenitsyn makes Armand out to be Lenin's mistress and the one person in the world on whom he is dependent and who might conceivably have humanized the grimly puritanical fanatic if she had not left him. Whether or not Lenin had an affair with Armand (Robert H. McNeal, *Bride of the Revolution: Krupskaya and Lenin* [Ann Arbor: Univ. of Michigan Press, 1972], p. 35, believes it is possible but not certain), it is clear from McNeal's biography of Krupskaya and from Bertram D. Wolfe's biographical essay on Armand (*Strange Communists I Have Known* [New York: Stein and Day, 1965], pp. 138–64) that Solzhenitsyn's depiction of the psychological relationships is completely off. His contrast between the compliant slavey Krupskaya and the strong-willed, independent Armand is false. Krupskaya was no mere drudge; she conducted a "remarkable one-woman operation as the center of a fairly complicated and effective network of agents" (McNeal, p. 101). Although she was not a political leader, she did not hesitate to disagree with Lenin on politics in public (McNeal, pp. 145, 173). Lenin did not merely put up with her, at times impatiently, as Solzhenitsyn has it; he behaved toward her solicitously and lovingly. Cf. McNeal, p. 148. Armand was not, as Solzhenitsyn presents her, a diversion from Lenin's revolutionary activity. She was as devoted to the revolutionary cause as he and Krupskaya. Far from being his tutor, she was his devoted pupil.
17. McNeal, pp. 148–49.
18. Deutscher, pp. 188–91.

19. Schapiro and Reddaway, p. 7.
20. Deutscher, p. 43.
21. Lunacharsky, pp. 43, 41.
22. Boris Souvarine, "Solzhenitsyn and Lenin," *Dissent*, 24 (1977), 234.
23. Williams, p. 173.
24. Gorky, p. 23.
25. Trotsky, *My Life* (New York: Charles Scribners Sons, 1930), p. 470; Trotsky, *Portraits: Political and Personal* (New York: Pathfinder Press, 1977), p. 59.
26. Trotsky, *Lenin: Notes for a Biographer* (New York: Putnam, 1971), p. 172.
27. Wolfe, *Three Who Made a Revolution*, pp. 482, 483.
28. Nikolay Valentinov, *Encounters with Lenin* (New York: Oxford Univ. Press, 1968), p. 82.
29. Schapiro and Reddaway, p. 62.
30. Gorky, p. 29.
31. Souvarine, p. 333.
32. *Lenin in Zurich*, p. 270. Solzhenitsyn is referring, as he makes clear elsewhere, to what he takes to be the decadent West's indifference to the dangers of communism.
33. Souvarine, p. 331.
34. Souvarine, p. 329.
35. Souvarine, p. 330.
36. Souvarine, p. 336.
37. Souvarine, pp. 325, 328, 329. Leaving aside Souvarine's simplistic description of Lenin's regime, which agrees with Solzhenitsyn's and which I have already discussed, one must state that Souvarine himself is here guilty of inaccuracy. Lenin did not entrust the state apparatus to Stalin: in his Last Testament, he warned that Stalin had gathered too much power into his hands and should be removed from his post as General Secretary.

# 5. The Prophet of Anti-Communism: Solzhenitsyn's Political Speeches and Writing

Solzhenitsyn's political speeches in the United States, with their questioning of democracy and their attacks on Enlightenment values, dismayed his liberal admirers. His call for a crusade against communism, on the other hand, endeared him to members of the American Right, but even they were ill at ease with his Russian messianism and worried that his critical observations on American society undermined the popularity and prestige he had gained as a prophet of anti-communism by his struggle against the Soviet bureaucracy and by the revelations in *The Gulag Archipelago*. Thus the arch-conservative *National Review* wrote after his Harvard commencement address: "Solzhenitsyn's great power resides in his fidelity to the truth. . . . Suspect assertions and faulty translations can only erode such authority."[1]

Nevertheless, although much of what he said was regarded as impolitic, the anti-communist clichés which he voiced were subscribed to by both liberals and conservatives. Volumes could of course be written on the issues he has raised, the issues of the Cold War, about which he was influenced by the United States radio stations beamed at the Soviet Union, to which he had been an avid listener. I shall seek, however, to be concise, merely indicating his shallowness, ignorance, and flagrant inaccuracy.

The chief themes with which Solzhenitsyn has been concerned are the intellectual bankruptcy and immorality of Marxism, its coming to power in Russia through an accident of history and its imposition on the Russian people of a system alien to it, the dangers of communism to the world, and the weaknesses and lack of resolve of the West that make it vulnerable to these dangers. I shall take these up in order.

102

Marxism, says Solzhenitsyn, claims to be a science. But all of its predictions based on its supposed scientific understanding have proven wrong. "[E]ven the social sciences can predict an event," but Marxism

> has never made any such forecasts. . . . [I]t was claimed that the conditions of the working class in the West would get . . . more and more unbearable until the workers would be reduced to total poverty. . . . Or the famous prediction that Communist revolutions would all begin in such advanced countries as England, France, America, Germany . . . Or the prediction that as soon as capitalism would be over-thrown, the state would at once wither away. . . . Or the prediction that . . . as soon as communism is introduced, all wars will come to an end.[2]

Marxism has been wrong in these and all its other predictions because its method is so crude. "All that is subtle in human psychology and in the structure of society . . . is reduced to crude economic processes" (*Detente*, p. 54). It is, in fact, "a discredited and bankrupt doctrine."[3]

What Solzhenitsyn presents as Marxism is really a caricature of it. Marxism is a far more sophisticated and complex method of analysis than simplistic economic reductionism. Without adding a disquisition to the many written on the subject, it is enough to quote Engels to demonstrate that the crudity Solzhenitsyn finds in Marxism is his own vulgarization of it:

> Political, juridical, philosophical, religious, literary, artistic, etc., development is based on economic development. But all these react upon one another and also upon the economic base. It is not that the economic position is the *cause and alone active*, while everything else has a passive effect. There is, rather, interaction on the basis of the economic necessity, which *ultimately* always asserts itself.[4]

Solzhenitsyn seems utterly unaware of the major contributions Marxism has made in the various academic disciplines, not only through the work of prominent Marxists but through that of those who, while not themselves Marxists, have been influenced by Marxism. Thus in the field of religious history, a subject which more than any other he thinks can only be hurt by Marxism's gross touch, there have been Max Weber's celebrated *The Protestant Ethic and the Spirit of*

*Capitalism* and R.H. Tawney's equally celebrated *Religion and the Rise of Capitalism*, books which, whatever disagreements Marxists may have with them, establish a relationship between a socio-economic formation and religion. They are, says Christopher Hill, a Marxist who is himself the leading living expert on Puritanism and one of the foremost historians in the world, indebted to Marx and Engels for their perception of Puritanism as the religion of the bourgeoisie.[5]

Marx and Engels spoke of their socialism as "scientific" to differentiate it from the socialist Utopias that had been constructed by Fourier and Owen and from earlier yearnings for socialism. Their socialism, they believed, was based on a study of the trends within capitalism that would eventuate in a working-class revolution leading to socialism. Just as natural science tests its theories, developing them or discarding them in accordance with experience, so they presented not a dogma, as Solzhenitsyn would have it, but a method of inquiry and a constantly evolving doctrine.

This was realized by the best of their followers. "We do not in any way," said Lenin, "regard Marx's theory as something final and inviolable, we are convinced, on the contrary, that it only laid the cornerstone of the science which socialists *must push* further in all directions, if they do not wish to be left behind by life."[6] Because life is always changing, discernible trends being superseded by other trends previously secondary but then gaining ascendancy, Marxism cannot be an unchanging dogma. Theory must always seek to catch up with life.

The main lines of development of modern capitalism analyzed in that youthful seminal work of genius, *The Communist Manifesto*, have been proven remarkably valid. These include the growth of big business, the concentration of wealth, the periodic breakdowns of the system in crises of "over-production," and the expansion of the world market, resulting in the shaking up of somnolent civilizations all over the world.

Today, according to the most recent available statistics, the twenty biggest manufacturing corporations in the United States hold 25% of all assets, and the 200 biggest corporations hold 56% of all assets.[7] A study commissioned by the Federal Reserve Board in 1983 found that "the wealthiest top 10 percent . . . own 84 percent of this nation's assets" and that "the richest one percent . . . own half of the country's wealth."[8] The crises of "over-production," of course, continue to recur, throwing millions of people out of work, although from time to time the economists employed by capitalism have announced that this problem has been solved[9]; indeed, millions of unemployed, formerly present in such numbers only during periods of depression, have become part of the economic scene in "prosperity" as well as depression. As for the expansion of the world market, this is self-evident, with the advanced capitalist countries benefitting from the unequal terms of trade with dependent capitalist countries in a system of neo-colonialism in which products costing enormous pain and sweat are exchanged for the products of automated factories.

While the accuracy of the main lines of development of capitalism sketched in *The Communist Manifesto* and elaborated on in Marx's *Capital* is unique in nineteenth-century literature, "this does not imply," wrote Trotsky on the occasion of *The Communist Manifesto*'s ninetieth anniversary, "that, after ninety years of unprecedented development of productive forces and vast social struggles, the *Manifesto* needs neither corrections nor additions. . . . However, as is evidenced by historical experience itself, these corrections and additions can be successfully made only by proceeding in accord with the method lodged in the foundations of the *Manifesto* itself."[10]

Among the corrections and additions to the *Communist Manifesto* that Marxists made were Trotsky's *Results and Prospects* (1906), developed and elaborated in *The Permanent Revolution* (1930), and Lenin's *Imperialism* (1917). Trotsky showed how the advanced capitalist countries, while introducing features of capitalism into the backward countries, blocked their development so that land reform, democracy, and the other characteristics of capitalist revolution could only be achieved there through working-class revolutions. "It is possible," he wrote in 1906, "for the workers to come to power in an economically backward country sooner than in an advanced country."[11] Working-class revolution in backward countries can set off the process of revolution in advanced countries, but to attain socialism there is needed the victory of working-class revolution in the advanced capitalist countries, for socialism is predicated on an economy of abundance rising from an internationally integrated, technically advanced economy.

Lenin's *Imperialism* showed how the "super-profits" derived from the exploitation of entire nations through the advanced capitalist countries' monopolistic position in the world market enabled them to "corrupt certain sections of the working class," a "labor aristocracy," and "win them over to the side of the bourgeoisie."[12] While, therefore, Trotsky found it entirely possible that working-class revolution would come first in backward countries, Lenin explained the existence of a brake on revolution in the advanced countries. This does not mean, of course, that they denied the possibility of revolution in advanced countries, any more than Marx, who speculated on the possibility of a proletarian revolution in Russia, ruled out the possibility of revolution in the backward countries.[13] For Marxism is not the schematic dogma that Solzhenitsyn regards it as being.

So too Marxism never predicted, as Solzhenitsyn alleges, an instant transformation of humanity "as soon as communism is introduced" so that "the state would at once wither away" and "all wars" would "come to an end." It does not believe in miracles by decree but in change occurring through processes. As early as *The Communist Manifesto*, imbued though it is with revolutionary optimism, Marx and Engels pointed out that, while "national differences and antagonisms between peoples" will disappear when "the proletariat," "of the leading civilized countries at least," becomes "the leading class of the nation," this will not come all at once. "In proportion as the exploitation of one individual by another is put an end to, the exploitation of one nation by another will also be put an end to. In proportion as the antagonism between the classes within the nation vanishes, the hostility of one nation to another will come to an end."[14]

Marx later wrote, "Bourgeois law . . . is inevitable in the first phase of communist society," and Lenin, commenting on this sentence, added, "[U]nder Communism not only will bourgeois law survive for a certain time, but also even a bourgeois state without the bourgeoisie!" Trotsky explained the paradox of a bourgeois state without a bourgeoisie: "Insofar as the state," in order to stimulate the economy,

> is compelled to defend inequality—that is, the material privileges of a minority—by methods of compulsion, insofar does it also remain a "bourgeois" state, even though without a bourgeoisie. . . . [T]he poorer the society which issues from a revolution, . . . the more crude would be the forms assumed by bureaucratism, and the more dangerous would it become for socialist development.[15]

This is why the victory of the proletariat in "the leading civilized countries at least" is necessary for the state to wither away and for wars to end, since its coercive powers will no longer be needed, as antagonisms within and without decline.[16]

Finally, as to Marx's supposed prediction that the workers in capitalist countries "would be reduced to total poverty," Marx never said this. "The 'theory of absolute impoverishment,' " says the Marxist economist Ernest Mandel in his *Marxist Economic Theory*, which was described by the London *Economist* as "by far the best popularization of Marx's economic theory that has appeared for forty or fifty years," "is not to be found in Marx." It was attributed to him by Social Democrats intent on revising him and by Stalinists intent on telling Russian workers that the workers in capitalist countries were worse off than they.

> What one finds in Marx is an idea of the absolute impoverishment not of the workers, the wage-earners, but of the section of the proletariat which the capitalist system *throws out* of the production process: unemployed, old people, disabled persons. . . . Periodical absolute impoverishment of the unemployed and other victims of the capitalist production process; more or less general relative impoverishment of the proletariat (i.e., increase in real wages which over a long period is less than the growth in social wealth and the average productivity of labour): these are the laws of development for the working class under the capitalist system.[17]

It is not from workers being "reduced to total poverty" that Marx and Engels expected revolution to occur. This would probably lead to demoralization rather than revolution. They expected revolution to come, as *The Communist Manifesto* clearly states, from the workers, despite the many things that set them in opposition to each other, being organized by capitalism itself into acting as a class that becomes conscious of its strength in unity, from the instability they are subjected to by recurring economic crises, from the manifest absurdity of unused industrial capacity and the enforced idleness of the unemployed in the midst of worldwide need.

Solzhenitsyn, then, can scarcely be said to have proven the intellectual bankruptcy of Marxism; he does not do better at proving its immorality. "*The Communist Manifesto*," he told the AFL-CIO chieftains, " . . . which almost no one ever takes the trouble to read, contains even more terrible things than what has actually been done. ... The whole world can read, ... but somehow no one wants to understand" (*Detente*, p. 52). One would think that, having said this, Solzhenitsyn would have gone on to enlighten his audience concerning the terrible things in *The Communist Manifesto* that have so escaped notice, but he simply dropped the subject without specifying the things that are apparently too terrible to describe.

Fortunately, however, a co-thinker of his, Igor Shafarevich, whose *Socialism* Solzhenitsyn has said to be "a brilliant book" and "a profound analysis" (*Detente*, p. 9), has been more explicit. In his "Socialism in Our Past and Future" in *From Under the Rubble*, a book which Solzhenitsyn edited and to which he contributed, Shafarevich wrote:

> [A]nybody reading *The Communist Manifesto* with an open mind will be surprised at the amount of space devoted to the destruction of the family, to the rearing of children away from their parents in state schools, to wife-sharing. In their arguments with their opponents the authors nowhere renounce these propositions, but try to prove that these principles are higher than those on which the bourgeois society of their time is based.[18]

This statement is remarkable on several counts. In the first place, the amount of space in *The Communist Manifesto* devoted to the subject of the family is only a little more than one page out of twenty-nine pages. This does not seem excessive, especially if we consider that Marx and Engels are answering one of the favorite canards of the time against communists, the canard that they would introduce "the community of women." In the second place, one could not tell from Shafarevich that Marx and Engels charge that "wife-sharing" is precisely the principle on which the bourgeois family of their time, in which capitalists impose their will on the wives and daughters of their workers and seduce each others' wives, is based. In the third place, they do not advocate "wife-sharing," Shafarevich drawing an unwarranted inference from a sentence and disregarding the context that contradicts the inference he has drawn.

The sentence to which Shafarevich attaches such significance is "Bourgeois marriage is in reality a system of wives in common and thus, at the most, what the Communists might possibly be reproached with, is that they desire to introduce, in substitution for a hypocritically concealed, an openly legalized community of women."[19] Shafarevich takes this as an admission that communists aim to have women become common property. But what Marx and Engels are saying is that all their bourgeois opponents could state if they were honest is that communists advocate what they themselves practice; this statement of their opponents, however, would be based, as Marx and Engels just before said, on a misconception of what communists advocate. It is a misconception that rises from the limitations of bourgeois thinking:

> The bourgeois sees in his wife a mere instument of production. He hears that the instruments of production are to be exploited in common and, naturally, can come to no other conclusion than that the lot of being common to all will likewise fall to the women. He has not even a suspicion that the real point aimed at is to do away with the status of women as mere instruments of production.

If this was not clear to Shafarevich, he could have gone to Engels's "Principles of Communism," a preliminary draft for *The Communist Manifesto*. There Engels says, "Far from inaugurating an era of communal ownership of women, communistic organization of society in fact abolishes it."[20]

Shafarevich's attribution to Marx and Engels of a desire for "the destruction of the family" and "the rearing of children away from their parents in state schools" is equally ill founded. They say nothing of the separation of children from parents but only call for (p. 34) "free education for all children in public schools." What they are opposed to is "the present family, the bourgeois family," which is a mechanism for the transmission of private property in the means of production and an authoritarian structure through which the husband, "the breadwinner" and "the head of the household," lords it over the wife and tyrannizes over the children, not monogamy as such. Again, if Shafarevich did not understand this, he could have consulted Engels's *Origin of the Family*, in which, arguing that under communism there will be no economic considerations in marriage and no male domination, he says: "Having arisen from economic causes, will monogamy then disappear? [F]ar from disappearing, it will on the contrary begin to be realized completely."[21]

Such is the "profound analysis" of *The Communist Manifesto* by the man Solzhenitsyn hailed as a brilliant thinker. The "terrible things" in that work, at which Solzhenitsyn hints, turn out not to be so terrible, after all. But Solzhenitsyn has other comments to make about the morality of Marxists. "Communism," he says, "has never concealed the fact that it rejects all absolute concepts of morality. . . . Communism considers morality to be relative, to be a class matter. Depending upon circumstances and the political situation, any act, including murder, even the killing of thousands, could be good or could be bad" (*Detente*, p. 55).

But Marxists are not alone in finding that the morality of an act depends on the circumstances. Churches, for example, using the doctrine of the "just war," have condoned mass murder through the ages. Solzhenitsyn himself said: "Your short-sighted politicians who signed the hasty Vietnam capitulation seemingly gave America a carefree breathing spell. . . . But if a fullfledged America suffered a real defeat from a small, Communist half-country, how can the West hope to stand firm in the future?" (*Detente*, p. 12). The United States released more explosives on the small peasant country of Vietnam—or "half-country" as Solzhenitsyn contemptuously calls it—than were released in all of World War II, killing close to two million Vietnamese, but Solzhenitsyn finds the discontinuance of this killing to have been not good but bad.

Although Marxists reject moral absolutes that hold for all circumstances, they find, in the words of Trotsky, that there is a "dialectical interdependence between means and end. . . . Seeds of wheat must be sown in order to yield an ear of wheat." "Precisely from this," says Trotsky, speaking of Stalinist methods,

> it flows that not *all* means are permissable. When we say that the end justifies the means, then for us the conclusion follows that the great revolutionary end spurns those base means and ways which set one part of the working class against other parts, or attempt to make the masses happy without their participation; or lower the faith of the masses in themselves and their organization, replacing it by worship for the "leaders."[22]

But Solzhenitsyn, although condemning Marxists for moral relativism, seems to say that any means is appropriate for fighting communism. "Communism is anti-humanity. . . . [T]hat which is against communism is for humanity" (*Detente*, p. 56). If "that which is against communism is for humanity," then Hitler, who proclaimed it his mission to save Germany from communism and sent great numbers of Communists to Dachau, which was built for them, is to be regarded as humane. Indeed in *The Oak and the Calf* Solzhenitsyn tells of how overjoyed he was in 1965 by the news of the suppression of the Indonesian Communist Party. This suppression was the occasion for one of the greatest massacres in history, in which, Amnesty International has estimated, more than a million people were killed.[23] Solzhenitsyn must have been aware of what the suppression of the Indonesian Communists entailed—*Pravda* could not have been sparing in its descriptions—but he makes no mention of it, as if it were a trifling matter.

Although communism is "anti-humanity," it triumphed in 1917, says Solzhenitsyn, in a country which had a "strong moral foundation" (*Letter to the Soviet Leaders*, p. 52). How did this come about? The answer is suggested in Solzhenitsyn's speeches as well as in *August 1914* and *The Gulag Archipelago*. Far from having been inevitable, as the Marxists say, it was, he alleges, a tragic accident of history. An incompetent government took Russia into a war it should never have entered, and an incompetent military leadership prolonged that war until the entire nation, despite its great inner strength, grew war-weary and ready to succumb momentarily to the blandishments of Bolshevik demagoguery. Seizing this fatal moment, the Bolsheviks imposed on the Russian people a regime at fundamental variance with its character. Indeed Lenin, the leader of the revolution, was not really a Russian. Aside from being an "Asiatic," he "spent most of his life in the West [and] knew the West much better than Russia . . ." (*Detente*, p. 23).

The Bolshevik regime almost immediately encountered great popular resistance, but it was too late, the revolution calling upon forces external to the Russian people. "Did not the revolution throughout its early years have some of the characteristics of a foreign invasion? When the organs of the Cheka teemed with Latvians, Poles, Jews, Hungarians, Chinese? When in the early critical years of the civil war it was foreign and especially Latvian bayonets that turned the scales and kept the Bolsheviks in power?" (*From Under the Rubble*, p. 126).

The revolution deflected Russia from its course. Western historians who depict a backward pre-revolutionary Russia "succumb to a persistent but fallacious tradition, thereby to some extent echoing the arguments of Soviet propaganda." Czarist Russia had "a flourishing manufacturing industry, rapid growth, and a flexible, decentralized economy," uncensored newspapers, an intelligentsia "not restricted in its activity," free universities, and a prosperous peasantry.[24]

As always in his political works, Solzhenitsyn does not present any evidence to controvert the historians to whom he refers but simply makes flat, categorical statements. It would seem, however, that he mistakes proclamations for reality. Freedom of the press had been proclaimed, but nevertheless the Czar decreed that no newspaper might mention Rasputin's name at a time when it was on everyone's lips.[25] The supposedly unrestricted intelligentsia in order to publish had to develop what it called an "Aesopian language," in which if it wanted to allude to the situation in Russia it spoke of the situation somewhere else that the perspicacious reader understood referred to Russia. Russia had an illiteracy rate of 76% and "what few schools and colleges there were dispensed obscurantist ideas rather than true knowledge."[26] The supposedly prosperous and contented peasantry, ten million families of which owned about as much land as belonged to 30,000 great landowners, was ready, stated a group of right-wing bureaucrats in 1916, warning the Czar to take stern measures, to "follow the proletariat the very moment the revolutionary leaders point a finger to other people's land."[27]

As for the industrial growth of which Solzhenitsyn speaks, it was shown by Trotsky to have taken place within the confines of Russian backwardness. In accordance with what he called the law of combined development Russia introduced the latest technological achievements into the economy without changing its basic nature. In 1914, far from having a flexible, decentralized economy, it had concentrated industrial production in a few giant factories (enterprises with more than 1,000 workers employed 41.4% of the country's workers as against 17.8% in the United States) while at the same time peasant cultivation of the land used the methods of the seventeenth century and the transportation system was similarly primitive (0.4 kilometers of railroad for every 100 square kilometers of land, as against 11.7 for Germany and 7 for Austria-Hungary).[28]

The traditional Western view of Czarist Russia's backwardness is indeed of long standing, but it is a view that was derived from the direct observation of Western commentators. It is not accidental that the Russian words taken into the English language include "czar" to refer to an autocratic official, "ukase" to refer to the order of an arbitrary authority, and "pogrom" to refer to an organized massacre, especially of Jews. Another word, "knout," is no longer in abridged dictionaries, having fallen into disuse since there is nothing comparable to it in the West or in the Soviet Union, but it is defined in the Oxford English Dictionary as "a kind of scourge, often fatal in its effects, formerly used in Russia for flogging criminals."

Solzhenitsyn's belief in the spiritual well-being of the Russian people under Czarism is as little grounded in reality as his belief in a flourishing, progressive Czarism. Russia, he says,

> preserved itself and its [physical and moral] health, . . . and for ten centuries millions of our peasant forebears died feeling that their lives had not been too unbearable. . . . The autocrats of earlier, religious ages, though their power was ostensibly unlimited, felt themselves responsible before God and their own consciences. . . . [A] man can live in such conditions without harm to his spiritual essence.

Communism, on the other hand, "demands of us total surrender of our souls" (*From Under the Rubble*, pp. 23–24).

With regard to Solzhenitsyn's statement that Russian peasants for ten centuries lived quite tolerable lives that enabled them to retain the integrity of their souls, it is sufficient to recall the seventeenth-century peasant revolt of Stenka Razin, celebrated in folk songs and legends, the formidable eighteenth-century peasant revolt of Pugachev, and the multitude of other peasant revolts. The Eleventh Edition of the *Encyclopedia Britannica* ("the scholar's edition") says of Razin's revolt, "It was not difficult to revolt the oppressed population by the promise of deliverance from their yoke" and of Pugachev's revolt, "The one thought of the destitute thousands who joined the new Peter [Pugachev] was to sweep away utterly the intolerably oppressive upper-classes."

As far as the beneficent moral effect of religion is concerned, we may quote from Solzhenitsyn himself: "The monstrous punishment of the Old Believers—the burnings at the stake, the red-hot pincers, the impalement on meat hooks, the dungeons—followed for two and a half centuries by the senseless repression of twelve million meek and defenseless fellow-countrymen . . . —all this is a sin for which the established Church has never proclaimed its repentance" (*From Under the Rubble*, p. 116).[29] Although the Church and the Czar "felt themselves responsible before God," it is doubtful that the Old Believers thought that they were not being asked for the "total surrender" of their souls.

The Old Believer sect influenced Pugachev. His revolt and the other peasant revolts set a tradition that was followed by the peasant-soldiers who cast off the authority of the army in 1917, but in 1917 the peasant revolt was conjoined with a proletarian insurrection, which made a revolution possible. The October Revolution, far from being an extraordinary aberration, grew out of the Russian soil.

Marxists, however, contrary to Solzhenitsyn, do not regard its occurrence as having been inevitable. "Dialectical materialism," says Trotsky, " . . . has nothing in common with fatalism. Without Lenin . . . it is by no means excluded that a disoriented and split [Bolshevik] party might have let slip the revolutionary opportunity for many years." If Lenin had died before reaching Russia in April 1917, it is possible that the October Revolution would not have occurred, but the revolutionary opportunity was there because of the historical forces governing Russia's development, and Lenin himself "was not an accidental element in the historic development, but a product of the whole past of Russian history."[30]

Solzhenitsyn's allegation that Lenin was not really a Russian is simply absurd. Lenin did not spend "most of his life in the West"; he spent a total of fifteen years in exile. Moreover, unlike Solzhenitsyn, who, in exile since 1974, has severed his ties with oppositionists in the Soviet Union and is quite isolated from the masses of people, he kept in close touch with events and the moods of the masses through the members of his party, who formed a network of observer-activists.

This party, far from being composed of intellectuals with foreign ideas alien to the Russian people, was intimately tied to the working class. "So many witnesses," says Liebman,

> have spoken of the close link between the Russian working
> class and Lenin's Party that there is no need to dwell on it
> here at greater length. . . . Party membership was 23,000 in

February; on the eve of the insurrection, Sverdlov [the Bolshevik General Secretary] was able to inform the Central Committee that the number had gone up to more than 400,000 members. ... Many workers followed the Bolshevik line without taking out membership cards. Moreover, the industrial proletariat did not exceed 2,500,000 workers at the time.[31]

The leadership of this party, in the grip of the mistaken idea that the revolution must be a bourgeois one, far from cunningly taking advantage of a moment of weakness on the part of the Russian people to seduce it, lagged behind the revolutionary consciousness of the masses. Souvarine, urging Solzhenitsyn to give up the idea of the October Revolution as a coup by a minority financed by the Germans, advised him to read the non-party socialist Sukhanov, "an attentive and impartial observer" of the February and October revolutions. There he would find that "Lenin was not wrong when he affirmed that 'the masses,' who wanted peace and land, were much further 'to the left' than the Bolsheviks."[32] It was not merely the authority and persuasive power of Lenin but the pressure of the worker-Bolshevik rank-and-file and of the masses that enabled him to win over the Bolshevik leadership to call for an insurrection. The almost bloodless victory of the Soviets throughout most of Russia within three short months after the Petrograd insurrection shows the popularity of the revolution.

The Russian people did not, as Solzhenitsyn says, turn against the Bolsheviks almost immediately after the insurrection. "I recently ... had reprinted," he told the AFL-CIO bureaucrats, "a pamphlet from the year 1918. This was a precise record of a meeting of all representatives of the Petrograd factories. ... I repeat, this was March 1918—only four months after the October Revolution—and all the representatives of the Petrograd factories were cursing the Communists, who had deceived them in all their promises" (*Detente*, pp. 19–20). But, comments Medvedev on this allegation,

> the pamphlet in question clearly states that it is the record of a meeting *not of all* the representatives of the Petrograd workers, but of those who supported the Mensheviks and Social Revolutionaries [in "a *number* of Petrograd factories"]. ... The meeting did not in any way reflect the state

of mind of the mass of Petrograd workers. Although in the spring of 1918 the workers of Petrograd had many good reasons to be dissatisfied, in particular with the economic situation, it is a historical fact that the overwhelming majority of workers in Petrograd and the other industrial centers in Russia supported the Bolsheviks and Lenin. It was of those workers that the *volunteer* units of the Red Guards and later the Red Army were formed in the first months after the Revolution.[33]

The revolution did not "have some of the characteristics of a foreign invasion." It is natural that many of the oppressed nationalities of the Czarist empire, who especially suffered under it, should have been in the forefront of the Revolution in numbers larger than their percentage of the total population, but they were outnumbered by the Great Russians.[34] Solzhenitsyn exaggerates the number of those who were not Great Russians in the Cheka and other revolutionary bodies and revealingly regards them as foreigners. At the same time he forgets all about the English, American, and other Allied forces who fought on Russian soil on the side of counterrevolution.

To be sure, Marxism came to Russia from the West, but ideas know no boundaries. The ideas of the American Revolution had their origin in the English Puritan Revolution and in the so-called Glorious Revolution that succeeded it, and the ideas of the French Revolution in turn were indebted to those of the American Revolution. Indeed the Russian Orthodox Church, which Solzhenitsyn regards as the nurturer of the Russian national spirit, itself made use—or misuse—of the ideas of a Middle Eastern Jew who lived 2,000 years ago.

Marxism took root in Russia because in accordance with the law of combined development Russia had produced an intelligentsia aware of the backwardness of its society and eager to revolutionize it and a proletariat which, concentrated in gigantic factories and drawn from the peasantry in a sharp break from the past, was receptive to revolutionary thought. The revolution struck a mighty blow against Russia's cultural backwardness, but it could not knock it out, and that backwardness made itself felt through Stalinism, which owes so much to Czarism.

Solzhenitsyn vehemently denies the indebtedness of Stalinism to its Czarist heritage, castigating the many historians of different political persuasions who have traced it. "The whole Stalin era, we are to believe," he says sarcastically, "is a *radical reversion* to the former tsarist era, and in no wise represents a consistent application of Marxism to contemporary realities." To derive the things "peculiar to communism" from "primordial Russian national characteristics established in some distant century" is "nothing less than a racist view" (*The Mortal Danger*, pp. 13, 8).

The accusation of racism is merely a diversion from the issue. As was said by Bertram D. Wolfe, one of those who explored the Czarist heritage of Stalinism, "In its formative period, its [Russia's] culture came from the Near East, from the 'Eastern Rome,' Byzantium, and from the Caliphate of Baghdad. This did not then spell backwardness, for in the tenth century when these Eastern cultures rippled through the Balkans and the Caucasus into Russia, their centers were not behind but ahead of Western Europe."[35] That the Near East, as earlier Africa, India, and China, witnessed a civilization far superior to that of Western Europe at the same time proves conclusively the fallacy of racism as an explanation of backwardness.

This is not to deny, however, that a cultural heritage of backwardness puts its stamp on the building of a new civilization. Backwardness supplied the explosive material for the revolution in Russia, but the weight of the past was a heavy burden in the construction that succeeded the revolution. Stalinism, however, was not a mere "reversion to the former tsarist era." Stalin in industrializing the Soviet Union changed it fundamentally from what Czarist Russia had been, but in using many Czarist ideas and practices to do so he incorporated new forms of retrogression into the system.

It is unnecessary to discuss in detail here the many features for which Stalinism was indebted to Czarism: an absolute autocracy, an overblown bureaucracy, a church that is the servile creature of the state, internal passports restricting movement, a secret police warring against dissidents, Siberian labor camps, and anti-Semitism, not so openly acknowledged as under Czarism, to be sure, but nevertheless made use of by the regime. Solzhenitsyn himself, as we have seen (page 27, above), pointed out some of Stalin's Czarist ideas and practices in *The First Circle*.

For Solzhenitsyn in his political works, however, there is no such thing as Stalinism. There is only communism, a demonic force that cannot really be explained. It is, he says in *Letter to the Soviet Leaders* (pp. 18–19), a "murky whirlwind" that "swept in on us from the West" and is "now veering away further east of its own accord." Elsewhere, however, when Solzhenitsyn is not speaking to the Soviet leaders, he finds that Communism is not a whirlwind that changes its direction of itself but has its source in these very leaders. "[T]he concentration of World Evil and the tremendous force of hatred is there [in the Soviet Union] and it's flowing from there throughout the world" (*Detente*, p. 47).

In *Letter to the Soviet Leaders*, in which he urges them to give up their Marxism while retaining their authoritarian rule, Solzhenitsyn at one point (p. 47) expresses his conviction that they do not really believe in Communism themselves. "This Ideology does nothing now but sap our strength and bind us. It clogs up the whole life of society—minds, tongues, radio and press—with lies, lies, lies. . . . And you, when you open your newspapers or switch on your television—do *you yourselves* really believe for one instant that these speeches are sincere? No, you stopped believing long ago, I am certain of it."[36] In his other political writing, however, Solzhenitsyn regards the Soviet leaders as fanatics driven by their ideology to seek world conquest. "Communism will never desist from its efforts to seize the world, be it through direct military conquest, through subversion and terrorism, or by subtly undermining society from within" (*The Mortal Danger*, p. 46).

It is a monolithic movement that cannot change and is everywhere the same.

> One mistake [of the West] is the failure to understand the radical hostility of communism to mankind as a whole—the failure to realize that communism is irredeemable, that there exist no "better" variants of communism; that it is incapable of growing "kinder," that it cannot survive as an ideology without using terror, and that, consequently to co-exist with communism on the same planet is impossible. Either it will spread, cancer-like, to destroy mankind, or else mankind will have to rid itself of communism. . . . (*The Mortal Danger*, pp. 1–2).

In the era of Gorbachev and the legalization of the opposition parties in Poland and Hungary, the ridiculousness of this view of Communism is obvious. The idea that Communism is the one thing in the universe immune to change, a totalitarian monolith frozen for eternity unless broken up from the outside, can no longer stand.

Far from the Soviet bureaucracy having been the center of world revolution, as Solzhenitsyn says, it sought to restrain revolutionary movements because it feared these could infect the Soviet workers. It gave limited aid to the liberation movements seeking to free their countries from dependence on the dominant capitalist powers, but it was always ready to sacrifice their interests in diplomatic bargaining, just as today it is giving up any aid at all in return for Western credits.

Thus, as Isaac Deutscher says, after World War II France and Italy, "where the authority of the old ruling classes was in ruins, the working classes were in revolt, and the Communist parties led the bulk of the armed Resistance," were ripe for revolution. However, "Stalin, acting on his diplomatic commitment, prevailed upon the French and Italian Communists to resign themselves to the restoration of capitalism in their countries from the virtual collapse and even to co-operate in the restoration."[37] If Solzhenitsyn had remembered the lamb-like meekness of the French Communist leadership, he would not have said that Communism is "a wolf" that cannot "stop eating meat and become a lamb," predicting after the uprising against the Portuguese dictator Salazar that the Socialist leader Soares would soon be gobbled up by the Communists and that "Olaf Palme . . . and Mitterand, and the Italian socialists will live to the day when they are in the position that Soares is in today" (*Detente*, p. 60).

The revolutions of our time have arisen not from conspiratorial trickery but from the indigenous conditions created by world capitalism. The societies established by these revolutions, if not manifestations of absolute evil, as Solzhenitsyn sees them, do suffer in their inherited backwardness from the evil of bureaucratism. In all of them democracy is not merely a luxury but vital to the proper functioning of the system.

Solzhenitsyn speaks of the Soviet Union's inefficient economy, but such things as the plenitude of shoddy unwanted goods and the shortage of desired goods that characterize the Soviet economy have nothing to do with the nature of socialism. They have everything to do, however, with the repression of democracy by the bureaucracy even when it has become more liberal. The necessity of democracy for the economic functioning of socialism was perceived fifty years ago by Trotsky, who wrote in an insightful passage:

It is possible to build gigantic factories according to a ready-made Western pattern by bureaucratic command—although, to be sure, at triple the normal cost. But the farther you go, the more the economy runs into the problem of quality. . . . Under a nationalized economy, *quality* demands a democracy of producers and consumers, freedom of criticism and initiative. . . . Behind the question of quality stands a more complicated and grandiose problem which may be comprised in the concept of *independent technical* and *cultural creation.* . . . No new values can be created where a free conflict of ideas is impossible. . . . Soviet democracy . . . has become a life-and-death need of the country.[38]

Gorbachev's "glasnost" campaign is an open admission of the need for democratization if Soviet society is to advance. But it is doubtful that bureaucratic resistance can be overcome and thorough-going democratization accomplished without independent movement from below. The prominent Soviet dissident Yuri Orlov, now living in the United States, told the Parisian French-language dissident magazine *La Pensée Russe* that "no bourgeois-type party will have any popularity among the Soviet workers. . . . [W]hat would be most suited to the Soviet Union would be socialist democracy, with all the freedoms."[39] This is essentially what the striking Soviet miners sought in July 1989.[40]

Equally far from reality as Solzhenitsyn's picture of a Stalinism frozen for eternity is his picture of the weakness and ineffectuality of anti-communism in a capitalist society. The United States has sent armed forces to Korea, Vietnam, the Dominican Republic, Libya, and Lebanon ("from the halls of Montezuma to the shores of Tripoli," as the U.S. Marines' song has it), to say nothing of a host of "covert operations" elsewhere.[41] These include the secret financing of foreign political parties in all continents,[42] assassinations (Lumumba in the Congo, General Schneider in Chile, and the repeated attempts on the life of Castro),[43] coups (Iran in 1953, Guatemala in 1954, Brazil in 1964, Chile in 1973), military aid to armies waging civil wars (Angola, Afghanistan). In the light of this record it is ludicrous for Solzhenitsyn to speak of United States governments as lacking in the will to fight communism.

Nor have United States governments shown what he regards as a deplorable squeamishness in supporting governments that are less than full democracies. Among the bloody tyrants they have supported with economic, military, and diplomatic aid have been the Somozas in Nicaragua, Chiang Kai-shek in China, the Shah in Iran, Rhee and Park in South Korea, Suharto in Indonesia, Marcos in the Philippines, the Duvaliers in Haiti, Trujillo in the Dominican Republic, Pinochet in Chile, and Botha in South Africa.

Solzhenitsyn, then, does not see the ruthless determination of the American ruling class to support the world capitalist system. He sees only its hypocritical declarations about democracy, which he deplores.

He is also ill-informed about other aspects of American society although some of the things he has to say have an element of truth.[44] In his Harvard address he finds the source of Western moral bankruptcy in

> the prevailing Western view of the world, which was first born during the Renaissance and found its political expression in the period of the Enlightenment. It ... could be defined as rationalistic humanism or humanistic autonomy: the proclaimed and enforced autonomy of man from any higher force above him. ... The West ended up by truly enforcing human rights, sometimes even excessively, but man's sense of responsibility to God and society grew dimmer and dimmer (*Detente*, pp. 14–15).[45]

The consequence has been the development of a materialistic and hedonistic society in which "[e]very citizen has been granted the desired freedom and material goods in such quantity and of such quality as to guarantee, in theory, the achievement of happiness, in the morally inferior sense that has come into being during those same decades." "[T]he constant desire to have still more things and a still better life," however, brings it about that "[a]ctive and tense competition permeates all human thoughts without opening a way to free spiritual development." Given over only to the satisfaction of one's own desires, no one wishes to "risk one's precious life in defense of common values" (*Detente*, p. 4).

The "destructive and irresponsible freedom" that holds sway in the West has made "society as a whole defenseless against certain individuals," pornographers, criminals, and terrorists. It is defenseless too against the mass media, which have tremendous freedom without obligations.

> [T]he press has become the greatest power within the Western countries. . . . By what law has it been elected and to whom is it responsible? . . . [W]ho has granted Western journalists their power . . . ? Enormous freedom exists for the press, but not for the readership, because newspapers mostly give emphasis to those opinions that do not too openly contradict their own and the general trend. . . . Nothing is forbidden, but what is not fashionable will hardly ever find its way into periodicals or books or be heard in colleges [*Detente*, p. 8].

In a revival of Russian messianism Solzhenitsyn finds hope for mankind to lie in the realm of the old Czarist empire, where the Dostoyevskian doctrine of redemption through suffering is being realized. "Six decades for our people and three decades for the people of Eastern Europe: during that time we have been through a spiritual training far in advance of Western experience. . . . After the suffering of decades of violence and oppression, the human soul longs for things higher, warmer, purer . . . " (*Detente*, p. 10).[46]

In speaking of American society as one in which "every citizen has been granted the desired freedom and material goods," Solzhenitsyn is writing as if from another world. Apparently, he does not know of the bleak existence of a numerous American under-class. He does not know of a great army of homeless whose freedom consists of the choice between freezing in the streets or seeking to find a roof in unsafe, dehumanizing municipal shelters. He does not know that workers fortunate enough to have jobs have just about every second of their working lives dictated by production-line efficiency experts. This is scarcely freedom.

"The constant desire to have still more things" is, however, very much a part of American life. It springs not from "rationalistic humanism" but from the nature of capitalism. The capitalist must seek to sell as much of the products of his workers as he can, just as he must, contradictorily, seek to pay his workers as little as possible. Therefore, "the entrepreneur," as Marx said, "accedes to the most depraved fancies of his neighbor, plays the role of panderer between him and his needs, awakens unhealthy appetites in him, and watches for every weakness in order, later, to claim the remuneration for this labor of love."[47]

So too "active and tense competition" indeed characterizes the American rat-race. It is the competition of a society in which it is every man for himself, where the main relationship between human beings is what Marx called "the cash nexus." This competition indeed closes off "free spiritual development." "Only in community with others," say Marx and Engels, "has each individual the means of cultivating his gifts in all directions; only in the community, therefore, is personal freedom possible." But the society characterized by class divisions (particularly, one may add, one of extreme economic individualism such as ours) is "not only a completely illusory community, but a new fetter as well." Only in a "real community," under the conditions of communism, will "individuals obtain their freedom in and through association."[48]

Criminality springs from the stifling of genuine human needs, including the need for social connectedness, and the stimulation of artificial dissatisfactions. Where people are alienated from each other and see every day on television images of enticing objects of which society deprives them, they turn to anti-social behavior. So too the media's sensationalism, salaciousness, and scandal-mongering, their regurgitations of trivia, and their invasions of privacy, to all of which Solzhenitsyn rightly objects, have their origin in the spiritual climate of capitalism, not in a failure to believe in God.

Some of the other points Solzhenitsyn makes about the media are, however, suggestive. The media do indeed have great power, but it is not the individual journalists, as he alleges, who have this power but the editors for whom they work and, even more, the publishers for whom the editors work. The media are highly monopolized, with small competitors barely managing a meager existence. They are generally governed in their commentary by common assumptions, indicated by such frequently used phrases as "our investments abroad" and "our markets," which identify the entire nation with a few giant corporations, and their differences are within a narrow range.

Although Solzhenitsyn perceives this narrowness of range and rightly deplores it, he himself would narrow it further in his authoritarianism. "[U]nlimited freedom of discussion," he says, "can wreck a country's resistance to some looming danger and lead to capitulation in wars not yet lost . . . " (*From Under the Rubble*, p. 22).

He is here undoubtedly thinking of the belated criticism of the war in Vietnam of the American press, which he elsewhere attacked for its publication of the Pentagon Papers. But this publication occurred only after the growth of conviction within the establishment élite that the cost of the war had become too high. Earlier the media had failed to report the savage bombing of Cambodia and Laos although there was ample evidence of it and had failed to question Johnson's false allegation that North Vietnam had sought to sink an American warship, an allegation that enabled him to get passed in Congress the Bay of Tonkin Resolution and thereby to carry on an undeclared war.

Finally, Solzhenitsyn's question as to who elected the media leaders and to whom they are responsible is pertinent. It can, however, be extended further, not only to the lords of the communications industry but to the lords of the other industries. Who elected them, concerned as they are only with their own profit and not with the common good, to make decisions that affect the lives of their work force and indeed the country at large? This is a question that Solzhenitsyn does not think to ask.

## NOTES

1. *Solzhenitsyn at Harvard: The Address, Twelve Early Responses, and Six Later Reflections*, ed. Ronald Berman (Washington, D.C.: Ethics and Public Policy Center, 1980), p. 32.
2. *Detente: Prospects for Democracy and Dictatorship* (New Brunswick, N.J.: Transaction Press, 1980), pp. 53–54.
3. *Letter to the Soviet Leaders* (New York: Harper & Row, 1974), p. 43.
4. "Letter to Heinz Starkenburg," Jan. 25, 1894, in Karl Marx, *Selected Works* (New York: International Publishers, n.d.), I, 392.
5. Christopher Hill, "The English Civil War Interpreted by Marx and Engels," *Science and Society*, 12 (1948), 154. For a synthesis and popularization of Marxist work on religion, see my *The Meek and the Militant* (Atlantic Highlands, N.J.: Zed Books, 1986).
6. Marx, *Selected Works*, I, xviii.
7. These are the figures given by Attorney General John N. Mitchell in 1969. Cf. Morton Mintz and Jerry S. Cohen, *America, Inc.* (New York: Dial, 1971), p. 16. It seems likely that the strength of big business has increased since then.

8. *The New York Times*, Sept. 23, 1986, Sec. A, p. 31.

9. Cf. the Nobel Laureate Paul A. Samuelson in *The New York Times*, March 14, 1973, p. 43.

10. Leon Trotsky, "*The Communist Manifesto* Today," Introduction to *The Communist Manifesto* (New York: Pathfinder Press, 1978), pp. 6–7.

11. Leon Trotsky, *The Permanent Revolution and Results and Prospects* (New York: Merit Publishers, 1969), p. 63.

12. V.I. Lenin, *Imperialism: The Highest Stage of Capitalism* (New York: International Publishers, 1939), p. 126.

13. Cf. Michael Lowy, *The Politics of Combined and Uneven Development: The Theory of Permanent Revolution* (London: Verso, 1981), pp. 23–27.

14. *The Communist Manifesto*, p. 32.

15. Trotsky, *The Revolution Betrayed*, pp. 53–55.

16. War has been so much a part of class society that doing away with it may seem a fantasy. However, twentieth-century anthropology has shown that it did not exist among the food-gathering tribes living in primitive communism before the advent of private property and that it cannot, therefore, be regarded as an inherent part of human nature. Cf. Bronislaw Malinowski, "War—Past, Present, and Future," *War as a Social Institution*, ed. Jesse D. Clarkson and Thomas C. Cochran (New York: AMS Press, 1966), p. 23 and M.F. Ashley Montagu, "The New Litany of 'Innate Depravity' or Original Sin Revisited," *Man and Aggression*, ed. M.F. Ashley Montagu (New York: Oxford Univ. Press, 1968), pp. 15–16.

17. Ernest Mandel, *Marxist Economic Theory* (New York: Monthly Review Press, 1970), I, 150–54. For the periodic absolute impoverishment of the unemployed, see *The Communist Manifesto*, p. 26; for the progressive relative impoverishment of the proletariat, see Marx, "Wage-Labour and Capital," *Selected Works*, I, 273.

18. Igor Shafarevich, "Socialism in our Past and Future," *From Under the Rubble*, ed. Alexander Solzhenitsyn (Chicago: Regnery Gateway, 1981), p. 30.

19. *The Communist Manifesto*, p. 31.

20. *Birth of the Communist Manifesto*, ed. Dirk J. Struik (New York: International Publishers, 1975), p. 186.

21. Frederick Engels, *The Origin of the Family, Private Property and the State* (New York: International Publishers, 1972), p. 139. It should be added that Engels anticipated many modern attitudes. Although, he said, it is impossible to say in detail how the family relationships will be altered under communism, he did think that there would be no fetish made of female virginity prior to marriage, no stigma attached to children born outside of marriage, and no restrictions on divorce. It is possible that Shafarevich and Solzhenitsyn would object to these ideas, but they do not constitute advocacy of "destruction of the family."

22. Leon Trotsky, *Their Morals and Ours* (New York: Merit Publishers, 1969), p. 37.

23. Noam Chomsky and Edward S. Herman, *The Washington Connection and Third World Fascism* (Boston: South End Press, 1979), p. 209.

24. Aleksandr I. Solzhenitsyn, *The Mortal Danger: How Misconceptions about Russia Imperil America* (New York: Harper & Row, 1980), p. 5.

25. Marcel Liebman, *The Russian Revolution* (New York: Random House, 1970), p. 38.

26. Liebman, *The Russian Revolution*, p. 41.

27. Leon Trotsky, *The History of the Russian Revolution* (New York: Simon and Schuster, 1937), I, 45, 31.

28. Trotsky, *History of the Russian Revolution*, I, 910. Cf. also his appendix to Volume I.

29. In this passage Solzhenitsyn regards "the soulless reforms of Nikon [Patriarch of the Russian Orthodox Church from 1652 to 1667] and Peter the Great" as having resulted in "the extirpation and suppression of the Russian national spirit." Elsewhere (*Letter to the Soviet Leaders*, p. 52) he says that "the ancient, seven-centuries old Orthodoxy . . . was battered by Patriarch Nikon and bureaucratized by Peter the Great." Consequently, "once this moral principle was perverted and weakened, the authoritarian order . . . gradually went into a decline and eventually perished." On the same page, however, Solzhenitsyn contradicts himself, saying that "at the beginning of the twentieth century both the physical and spiritual health of her [Russia's] people were still intact." He can't seem to make up his mind whether Russia's spiritual health endured for seven centuries or ten centuries.

30. Trotsky, *History of the Russian Revolution*, I, 330.
31. Liebman, *The Russian Revolution*, p. 288 and n.
32. Souvarine, p. 336.
33. Medvedev, *Political Essays*, p. 145.
34. Mark Perakh, "Solzhenitsyn and the Jews," *Midstream*, 23 (1977), 9.
35. Wolfe, *Three Who Made a Revolution*, p. 15.
36. Solzhenitsyn's assertion that the Soviet leaders do not really believe in Marxism has a great deal of truth, as has been demonstrated recently under Gorbachev. It is similar to the lack of belief in the Bill of Rights by American governmental officials despite their ritualistic invocation of the Constitution. Cf. Lakshin, p. 71: "[W]hat currently passes for ideology in the USSR today contains so much that is hollow and purely ornamental . . . that it is doubtful whether 'Soviet ideology' has much in common with Marxism. . . . There is no sign that the 'leadership' ever read Marx at all (in general, they prefer reading typewritten reports and 'extracts' summarized for internal Kremlin circulation)."
37. Isaac Deutscher, *The Prophet Outcast* (New York: Oxford Univ. Press, 1963), p. 518. General de Gaulle himself testified to the Communist leadership's role in restoring French capitalism. Cf. Charles de Gaulle, *Memoires de Guerre* (Plon, 1959), Vol. 3: *Le Salut*, pp. 118-19: "Immediately following his [Maurice Thorez, the Communist Party leader] return to France [from the Soviet Union], he helped eliminate the last vestiges of the 'patriotic militias' that some of his people were trying to maintain in a new clandestinity. . . . To many workers, in particular miners, who listened to his harangues he continually gave the order to work to their utmost and to produce no matter what the cost. Was this out of a political tactic? There is no reason for me to try to unravel it. It is enough for me that France is served." Quoted by Ernest Mandel, "Peaceful Co-Existence and World Revolution," *Revolution and Class Struggle*, ed. Robin Blackburn (Atlantic Highlands, N.J.: Humanities Press, 1978), p. 296, n. 28. For attempts by Stalin to avert revolution in Yugoslavia and China, see the dissident Milovan Djilas, formerly Tito's second in command, and Jack Belden, the American correspondent who was the John Reed of the Chinese Revolution: Milovan Djilas, *Conversations with Stalin* (New York: Harcourt, Brace & World, 1962), pp. 6, 74, 82 and

Jack Belden, *China Shakes the World* (New York: Monthly Review Press, 1970), pp. 69, 168–69.

38. Trotsky, *The Revolution Betrayed*, p. 276.

39. *Socialist Action*, June 1987, p. 13.

40. Cf. *The New York Times*, July 25 and 26, 1989.

41. For a detailed, heavily documented account of U.S. global intervention, see Chomsky and Herman's *The Washington Connection and Third World Fascism*.

42. Cf. *The New York Times*, Oct. 24, 1984: "[U.S. Central] Intelligence officials said . . . Nicaraguan business leaders had had a close association with the agency since 1980, when the Carter Administration . . . initiated a program of covert aid to moderate business and political groups in Nicaragua. . . . The United States has covertly attempted to influence the outcome of foreign elections in the past. Earlier this year, the C.I.A. secretly gave $1.4 million to two political parties in El Salvador . . . , according to intelligence officials and members of Congress. The United States, usually through the C.I.A., has also funneled money to moderate political parties in Europe, Africa and Asia in hopes of promoting the election of pro-American candidates. During the 1950's the C.I.A. covertly gave millions of dollars to Italian political parties to prevent the election of Communist candidates, former intelligence officials have said."

43. Cf. Chomsky and Herman, p. 50.

44. His views on American society, essentially derived from nineteenth-century Slavophiles, have remained unchanged from those he expressed in *Letter to the Soviet Leaders* before he came to the United States. However, before his Harvard address, in which he returned to his theme of Western moral weakness, he for a time in courting public opinion soft-pedalled his views. During his tour of the United States, of which an aide stated, "He simply stays in his room and works," he said (*The New York Times*, Mar. 5, 1974, p. 9) he was "impressed with the freedom and vitality of American life."

45. Lakshin accurately forecast the direction of Solzhenitsyn's thought (p. 68): "Yesterday, everything was the fault of Stalin; today Lenin is the culprit; tomorrow it will be the whole of nineteenth-century society and its thoroughly atheistic literature . . . ; and then before we know where we are it will be the *philosophes* of the French

Enlightenment who are to blame. ... Thought itself is evil; the sole good is faith."

46. Sometimes, however, in a mood of nationalistic breast-beating rather than of nationalistic fervor, Solzhenitsyn says the opposite. In *From Under the Rubble*, he asserts (p. 118): "This realm of darkness, of falsehood, of brute force, of justice denied and distrust of the good, this slimy swamp was formed by *us*, and no one else. We grew used to the idea that we must submit and lie in order to survive—and we brought up our children to do so."

47. Karl Marx, *Economic and Philosophical Manuscripts* in Erich Fromm, *Marx's Concept of Man* (New York: Frederick Ungar, 1961), p. 142.

48. Marx and Engels, *The German Ideology* in *Reader in Marxist Philosophy*, ed. Howard Selsam and Harry Martel (New York: International Publishers, 1973), p. 270.

# 6. Politics and Art in Solzhenitsyn's Novels

In his political odyssey Alexander Solzhenitsyn has gone from an ardent Leninism to an eclecticism combining Leninism and Tolstoyism to a bitter anti-communism that not only rejects Lenin but all forms of radicalism, including the radical aspects of Tolstoy. His present politics, as we have seen, are highly simplistic and falsify history. His method of inquiry is that which he satirically attributes to Lenin: "He had all his findings clearly in mind long before he had filled his twenty notebooks. His foresight had become so acute of late that he knew remarkably early, before he sat down to write, what his conclusions would be" (*Lenin in Zurich*, p. 90).

At the same time the subject matter of his novels has changed from his concentration-camp experiences to the history of a time before he was born. The project which has long occupied him is one that he had cherished from early manhood, but now, instead of celebrating the October Revolution and its leader, as he had intended to do, he is presenting that revolution as a disaster for Russia and all of mankind unloosed by the demonic force that was Lenin. He is therefore engaged in research in accordance with his method of inquiry that will give him the materials to provide a picture of the past that will conform to his vision of what it was.

The results for his art of the change in Solzhenitsyn's politics and subject matter were foreshadowed by the remarks made by two Russian dissidents. The first was by Solzhenitsyn's prison-camp friend, the literary scholar and critic Lev Kopelev. In a letter to Solzhenitsyn about the manuscript of *The First Circle*, he wrote, says Scammell (p. 500), that "the scenes in which Solzhenitsyn had written out of his own experience were immeasurably stronger than the rest" and that "he found it difficult to believe in 'those homunculi who perforce are conceived in newspaper and archival test-tubes.'" Moreover, he added, Solzhenitsyn, in writing about what lay outside of his own experience, "appeared to be imbued with a dangerous certainty that he held 'all the truths in the hollow of his hand.'"

The second dissident, Pavel Litvinov, expressed in an open letter the outrage many dissidents, both those who, like Litvinov, had emigrated and those who remained in the Soviet Union, felt about the public utterances critical of his former associates that Solzhenitsyn made shortly after being exiled. Litvinov, Scammell states (p. 908), condemned Solzhenitsyn's

> harshness of tone, intemperate language, and intolerance of the opinions and actions of others. . . . He also suggested that a distinction existed between Solzhenitsyn's literary and polemical works: "In your books you destroy the myth that there are quick and obvious solutions to the various problems that people face, yet in your public statements you create the impression that a single solution exists and that you know what it is. And then you start to believe it yourself."

In his later fiction, in contrast to his earlier fiction, Solzhenitsyn has indeed tended to reduce the complexity of reality to the simplicism of the propagandist, and his characters, conceived in "archival test-tubes," too frequently fail to come convincingly alive.

It is not that Solzhenitsyn's art has deteriorated because his political views have become reactionary. As Rosa Luxemburg pointed out, the doctrinal content of Dostoyevsky and (at least in some aspects) of Tolstoy is reactionary, but "the writings of both have, nevertheless, an inspiring, arousing, and liberating effect upon us. And this is because . . . theirs is the warmest love for mankind and the deepest response to social injustice. . . . [W]ith the true artist, the social formula that he recommends is a matter of secondary importance; the source of his art, its animating spirit, is decisive."[1] It is Solzhenitsyn's animating spirit, not merely the ideological content of his novels, that has changed.

Solzhenitsyn himself has given the clue to this change. Speaking of his concentration-camp experience in *The Gulag Archipelago*, he wrote (II, p. 268), "I now know that a writer cannot afford to give in to feelings of rage, disgust, or contempt. Did you answer someone in a temper? If so, you didn't hear him out and lost track of his system of opinions. You avoided someone out of disgust—and a completely unknown personality slipped out of your ken . . . ." In *The First Circle* and *Cancer Ward* the ability to "hear out" his characters even though he condemns their views and way of life is constantly present. It enables him to understand them and to perceive what made them what they are. This understanding generates both compassion and irony. In *August 1914* and still more in the chapters from the later novels in *Lenin in Zurich*, Solzhenitsyn's ability to "hear out" his characters is impaired by his feelings as a fanatical anti-communist. In not listening to them, he deprives many of them of their human voices, and the characters, the puppets of the author-ventriloquist, instead of undergoing development, are static and predictable. Surprise, irony (except of the most obvious and insistent sort), suspense are lost.

I shall examine in turn the aesthetic patterns of *The First Circle*, *Cancer Ward*, and *August 1914* and the features revealed in *Lenin in Zurich* to substantiate these observations. They explain why American and English critics, well disposed to Solzhenitsyn, who had been lauded to the skies and who was still in the Soviet Union when *August 1914* appeared, greeted it with "decidedly mixed" reviews and an "over-all response" that was "one of respectful bewilderment." "Comparisons to Tolstoy or Dostoyevsky now struck the reviewers as grotesquely inflated. Margaret Mitchell, Pearl Buck, James Michener, and Maxim Gorky were the names now invoked" (Scammell, pp. 791, 792).

The action of *The First Circle* takes place within four days during Christmas time in 1949. The novel begins with the diplomat Innokenty Volodin, who has learned that his former family physician had promised French fellow-scientists while abroad that he would send them a medicine, telephoning to warn him that he is being watched and will be arrested if he does so. Volodin has undergone an agonizing inner struggle before making the call, knowing that he is putting himself in danger by doing so, but he reasons to himself that a call from a public telephone booth cannot be traced. It is 270 pages later before Volodin reappears; however, he has not only initiated the action but is the first of numerous characters to be confronted with a moral choice. It is the theme of moral choice that holds together this polyphonic novel with its enormous cast of characters, each of whom is unaware or only vaguely aware of how his fate interlaces with that of the others.

Most of the action takes place in the Mavrino Institute, the special camp for scientists, which is similar to Dante's "first circle," the best and highest circle of hell. Here a search for a method of identifying voices, as a person's identity is revealed by his or her fingerprints, is being made. It is through the work done at this camp that Volodin will finally be apprehended. However, we also see the "free" world outside of the camp, even up to the living quarters of the man at the pinnacle of Soviet society, Joseph Stalin. The irony is that the "free" world is seen to be as lacking in genuine freedom as the world of the concentration camps.

The most obvious instances of those who make moral choices under conditions of extreme constraint are the labor-camp prisoners who become informers. Solzhenitsyn in *The Gulag Archipelago* described the tremendous pressure on the "zeks," as the prisoners called themselves in their lingo, to become informers and confessed that he himself had agreed to become one. In *The First Circle*, although he condemns them, he does not withhold sympathy from them.

One of the informers is Victor Lyubimichev. Young, handsome, athletic, with "the candid eyes of a deer," he is popular among the other prisoners. But as a prisoner of war in a Nazi concentration camp, Lyubimichev had seen men dying all about him, the only ones surviving being those who in one way or another sold out their fellow prisoners. "With all the yearning of his young body, Victor Lyubimichev wanted to live. He resolved that if he had to die he would be the last." When a recruiter for the Nazis who had been a political officer in the Red Army urged the prisoners to join the Vlasov forces, the prisoners, including Lyubimichev, did so.

When he was caught by the Soviet security forces after the war, he was given exactly the same sentence as those who had fought in the resistance movement but had seen too much of foreign countries. Lyubimichev was thus reinforced in his belief that there was no point in having convictions. But when the sharashka prisoners discover that he is an informer and reject him, there is an authorial comment, "He was ready to assure anyone that he understood life, but it had turned out that he didn't" (pp. 542, 544).

Another one of the informers is Isaak Moiseyevich Kagan, a Jew with a great love of money who worked in the cellar battery room. In freedom Kagan had been asked by the State Security to become a secret informer. "That proposal was repulsive to Kagan. He had neither the candor nor the boldness—who did?—to tell them to their faces that what they were suggesting was vile," but he cleverly squirmed his way out of it. "It was not that he was incapable of informing. Without a tremor he would have informed on anyone who had harmed or humiliated him. But it would have nauseated him to inform on people who had been good or even indifferent to him" (p. 341).

And yet the prisoners discover that in the sharashka he is an informer. His bunkmate could not "find the strength to be angry with him. He only said, 'Oh, Isaak, you're a pig, just a pig! In freedom you turned down their offer of thousands, and here you went along with them for hundreds.' Or had they scared him by threatening him with the prospect of camp?" (p. 547). Kagan, not an exemplary human being, was not an entirely bad sort. Had he succumbed to his master passion of the desire for money or had he, who in freedom wanted nothing more than to be obscure in order to avoid being struck down during a time of turmoil, finally been unable to escape his fate?

Then there is Ruska Doronin, who is as impulsive and reckless as Kagan is adroitly wary and cautious. Twenty-three years old, amiable, outgoing, full of youthful enthusiasm, he is liked by everyone. As a youngster he had been imprisoned for having become friendly with visiting Americans. Then when he was released, he realized it was in order that he might be kept under surveillance. He bolted and lived for two years on forged passports before he was caught again. In knocking about, he acquired a shrewd cynicism and the ability to fend for himself, but he has retained his engaging ardor. His animated face is "sometimes simple-hearted and boyish, sometimes the face of an inspired confidence man" (p. 76).

When Ruska was asked by the sharashka security officer to become an informer, the cynicism he had learned from his experience and from his education as a young person in Soviet society might have led him to accept. However, he realized that in the long run it might be as dangerous to cooperate as not. Moreover, he was a confirmed gambler. He therefore agreed to be an informer but then told the most influential prisoners about it, saying that he had done so out of sport and to help expose the real informers.

The prisoners believe him, but in order to maintain his credibility as an informer Ruska has to divulge to the security officer information which he tells himself is inconsequential. Seeing this, the prisoners now avoid him. It is indeed a dangerous game the double agent is playing, not only as far as his physical fate is concerned but as far as its moral consequences are concerned. The question is whether the youthful innocence that is still partly unsullied or the cynical trickiness he has acquired will prevail.

There are prisoners who refuse to become informers, but they are not conventional story-book heroes. The engineer Potapov has had all his life no thought about anything but work, hating even to take vacations. He was in the Nazi prisoner-of-war camps where prisoners had to resort to eating bark, grass, and their dead comrades. Taken from there, he was interrogated by a Russian agent of the Nazis, who offered him freedom, food, money, and the opportunity to engage in his beloved work if he would reconstruct the plans for the Dnieper hydroelectric station. Potapov, whose "coarsely furrowed face" and "deep, dark eye cavities . . . almost like a corpse's" are in contrast with the youthful face and deer eyes of Lyubimichev, diffidently and without heroics explained that he could not do so because he had taken an oath not to divulge information.

This did not prevent him, however, from being convicted by the Soviet secret police of having informed the Germans of military secrets. Potapov, who had never concerned himself with politics, now begins to have some doubts about the system. "[T]he robot became puzzled for the first time, something which, it is well known, is not recommended for robots." He still does not regret having served in the Soviet forces or having refused the German offer, but "[s]omehow, he could not understand why they jailed people whose only guilt was that they had constructed Dneproges" (pp. 185, 186).

Gerasimovich is a physicist, a specialist in optics, "a short, narrow-shouldered man with an emphatically intellectual face, wearing a pince-nez like a spy in a poster" (p. 229), the typical Soviet poster warning against engineer-saboteurs. A mournful-looking man whose vitality seems to have been killed, he retains a bitterly independent spirit. When the Head of the Special Equipment Section of the Ministry of State Security asks him to work on a camera that could be fitted into a door frame, photographing all those who enter, Gerasimovich hesitates. He knows that the extension of his prison term upon his refusal would mean the end of his long-suffering wife and with it the end of his own existence. Why should he concern himself with those outside of the camps who "made stupid and greedy use of the freedom they were allowed to enjoy"?

When he is told, however, "But what is there to think over? It's right in your field," Gerasimovich stands up. "He glared contemptuously at the fat, double-chinned stupid mug in a general's astrakhan hat. 'No! That's not my field! I don't set traps for human beings! It's bad enough that they put *us* in prison'" (pp. 582, 583). The man who looks like "a spy in a poster," whose intellectual face contrasts with the "stupid mug" of the spy chief, does not regard spying as a field for those with any self-respect.

It is not only in the sharashka that spying takes place. It is omnipresent in the "free" world outside of the sharashka. Muza, a graduate student in humanities living in the same student dormitory as Nadya, the autobiographical Nerzhin's wife, has been approached by the secret police to become an informer. She is in agony. If she does not accept, her academic career will be ruined. She has no one to consult in making this "decision of a lifetime," not even her parents, with whom she is very close, but whom she cannot possibly write about her problem. While, unknown to the other girls, she is struggling with herself, another girl is reading a novel that presents "a clear, beautiful world, where all suffering was easily conquered. Galakhov's characters were never shaken by doubts: whether to serve one's country or not, whether to sacrifice oneself or not." The implied comparison between Solzhenitsyn's own novel and the novel by Galakhov, one of the characters in *The First Circle*, suggests the difference between literature and propaganda.

Muza, after her encounter with the secret police, feels "as if she had been smeared with something dirty and shameful, something which could not be washed off, hidden, or shown to anyone—and which it was also impossible to live with." In her suffering she does not listen to a girl who is inanely chattering away about how she is deceiving a suitor, a young Spanish poet, into believing that she is a shy virgin. "'And I said, "You Spaniards, you make so much of a person's honor, but since you've kissed me on the lips I have been dishonored."'" The attractive though hard face of the light-haired Lyuda communicated the despair of a violated girl." Muza, "excessively plump, coarse-featured, and wearing glasses," does not have the "attractive" face of Lyuda, but it is she who genuinely feels that she has been violated. But now that she has been violated, "[W]hat miserable choice did they leave her" but to accede to their insistent demand? (pp. 308, 309).

However, although it is clear that Muza has in any event been crushed, it is not certain as to what decision she will come.

Complex characters, unlike those of Galakhov, are not always predictable. Indeed they often do not understand themselves or each other. This is illustrated by Nadya and Nerzhin. Nadya has been so devoted and faithful to Nerzhin that, overwhelmed by love and gratitude, he wonders if he could have been as steadfast as she. He had urged her to divorce him, but her only thought on hearing this was that he was rejecting her. But then, after a long separation, when they have a brief visit under the surveillance of a guard, despite their love each ironically is unable to communicate with the other. She suggests a nominal divorce, as his prison sentence has been blighting her academic career and her whole life, assuring him that she will remain true to him. Instead of the expression of forgiveness and understanding for which she yearns, he heartily tells her, "Good girl. You should have done it long ago!" She does not know that inwardly he is trembling with doubt and fear.

He for his part feels that he must warn her that his term may be extended. He does not know the devastating effect his words will have on her. "He did not understand that his wife even now continued, as at the beginning, to count off methodically the days and weeks of his term. For him the term was a bright, cold endlessness . . . ." Looking at him, she thinks—and here she is in good part right—that he has come to terms with his life. "He never needed anyone's sympathy . . . . Did he really need a woman's loyalty?" (pp. 255, 256, 257). But Nerzhin does not guess these half-formed doubts that are assailing Nadya.

Without quite realizing what she has been doing, Nadya in her loneliness has been flirting with a man who is interested in her. Now in her despair she tells him of her visit with her husband. What will be the outcome of this new intimacy remains uncertain. Nerzhin, on the other hand, has made a rendezvous in a locked acoustic booth with Simochka, a free employee who has fallen in love with him. The visit has an opposite effect on him than it has on Nadya: he tells Simochka that he has had an unexpected visit from his wife and that he feels now that he cannot keep the rendezvous. "Nine out of ten men would have ridiculed Nerzhin for his renunciation—after so many years of deprivation. . . . But he was happy he had acted as he had. He was moved . . . as if it were someone else who had made the great decision" (p. 603). Unknown to him, he makes his renunciation as the long-faithful Nadya is perhaps on the verge of giving up hers.

It is not alone those who face moral decisions who do not know themselves. Major Shikin, the security officer at the Mavrino Institute, has the soul of a bookkeeper. He prides himself on the completeness and tidiness of his records as well as on the general deference he receives. "If anyone had said to Shikin (as no one ever did) that he inspired hatred, that he tortured other people, he would have been genuinely outraged. For him torturing people had never been a gratification or an end in itself. . . . Shikin only carried out his duty, and his sole purpose was that no one should think or do anything harmful" (p. 510). He is not aware that it is he who is doing harm.

So too Lieutenant Colonel Klimentiev, the head of the Mavrino Special Prison, a military martinet, "brought to prison, he believed, not a degrading discipline but rational military order." The rationality of his regime can be judged from his briefing to the guards who are to supervise the visits of the prisoners' wives. In it he emphasizes that the prisoners' "single-minded wish" is "to use this particular visit to transmit state secrets in their possession through their wives directly to the U.S.A." and that "a scrap of paper, transmitted from Mavrino, might destroy the whole country."

Colonel Klimentiev, having consulted the regulations and considering it advisable to be magnanimous during the holiday period, which is always a difficult time for prisoners, has granted the prisoners' petition that they be permitted to have a New Year's tree. "Getting on the subway, he had thought about himself with satisfaction; after all, he was essentially an intelligent, businesslike person, not a bureaucratic clod; a kind person, even; but the prisoners would never appreciate that . . . ."

On the subway, recognized and accosted by Nadya, who urgently inquires about her long-standing application for a visit, he is taken aback by her intensity and embarrassed by such a conversation taking place in public. On impulse he tells her that the visit has been approved. When her eyes fill with tears, "[a]voiding those tears, that gratitude, and all such nonsense, Klimentiev got out. . . . He was surprised that he had said what he had, and was annoyed with himself" (pp. 173–80). Even the Colonel has his "weaknesses."

Other executive officers are less robotized than Shikin and Klimentiev. They are human beings, not stereotyped villains, but they have degenerated as a result of having made the wrong choices in life. Solzhenitsyn in *The Gulag Archipelago* tells of how he was once approached in his youth to enter a training school for secret police. If enough pressure had been exerted, he says, he thinks he would have given in and become an NKVD man like others. Underlying the depiction of the Mavrino officers is the sense that "there but for the grace of God go I."

Lieutenant Nadelashin, Klimentiev's junior officer, is his opposite. "[R]ound-faced, ridiculous, not at all a military type," with his fresh face and cheeks that take on spots of red at moments of anxiety in front of his superior, he looks younger than his thirty years. Klimentiev too looks younger than his age, but that is because "at forty-five he carried himself like a young, well-built military man" and because his flat hair is shiny black like "painted cast iron." The unsmiling "dark moroseness of his face" is also like cast iron, unlike the face of the constantly smiling Nadelashin.

Nadelashin's "natural good nature had long been a handicap to him in the security organization. Had he not managed to adapt himself, he would have been expelled a long time ago or even imprisoned." Because he smiled upon the prisoners "with honest goodwill" and did what he could for them, they loved him and talked freely in front of him. These conversations he wrote up afterward in a special notebook and "reported the contents of his notebook to his superiors, thus making up for his shortcomings" (pp. 166, 172–73).

Colonel Yakonov, chief of operations at the Mavrino Institute, and his deputy, Major Roitman, differ entirely from each other. Yakonov is tall and impressive-looking, with "majestically assured movements" (p. 44), while Roitman has an "unfortunate appearance; his thick lips always parted for breath because of the polyps in his nose" (p. 586). From their very first meeting, they do not like each other. They engage in bureaucratic infighting, each backing a different project for solving the problem of identifying voices on the telephone.

Yakonov came from an upper-class background. Therefore, as a young man he was all the more zealous to prove his devotion to the Revolution. He defended the actions of the regime to his fiancée, no doubt half-believing what he was saying, but the chief determinant of his behavior was the fact that the disadvantage of his social origin caused him to keep his eyes open for the main chance. When, after an official trip abroad, he wrote at the behest of the regime an article on the capitalist world that was full of half-lies, his fiancée left him. Without her constant criticism, he breathed easier and was able to pay better attention to his career.

Yakonov is content to have the reputation of being an expert while being at a considerable remove from the work being done and, without giving any real direction, imperially presiding over the Institute. He is old enough and experienced enough to avoid the struggle over a Gold Star or a Stalin Prize, knowing that with ambition there comes anxiety. The maintenance of his comfortable and prestigious position is sufficient for him.

Roitman, on the other hand, as a Jew whose people had been relieved by the Revolution from pogroms and settlement restrictions, was as a child genuinely devoted to the new regime. Following the herd in the manner of children, he had participated in the baiting of a boy of upper-class origin. The baiting culminated in the accusation without any real basis in fact of anti-Semitism, in those days a grave offense, and the expulsion of the boy from the Young Pioneers and the Soviet school system. Roitman has continued to retain within himself the half-suppressed memory of this incident as a shameful action on his part.

Roitman has an advantage over Yakanov in their bitter contest in that he is a Communist Party member and Yakanov is not. The "Young Turks" at the Institute, all in the party, are afraid that Yakanov will get the Stalin Prize solely for himself, not realizing that he has no desire for it. They adopt resolutions at their meetings that undermine his position by suggesting that he is doing things wrong. At times Roitman even feels sorry for Yakanov but he does not know how to put an end to the struggle. He is not aware of the similarity between the castigation of the Young Pioneer and the criticism of Yakanov, and Solzhenitsyn, as he often does, leaves it to the reader to perceive the irony.

What drives Roitman on is his ambition. Only at rare moments does he realize that he hates the cut-throat competition to come out on top and that he has stopped enjoying his job. Without even having noticed it, he has slipped from being a creator into being a boss of creators. But although the enthusiasm of inquiry is no longer his, his ambition does not permit him to give up the role that has become his.

Each of the two has a major vulnerability. Yakanov was once in a prison camp for six years: ironically, the trips abroad that had been the basis for his article, through which he had thought to get ahead, had made him subject to accusations of dealing with the West. This experience only made him stay away from all who had been in the camp with him so that he might incur no suspicion. Although his prison-camp record does not permit him to become a Communist, he feels secure in his present high position. He does not, however, wish to be reminded of the past and has no sympathy for the prisoners in the sharashka, by whom he is hated, unlike Roitman, who is liked for his decent behavior toward them.

Roitman's vulnerability is that he is Jewish. The Stalinist campaign against "cosmopolitans," a code word for Jews, takes him by surprise. He is now victimized for his racial origin, as the Young Pioneer was victimized for his social origin. Most of the "Young Turks" are Jewish, and their position is destroyed by this fact. Yakanov seizes the occasion to denounce "cosmopolitanism" pitilessly at every opportunity.

Although Roitman is a much more sympathetic character than Yakanov, it is not only Roitman who evokes compassion in his suffering. Yakanov has been told that, because of the failure of the project and his lies about it, unless it becomes successful within the seemingly impossible time of a month, it will be inferred that his prison record indicates he is engaged in willful sabotage and he will become a prisoner in the sharashka. So pitifully transformed is he that his chauffeur, who has been waiting hours for him, angrily remembering all of Yakanov's nasty actions in the past, feels his anger evaporate when he sees Yakanov's face. It is at this time too that we learn of Yakanov's love for his wife and two children, just as, in the chapter in which Roitman lies awake tormenting himself with his fears and painful memories, we see his tenderness toward his wife sleeping by his side.

It is not only characters which contrast with each other. There are parallel and contrasting situations. In the main they serve to suggest that some zeks through their very suffering are able to attain higher moral values than people in the outside world. Nerzhin's birthday party, with its improvised "delicacies" and highly diluted spirits obtained from the chemical laboratory, which are nevertheless eagerly awaited, contrasts with the lavish dinner party of the prosecutor Makarygin, where the guests are "caught up in their social duties, talking, joking, and showing a careful lack of interest in the food" (p.

403). Makarygin's party begins with "formal toasts: to Comrade Stalin, to officials of the judiciary, and to the host—that this honor might not be his last" (p. 402). Nerzhin, however, interrupts the traditional toast to the birthday celebrant to say, "Let's not burden ourselves with ceremony. Let's raise a toast to the friendship which thrives in prison vaults!" (p. 370). Moved by "the men's warm feelings, showing in their eyes," Nerzhin exclaims, "This happiness we have right now—a free banquet, an exchange of free thoughts without fear, without conceal-ment—we didn't have that in freedom." Indeed this is so, and it is another contrast with Makarygin's party.

At each party the conversation turns to art. The zek painter Kondrashev-Ivanov speaks exaltedly of an aspiring art that goes beyond surface realism; the equable young critic Lansky, already an ornament of the literary establishment, speaks of drama that will portray real life (as seen through official eyes) and that will contain the proper conventional sentiments. Dinera, the daughter of Makarygin and wife of the novelist Galakhov, takes issue with Lansky. She is well known for the daring of her judgments, of her dress, and of her life, which makes her excitingly different, but her criticism is "always just within the bounds." Speaking of the insipid plays on the stage, she says, "I promise you, someday I won't hold myself back, I'll put two fingers in my mouth and give such a whistle—" But this pampered intelligentsia, even at its most "daring," is incapable—"someday" or ever—of protesting with derisive whistles that which is false and hollow: "She pursed her lips very daintily to show how, from which it was clear that she didn't know how to whistle."

In this society it is impossible for there to be a free exchange of thoughts. Galakhov, speaking to Makarygin's other son-in-law, the diplomat Volodin, is "longing to speak out, to say what he could not say in literary circles," but he is guarded. Even Volodin, though more honest and somewhat under the influence of the dinner wine, is not entirely free of caution.

Another parallel situation is that of Sunday evening in the women's dormitory and Sunday evening in the zek barracks. Lyuda provokes a quarrel with the other students. "All five of them were shouting at once, no one listening to anyone, no one agreeing with anyone." When Lyuda and another girl go out on dates, the room becomes dispirited. "It was unbearable to think that they were going to kill Sunday night in this hole of a place." When the current goes down and the electric light dims, one of the girls groans, "You could hang yourself in a place like this!" (pp. 325–26). In order to be "doing something," they go to a movie that they know is trashy.

Sunday evening is the one time of the week that the sharashka zeks do not have to work. There are no movies or other recreation for them since the prison administration feels it has to maintain extra vigilance on Sundays. Their only recreation, therefore, is lying down, lounging about, or talking. Nevertheless, Sunday evening is a special time. "The feeling of plenitude during the Sunday rest came from the fact that the time belonged to them, not to the government. Therefore the rest period was appreciated as something real."

The rest period means for the zeks that "the entire outside world . . . had sunk into nonexistence." It was as if they could look into the depths of life, their minds illuminated by the bright lights that contrast with the dim bulb in the dormitory.

> The light of bright bulbs reflected from the white ceilings, from the white-washed walls, flooded their lucid minds. . . . In these Sunday evening hours solid matter and flesh no longer reminded people of their earthly existence. The spirit of male friendship and philosophy filled the sail-like arches overhead. Perhaps this was, indeed, that bliss which all the philosophers of antiquity tried in vain to define and teach to others (339–40).

Another instance of a parallel situation is when Yakanov wants Nerzhin to move from the acoustics laboratory to cryptography. A former teacher of Nerzhin's, now employed by state security, who is to be his superior, tells Nerzhin that if the work is successful he will be freed and the conviction removed from his record. "They'll remove the conviction from my record!" Nerzhin exclaims to his former teacher. " 'You've worked well, so we'll free you, forgive you.' . . . Let them admit first that it's not right to put people in prison for their way of thinking, and then *we* will decide whether we will forgive *them*."

In the next chapter we are told of how Yakanov, when selected for the telephone project, true to his principle of avoiding such risky projects, sought to argue that he was overloaded with work and could not undertake it. "The head of the section, Foma Guryanovich Oskolupov, stared at Yakanov with his green, feline eyes—and Yakanov remembered the stain on his official security record. . . . So he kept his mouth shut" (pp. 50–52). The zek, offered a job he doesn't want with the enticement that his conviction will be expunged from his record, is indignant at the supposed magnanimity; the chief of operations, offered a job he doesn't want, is fearfully silent at the recollection of his vulnerability because of his conviction.

In addition to parallel situations there are ironic juxtapositions between the conclusion of one chapter and the beginning of another chapter. Thus at the conclusion of Chapter 23 Yakanov, who has been walking about aimlessly in his agony, finds himself at the site of a beautiful church that, twenty-two years before, his fiancée had brought him to so that he might admire it. Now it is in the process of being demolished to be replaced by a skyscraper. As he rouses himself from his reverie about his past life, the terror of the threat he has received strikes him again. "Yakanov . . . held high rank in a powerful ministry. . . . Yet he . . . did not want to live any longer. Everything was so hopeless within him that he had no strength to move. It was growing light . . . . Abundant hoarfrost furred . . . a stretch of the long, circular fence around the construction site of the future skyscraper."

The beginning of the next chapter echoes these words but offers an ironic contrast in its description of Sologdin, the zek who has come to saw wood because of the excess of vitality he is experiencing, now that his muscles, which had become like dry strings during his interrogations, have grown solid once more. "It was growing light. The regal, lavish hoarfrost covered not only the fence posts . . . but also the barbed wire, twisted into a thousand tiny stars. . . . Dmitri Sologdin gazed wide-eyed at this miracle and took delight in it. . . . He was an insignificant slave with no rights. . . . Yet there was an inviolable peace in his soul. . . . His chest bared to the frost rose with the fullness of life" (pp. 149–51). It is the zek, not the powerful administrator, who has peace of mind and contentment.

So too the first sentence of Chapter 60 tells of Ruska's happiness at the half-promise Clara Makarygin had given him that morning to wait for him until his prison term was completed. A free employee at the sharashka, she had been attracted to him by his personality and by his novel ideas, which appealed to her rebelliousness. He does not know that at this very moment, as we have been told in the final paragraph of the preceding chapter, Clara is agreeing to a New Year's Eve date with her suitor Lansky that will eventuate in their engagement. Overflowing with youthful vitality, carried away by the gaiety of the young people at her father's party, she does not have the fortitude to wait for a zek.

Ironically, in the intoxication of his love, Ruska both dooms himself and at the same time possibly saves himself. Wanting to rehabilitate his reputation with his comrades and to impress Clara, he devises a clever scheme that will expose the other informers. It succeeds, but it causes him to be revealed to the authorities as a double agent, and he is sent at the conclusion of the novel to a regular labor camp in the company of Gerasimovich and Nerzhin. The camp will furnish him the opportunity, if he is able to take advantage of it, for undergoing a rehabilitation not just of reputation but of character.

Gerasimovich is being deported because of his refusal to work on the camera for door frames. Nerzhin is being deported because he refuses to save himself by accepting Sologdin's offer to have him assigned to a special project Sologdin is heading. The refusal, however, stems not so much from a desire not to cooperate with the authorities (he does not know the nature of the project) as from a desire to test himself through hardship and in doing so to rise above the petty circumstances of life that submerge our best intentions. "Thank you, Dmitri," he tells Sologdin (p. 658). ". . . But for some reason I'm in a mood to try an experiment for myself. The proverb says: *'It's not the sea that drowns you, it's the puddle.'* I want to try launching myself into the sea."

Nerzhin in his search for meaning has been growing in moral strength. After his imprisonment he was horrified to observe "delicate, sensitive, highly educated persons who . . . degenerated into traitors, beggars, and hypocrites. And Nerzhin had just barely escaped becoming like them" (p. 450). "Everyone," he learned, "forges his inner self year after year. One must try to temper, to cut, to polish one's soul so as to become *a human being*" (p. 452). The conclusion marks the final tempering of Nerzhin's soul into a diamond's brilliance.

He has learned from the peasant Spiridon, the artist Kondrashev-Ivanov, and the individualistic intellectual Sologdin. Nerzhin, however, goes beyond his teachers. From Sologdin he learns what Sologdin does not himself really assimilate. He continues to strive to improve himself, as Sologdin does not. In the humility of his truth-seeking Nerzhin is conscious of his weaknesses. "I try to have only lofty thoughts," he exclaims (p. 41). "But circumstances overcome me and I get dizzy; I fight back in outrage." Sologdin, on the other hand, has a self-deprecatory manner, but this is ironic and simply the expression of his sense of superiority over everyone else. Thus Nerzhin's renunciation of Simochka contrasts with Sologdin's succumbing to Larisa, a free employee who is the wife of a lieutenant colonel in the MVD, after having given himself in his eccentric systematic fashion a number of "penalty marks" for desiring her and after having told her, "A man must develop unwavering will power subject only to his reason" (p. 210).

So too, when Nerzhin and Sologdin are sawing wood together, each holding one end of the saw, Nerzhin thinks to himself that "it was Sologdin who had first nudged him into thinking that a person shouldn't regard prison solely as a curse, but also as a blessing." At the same time "his partner . . . was thinking of prison as nothing but an unmitigated curse from which one must surely escape someday" (p. 158).

Sologdin and Rubin, who have completely different philosophies, find it hard to get along together. Sologdin is cold and arrogant; Rubin is warm-hearted but wrongheaded in his adherence to Stalinism. Yet extremes meet, and the two are in many ways alike, both of them contrasting with Nerzhin. Each regards Nerzhin's friendship with Spiridon as a repetition of the nineteenth-century idealization of "the people" and as a vain search for some "great homespun truth." "Rubin and Sologdin didn't bother looking for this homespun truth themselves because they were in firm possession of absolute truth." Rubin knew that the term "the people" covered many social classes, of which only the proletariat counted in enabling one to attain life's highest significance, and Sologdin "knew equally well that 'the people' is an over-all term for a totality of persons of slight interest," with "only unique personalities" being capable of "supreme understanding" (pp. 448–49). But Nerzhin does not idealize either the Russian people at large or a single class or an intellectual élite. One becomes a true human being only by working at it, and then one becomes a member of a fellowship of kindred souls. These constitute the true "people."

But Rubin and Sologdin, in possession of absolute truth, do not engage in a search for it or in an exploration of their inner selves. In a violent quarrel they tell each other some home truths. Rubin accuses Sologdin of being a poseur with a philosophy on which he does not act. Sologdin accuses Rubin of intellectual inconsistencies with moral consequences in his defense of an indefensible society. Each charges that the other will accommodate himself to the wishes of the authorities while rationalizing his action.

This is indeed what happens. Sologdin creates a design for an encoder that will enable telephone voices to be identified. Even though he realizes that it will be used by an unscrupulous regime to trap innocent human beings, he uses it to bargain for and gain his freedom from Yakanov. Rubin, comparing the voice prints in the recorded telephone conversation between Volodin giving his warning and the voice prints of the recordings of five suspects, is carried away by the excitement of developing a new science of phonoscopy. He convinces himself that Volodin's innocent-sounding warning must really be the coded message of a spy.

Volodin, apprehended near the end of the novel, is abruptly reduced from a member of the Soviet élite to a zek. In the shock of his fall he realizes more deeply than ever the inadequacy of the hedonistic philosophy that had guided him. His fate converges with that of Nerzhin, Gerasimovich, and Ruska, who have never met him. In the cruel land of the zeks, most become hardened, cynical, and self-seeking, but some grow in moral stature. It all depends on the moral choices they make. This underlying theme emerges strongly in the conclusion.

The greatest weakness in this towering novel is the character of Stalin, who is the center of four chapters. It is to Stalin that Kopelev was, it seems, referring when he deplored the characters "conceived in newspaper and archival test-tubes." Other critics have disagreed among themselves as to the artistic success of Solzhenitsyn's Stalin. Actually, there is truth on the side of both those who regard the portrait as a success and those who regard it as a failure. Convincing and masterfully executed as it is in many respects, it is finally only a partial success as a result of Solzhenitsyn's hatred, which causes him to depart from complete accuracy of portraiture and to err artistically by making Stalin to be in some respects unbelievable.

To begin with what is successful, Solzhenitsyn, taking us into the mind of Stalin and showing us how things seem to him, conveys the megalomania that compensates for his abiding sense of inferiority with regard to other party leaders and his intense envy of them. Indebted to the Secret Speech in which Khrushchev gave as an example of Stalin's extraordinary vanity his supervision of a biography of himself, strengthening its grossly fulsome adulation and personally adding a statement about his own great modesty, Solzhenitsyn makes this biography Stalin's favorite reading. He savors the adulation and acknowledges to himself the truth of it all, including the statement about his modesty.

At the same time, even as he is thinking, "How could he leave humanity? In whose care? They'd make a mess of everything" (p. 131), there is a gnawing awareness within him that the party antagonists he defeated were intellectually superior to him. Vindictively hating "especially those who spoke well" (p. 122), he had annihilated them. But "[f]or some reason it always happened that annihilated opponents turned out to have been right about something. Fascinated by their hostile thoughts, Stalin listened wearily to their voices from beyond the grave" (p. 110).

Similarly, still operating from within Stalin's mind, Solzhenitsyn conveys his loneliness, brutality, crudeness, morbid suspiciousness, and mediocrity of intellect. So greatly deluded is he about himself that he may be said to be half-mad, even coming close to regarding himself, like another Nero, as a god. We can see how the sense of absolute power and the atmosphere of adulation were enough to make anyone lose contact with reality, and indeed Khrushchev's allusion to "the sickness which began to envelop Stalin's mind in the last years of his life,"[2] manifested in his belief in his infallibility and his paranoid suspicions, bears Solzhenitsyn out.

Thinking to die as "Emperor of the Planet," "the Greatest of the Great, without equal on the history of the earth" (pp. 130–31), Stalin is yet a prisoner of his own system. Deathly afraid of assassination, he spends the lonely night in a "small and low" windowless room, most of whose space is "taken up by a low, dark ottoman." The uncurtained heavy door is bolted, the bolt operating by a remote-control switch beside his couch. In another room there is a "tiny window" with bulletproof glass through which one cannot see and a steel shutter. Behind the walls there is armor plate and, on the outside, stone. Outside there is "a small, fenced-in garden where, mornings only, the gardener went about under the eyes of a guard." About the grounds of the house are three circles of fencing. The room is small because Stalin is afraid of space; there are no curtains so that no one may hide behind them; the ottoman has flower-patterned pillows, and the rooms are air-conditioned. Nevertheless the rooms are nothing so much like cells in a prison, with prisoners' cots, shuttered windows, an enclosed and guarded recreation area outside, and barbed wire around the area.

Stalin is at the topmost rung of the hierarchical ladder, which is governed to the *n*th degree by the principle that General Cummings in Norman Mailer's *The Naked and the Dead* says is the guiding principle of the United States Army: "The Army functions best when you're frightened of the man above you, and contemptuous of your subordinates."[3] There is no one above Stalin for him to fear; instead, he is afraid of everyone.

The irony underlying the portrait of Stalin receives powerful expression in the description of his savoring of the book on Tito that he has had written. This, like his own biography, was published in millions of copies. "How many eyes," he thinks, "it would open to this self-adoring, cruel, cowardly, perfidious, evil tyrant! This loathsome traitor! This hopeless blockhead!" (p. 106). Of course, these words apply to Stalin himself, and the biography of Tito is what an honest biography of Stalin would have been.

At times, however, the irony becomes too insistent. Stalin is repeatedly referred to by Solzhenitsyn as "the Greatest of all the Great," "the Wisest of the Wise," "the Nearest and Dearest," and similar epithets. This comes to seem heavy-handed, as overdone as the italics and exclamation points that abound in Solzhenitsyn's polemical works.

More than this, some aspects of Solzhenitsyn's portrait of Stalin raise doubts in the reader's mind. Solzhenitsyn contrasts throughout the mediocrity of the man and the immense power he attained. He does not explain how this mediocre person attained that power. The consequence is that the reader senses elements of implausibility in the picture. Solzhenitsyn, furthermore, contrasts Stalin with Lenin throughout the novel, Stalin comparing Lenin unfavorably with himself, and Nerzhin, who deeply admires Lenin and hates Stalin, finding that the different prose styles of the two men proclaim the difference between the greatness of spirit and intellect of Lenin and the dull brutishness of Stalin. But then how did Stalin rise to the position that he did in Lenin's party? Again, Solzhenitsyn does not explain this.

Solzhenitsyn does not show Stalin as having undergone any change. He is unwilling to concede that he had any positive qualities at any time. In this he is quite unlike Leon Trotsky, who, stalked by Stalin's assassins as he was, with his children killed before him by Stalin's vindictiveness, and calumniated by a huge propaganda machine on an unprecedented scale, was more objective than Solzhenitsyn. Thus Solzhenitsyn treats the words of Stalin's biography about his "iron will" as ironically as he does its words about his modesty. His will is really a practiced pose. He takes a nip of liqueur to buck himself up and then looks in the mirror to insure that his eyes appear "incorruptibly stern" before he summons his orderly. "Even to those close to him he appeared as he would to history. His iron will. His inflexible will" (p. 108). Trotsky, on the other hand, speaks of "the strength of Stalin's will" and even says that it "is not inferior perhaps to that of Lenin's."[4]

Solzhenitsyn makes Stalin subject to ungovernable terrors. In 1937, on visiting the Museum of the Revolution, he comes upon the portraits of two terrorists of Czarist days. Their faces seem to him to proclaim: "Kill the tyrant!" "Stalin, struck by their twin stares as by two shots, drew back, wheezed, coughed. His finger shook, pointing at the portraits. They were removed immediately" (p. 124). Trotsky, however, while saying, "The mainspring of the policy of Stalin himself is now his fear of the fear which he has engendered," adds, "Stalin personally is not a coward, but his policy reflects the fear of the privileged parvenus for their own future."[5]

Finally Trotsky, like Solzhenitsyn, speaks of Stalin's mediocrity as far as intellectual creativity is concerned, but, unlike Solzhenitsyn, he gives him credit for some kinds of intellectual ability to a high degree. There is in Stalin, he says, an "extreme development of practical sagacity and cunning at the expense of the ability to generalize and of the creative imagination. . . . A shrewd tactician, he is not a strategist." But Stalin is not content with the abilities he has; his "consciousness of his mediocrity" as a theoretician, writer, and orator explains "his need for flattery."[6]

Trotsky's comments are corroborated by others. General Zhukov, who, demoted by Stalin because of his jealousy of his war-time popularity, had no reason to love him, said of Stalin, "You can say what you like, but that man has got nerves of steel."[7] To be sure, according to Khrushchev's and other accounts, he was paralyzed by depression during the first weeks of shocking defeats after Hitler's invasion; yet he recovered and presented to the world an imperturbable face. Averell Harriman and other Allied visitors were greatly impressed by his organizational and administrative ability and by his mastery of detail in managing military, political, and diplomatic matters. The other side of it was that, as Khrushchev revealed, his centralized control hamstrung his commanders and his false belief in himself as a great military strategist was the cause of many disasters. Managerial ability and firmness of will could not take the place of creative imagination and democratic procedure.

Solzhenitsyn's Stalin, without ability in any sphere, terror-ridden, a poseur without genuine strength of character, could not possibly have gained power. The character traits of Stalin that Solzhenitsyn shows could not by themselves have enabled him to do so. In combination, however, with the willpower and organizational ability of the real-life Stalin whom Trotsky describes, they did under the given social circumstances bring about his victory. As Trotsky says,

> Such attributes of character as slyness, faithlessness, the ability to exploit the lowest instincts of human nature are developed to an extraordinary degree in Stalin and, considering his strong character, represent mighty weapons in a struggle. Not, of course, any struggle. The struggle to liberate the masses requires other attributes. But in selecting men for privileged positions, in welding them together in the spirit of caste, in weakening and disciplining the masses, Stalin's attributes were truly invaluable and rightfully made him the leader of the bureaucratic reaction.[8]

This understanding of the interrelation of personality and social forces is lacking in Solzhenitsyn's portrayal of Stalin and weakens his characterization.

This characterization is further weakened by Solzhenitsyn's failure to show Stalin's degeneration, as he shows that of Makarygin and Yakanov. As a revolutionist Stalin displayed the virtues of courage, determination, and perseverance necessary for underground opponents of the Czarist regime. Like other revolutionaries, he hated the rulers of his society, but in hating the oppressors the cold, calculating Stalin was not animated, as were his ardent young comrades, by sympathy for the oppressed. He masked his envy, vindictiveness, and malevolence, but about no other Bolshevik were there rumors about intrigue and duplicity as there were about him at all stages of his career. Nevertheless, these were only rumors that were at the time dismissed.

Like Iago, he had the exterior of a plain dealer, a blunt, unpolished man without airs or pretensions, and he was generally regarded by those who knew him in the party as a rough diamond in his hardness.[9] The poisonous flower of evil in him, which had its seed in his harsh, meager childhood and his resentment of his inferior social position among his seminary classmates, was present in bud from his early years, but it only fully blossomed in the struggle for power and reached giant size after the attainment of power. Solzhenitsyn shows his moral monstrosity but not how it came into being and developed.

In *Cancer Ward*, instead of showing the chain of command in Soviet society reaching up to the very top, as he does in *The First Circle*, Solzhenitsyn shows a cross-section of Soviet society two years after Stalin's death, the action taking place in February and March of 1955. The patients in the ward are drawn from all classes and nationalities. In some ways they are like the zeks of *The First Circle*. All of them are under sentence—the sentence of death. Entering the cancer ward is like undergoing imprisonment. The bureaucrat Rusanov looks with dismay upon "the eight abject human beings who were now his 'equals'" in their uniformly faded hospital pajamas. "In a matter of hours he had as good as lost all his personal status, reputation, and plans for the future" (pp. 9, 10), just as Volodin had suddenly dropped as though through a trapdoor from his high position into the world of the zeks.

The doctors live in a different world from that of their patients. They constitute a little society of their own, meeting at planning sessions presided over by the head of the hospital, an imposing-looking incompetent who has loaded the staff with incompetents like himself. We are reminded of the statement in *The First Circle*, "Just as King Midas turned everything to gold, Stalin turned everything to mediocrity" (p. 123). The head of the hospital is typical, as the surgeon on whom the hospital depends realizes. "He knew that administrators were seldom efficient in their actual profession" (p. 355).

There are, however, many devoted doctors who are sympathetic and caring toward their patients. But even these cannot really enter the world of the patients. This is illustrated by Dontsova, the radiologist who in her devotion to her work has overly exposed herself to X-rays and contracted cancer. When she consults her old professor about her symptoms, she feels as if she is at the bar of judgment. "[H]aving confessed to being ill was like having confessed to a crime . . . . By her confession she had excluded herself from the noble estate of medical men and transferred herself to the tax-paying dependent estate of patients" (p. 419). Waiting to hear the decision he and her colleagues have come to, she reflects, "How many times had patients sat there waiting for her to announce her decision after a similar moment of respite? . . . What a cask of horrors, she now thought, lies concealed in this moment of respite!" (p. 448).

It is not only doctors and patients who cannot enter each other's worlds. People who have not been zeks, it appears, cannot understand what it means to have been one. Ahmadjan, a young Uzbek who speaks only broken Russian, happy at being released from the hospital, holds forth about the zeks over whom he had been a guard. They eat well, he claims, and don't do any work. The ward accepts what he has to say without question—except for the former zek Kostoglotov. Kostoglotov is amazed to learn that the simple, cheerful Ahmadjan had been a concentration-camp guard and that the ward is ready to believe his description of zek life. "Ahmadjan was uneducated above the checker-playing level, but he was sincere and straightforward. If decade after decade no one tells the true story, each person's mind goes its own separate way. One's fellow countrymen become harder to understand than Martians" (p. 458).

Yet Kostoglotov himself is able to understand and forgive those who without protest went along with Stalin's witch-hunts. Shulubin, who for the sake of his own skin did so, cannot forgive himself or the rest of the country, but Kostoglotov, who was thrown into labor camp for having criticized Stalin, does forgive Shulubin and, except for those who played active roles as denunciators and witnesses, the others. "[I]t all depends on the number you draw," he tells Shulubin. "If the position had been reversed it would have been just the opposite: you'd have been the martyrs, we'd have been the time-servers." Here, even more clearly than in *The First Circle*, is expressed the idea "There but for the grace of God go I." As for the country at large, an entire nation cannot be condemned for bowing to force. "A storm breaks trees, it only bends grass. Does this mean that the grass has betrayed the trees? Everyone has his own life. As you said, the law of a nation is to survive" (pp. 433, 435).

Kostoglotov's understanding and compassionate attitude toward Shulubin has some similarity to Solzhenitsyn's attitude toward the patients. With the exception of Kostoglotov and the sixteen-year-old

Dyomka, who have other functions, each of the major characters among the patients has a cancer that is related to a life that is in some way inadequate. In *The First Circle* the thematic framework that holds the novel together is that of the moral choices the characters have to make; in *Cancer Ward* the thematic framework is the manner in which their cancers act as a comment on their false values. The connection between cancer and character, sometimes explicitly stated and sometimes not, creates an ironic effect, all the more powerful when the significance of the cancer is suddenly perceived. Accompanying the irony, however, is Solzhenitsyn's compassion, which more or less extends to everyone but Rusanov.

To begin with those where the connection between cancer and character is most obvious, Yefrem Podduyev, a construction foreman who has knocked about all over the Soviet Union collecting fat bonuses for his work, has cancer of the tongue. His only thought in life had been to revel in his physical strength and his self-assurance and to have a good time. Reading for anything but practical purposes seemed to him ridiculous: he never found a book "for a man with an intelligent turn of mind." When Yefrem found his tongue swelling within his mouth, he was secretly terrified although he tried to swagger among his workmates with his old bravado. "The whole of his life had prepared Podduyev for living, not for dying." But when he finally has to acknowledge to himself that he has cancer, he has no idea how to face death.

During his lifetime Yefrem has given his tongue a lot of exercise, talking his way into pay he never earned, standing up to the bosses over him, and shouting insults at the workers under him. With it he "lied to hundreds of women scattered all over the place, that he wasn't married, that he had no children, that he'd be back in a week and they'd start building a house. 'God rot your tongue!' one temporary mother-in-law had cursed him, but Yefrem's tongue had never let him down except when he was blind drunk" (pp. 97, 94). But now his tongue had finally failed him.

In contrast to the rough-and-ready Yefrem is the man of books, a lecturer in philosophy who has cancer of the throat. Yefrem is familiarly called by his first name by everyone, even the younger patients, but the lecturer is not named at all. The "thickset, broad-shouldered" Yefrem has a "heavy block of a head" with a "great, wild, fox-colored thatch" of hair and a "broad, pock-marked sullen face" (pp. 8, 9); the lecturer is "quite a presentable man" (p. 132) with a "portly frame" that makes him look like "some sort of banker or minister" and "gray, sleek hair" (p. 148). Different as they are, however, they are united by their cancer: Yefrem speaks with a "throaty voice" (p. 8) and the lecturer speaks in a wheezing whisper. "Diseases of the tongue and throat, which made it impossible to talk, are somehow particularly oppressive" (p. 138).

Formerly a man of dignified professorial bearing, the lecturer wanders about the ward, abjectly frightened, asking other patients, all of them ignorant, what they have picked up about the progress of the disease. The learned academician is eager to grab at any comforting bit of misinformation he can. Kostoglotov exclaims on learning the man's profession, "A lecturer, and it's your throat!" and thinks to himself: "What did he churn out in his lectures anyway? Perhaps he was just clouding people's brains? And what was the point of all his philosophy if he was so completely helpless in the face of his illness? . . . But what a coincidence—in the throat, of all places!" (p. 149).

Shulubin, as gloomily taciturn as the lecturer is nervously talkative even with his barely audible voice, is also a man of books, a provincial librarian. He too had been a university lecturer, but, although he had done nothing to call attention to himself, he had been caught up in the academic purges and demoted to his obscure post. He does not engage in the conversation of the ward, says nothing of himself, and won't even say what his ailment is. A strangely disconcerting figure, he sits in a strained position and walks about with an oddly unnatural gait.

Just before his operation, when he is facing death and there is no other auditor, he tells Kostoglotov the bitter story of his silence during the Stalinist purges, a story he would not tell at any other time. "First I kept silent for my wife's sake, then for my children's sake, then for the sake of my own sinful body. But my wife died. . . . And my children have grown up so callous it's beyond my comprehension." Shulubin has cancer of the rectum, the explanation of his peculiar walk and sitting position, and now that body for the sake of which he had kept silent "is a bag full of manure—they're going to drill a hole for it on one side" (p. 437). His shame and self-disgust for the life he has led is expressed in the way he regards his illness: "My disease is something especially humiliating, especially offensive. . . . If I live—and it's a very big if—simply standing or sitting near me, like you are now, for instance, will be unpleasant. Everyone will do their best to keep two steps away. Even if anyone comes closer I'll still be thnking to myself, 'You see, he can hardly stand it, he's cursing me' " (pp. 431–32).

In contrast with Shulubin is the black-market operator Chaly, who enters the ward the same day he does. Shulubin is "a tall man" with "a terrible stoop" and a "crooked spine," the physical symbols of the moral twists and turns he has had to make. He has "a worn face like a very old man's" that gives him the appearance of "an exhausted actor" who has "just taken off his makeup," the face of one who has repressed his outrage and concealed his self-loathing most of his life. His distinctive feature is his "great, round, fixed eyes," which look upon everyone with "an unpleasant, attentive gaze" (pp. 299, 302, 320).

Chaly, on the other hand, is a "shortish, energetic-looking man" who walks "briskly and healthily into the ward." There is "nothing of the exhaustion of cancer on his face" and his smile twinkles "with confidence and *joie de vivre*." His "quick eyes" dart everywhere. His distinctive feature is his "great, soft, reddened nose." It is this that gives his "artless face" its "simple-hearted, attractive and open quality" (pp. 304–05, 316). He is as prepossessing as Shulubin is unprepossessing, but his clown's face is the expression of his moral vacuousness whereas Shulubin's tragic mask is the expression of the moral understanding he has gained through his suffering.

Both Shulubin and Chaly have their cancers in their digestive systems, Chaly's being in his stomach. Unlike the reticent Shulubin, he cheerfully announces at his arrival that three-quarters of his stomach will have to be hacked away, but he makes nothing of it. "If you don't want to croak, you shouldn't get yourself upset" (p. 307). He has no real idea, however, of what is entailed, saying that he has polyps in his stomach and voicing the maxim that vodka, which has been strictly forbidden to him by the doctors, is the cure for all illnesses. He is of course mistaken in his belief that vodka will cure his present illness, and it is not fortuitous that he, who so loves eating and drinking, has cancer of the stomach. "Life will always conquer," he asserts (p. 319), telling of how he is able to circumvent the Soviet authorities in his black-market operations by bribing all and sundry. He thinks to get around the doctors' orders in the same way, not realizing that in this instance life will not conquer.

The same kind of irony pervades the description of the seventeen-year-old Asya's discovery that she has cancer, but with it is a compassion that is more poignant than for any of the other patients. In the hospital for a check-up, she speaks to the sixteen-year-old Dyomka and is surprised and amused to infer that he is still a virgin. In his serious-minded way he tells her of Yefrem's repetition of Tolstoy's question, "What do people live for?" and she responds without having to think about it, "For love, of course." It is the same answer Tolstoy had given, but love for Asya is sexual gratification, not what it meant for Tolstoy. "The earlier you start," she exclaims, "the more exciting it is . . . . Why wait? It's the atomic age!" (pp. 130–31).

It is to this girl, who has urged Dyomka not to allow the amputation of his leg—"What sort of life is it for a cripple, do you think? Life is for happiness"—that there comes the news that she must have a breast removed. Beside herself with grief, she bursts into the room Dyomka now has after his amputation. Always mature for his age, he seems to have grown even older, soberly planning for the life that lies ahead of him. Asya, however, is utterly crushed. "No longer Dyomka's senior by a full year in school, she had lost her advantage of extra experience, her knowledge of life and the three long journeys she had made." Her "knowledge of life" has proven inadequate. It is he who is the mature and experienced one, as he feels more pity for her than he has ever felt for himself. But nothing he says can console her; indeed, nothing anyone could have said would have consoled her. "Her own experience led to only one conclusion: there was nothing to live for now" (pp. 392–93). It is the logical conclusion of her answer to Tolstoy's question, "What do people live for?"

The values of the twenty-three-year-old Vadim seem superior to those of Yefrem, the lecturer, Chaly, and Asya, but they too prove inadequate. A student of geology, he is entirely devoted to his science. He plans to spend the few months that he knows are all he has to live working to find the new method of discovering ore deposits for which he had done the field work. Thus he will atone for his early death and die reconciled. He is sure of himself and prides himself on his self-control. He is, however, unconsciously selfish, concerned only with doing his work without regard for others. The inadequacy of his values is pointed up by Shulubin, who, in response to Vadim's statement that his work is the most interesting thing he knows in the world, replies, " 'Interesting'—that's no argument. Business is interesting too . . . . If that's your explanation science becomes no different from the ordinary run of selfish, thoroughly unethical occupations" (p. 378).

Vadim is a member of the scientific élite and of the Communist Party. Like Rusanov, he is dismayed when on the second anniversary of Stalin's death the newspaper has only a brief article on him, not even on the front page and without the customary encomia.

> [A]ll reasonable considerations demanded that one honor the great man who had passed away. . . . He had exalted science, exalted scientists and freed them from petty thoughts of salary or accommodations. Science itself required his stability and his permanence to prevent any catastrophe happening that might distract scientists or take them away from their work, which was of supreme interest and use—for settling squabbles about the structure of society, for educating the underdeveloped or for convincing the stupid (pp. 311–12).

For Vadim the struggles against autocracy and special privileges are mere "squabbles." A strong leader is necessary to prevent "the underdeveloped" and "the stupid" from jeopardizing the stability that allows scientists to enjoy their precious work—and their high salaries and comfortable accommodations.

Like Dyomka's, Vadim's cancer is on his leg. His, however, is a melanoblastoma, which sends secondaries throughout the body, invariably resulting in death. Ever since childhood he had had a large patch of pigmentation on his leg, and his mother, a physician, aware of the danger of a malignancy setting in, was constantly probing it and once insisted on having a top surgeon conduct a preliminary operation. It was the wrong thing to have done, causing the tumor to flare up. Her pampering and interference, which may be said to resemble Stalin's pampering of the scientists and his interference in their field, brings disaster upon him.

Now his mother is engaged in pulling strings, invoking the memory of his war-hero father, to obtain colloidal gold to combat the secondaries. Vadim at first disliked this making use of privilege, but now he is waiting eagerly for a telegram announcing that she has been able to get the gold. His confident plans for his last months have not worked out. Not only his pain but his thoughts prevent him from working.

> For him to die before his talent had burst forth would be a much greater tragedy than an ordinary man's death, in fact

> more tragic than the death of any other man in the
> ward. . . . These hopes and despairs beat so insistently in his
> head that he found he was no longer fully grasping what he
> read. . . . [H]e could no longer scale other people's thoughts
> as a goat scales a mountain. . . . His leg was in a trap, and
> with it his whole life (p. 377).

His cancer had prevented him from going up into the mountains to
do his field work and now it has prevented him from scaling the
mountains of other people's thoughts. He does not face death as he
expected he would; although, unlike Asya, he outwardly maintains his
self-control, inwardly he is as a trapped animal.

Finally, there is Rusanov. Rusanov had started out as a worker but
has ascended the bureaucratic ladder. For the last twenty years he has
been in personnel records administration. He well knows how to
intimidate people, assuming a severe, authoritative manner and
making appointments with his victims for the following day so that
they have time to agonize over what incriminating matter in their
records he may have been able to find.

Rusanov likes to believe that he himself is afraid of nothing. After
all, in the security of his position what does he have to fear?
Nevertheless, although he tells himself that he loves the People and
would give up his life to serve it, he has found himself "less and less
able to tolerate actual human beings, those obstinate creatures who
were always resistant, refusing to do what they were told and, besides,
demanding something for themselves." Especially has he become wary
of those who are poorly dressed, impudent, or somewhat drunk. Such
louts are likely to bash his face in just for the fun of it, just as his sixth-
grade classmates had once beaten him up. "So although there was
nothing in the world Rusanov feared, he did begin to feel a totally
normal, justifiable fear of dissolute, half-drunk men, or, to be more
precise, of a fist striking him a direct blow in his face" (pp. 193–94).

When his wife tells him of how labor-camp prisoners are being
released, Rusanov is fearful that a former friend whom he had secretly
denounced early in his career in order to get full occupancy of the
apartment they had shared will also be freed. This former friend had
become obnoxious, laughingly telling Rusanov: "Look at you, you've
become such a weakling you'll wither away behind that leather door of
yours. Come down to the factory and I'll get you a job on the shop

floor, eh?" Who knows but that this robust athlete may have surmised who denounced him and will come charging into the ward to "punch him in the face" (pp. 185, 194).

Rusanov is made uneasy by the hard, accusatory stare of Shulubin, which feels "like a stubborn, reproachful pressure on the side of his head" (p. 308). That accusatory stare is like the tumor on the side of his neck, "pressing against him like an iron fist." His cancer is the fist of retribution of which he is terrified. "The terrible thing stuck to his neck was pressing up against his chin and down onto his collarbone. . . . His fate lay there, between his chin and his collarbone. There justice was being done. And in answer to this justice he could summon no influential friend, no past services, no defense" (pp. 195–96).

Counterposed to Rusanov is Kostoglotov. They instinctively dislike each other and get into an argument even before each knows who the other is. Rusanov sees Kostoglotov, who has a facial scar, black, dishevelled hair, and what seems to Rusanov to be a "coarse, tough expression," as having "a villainous cutthroat's mug" (pp. 10–11). In reality Kostoglotov's tough exterior reflects his experience as a zek (he had acquired the scar in a fight between the criminals and the political prisoners), but he has great sensitivity and compassion. Rusanov, seen through the eyes of the rough-hewn Yefrem, is a "milksop" and a "pipsqueak," a "scrubbed little man" with a "small, bald head" and gold-rimmed spectacles that give him the look of a professor (pp. 101, 104). However, although Rusanov may seem insignificant in the hospital bed, in his office those gold-rimmed spectacles, through which he could gaze coldly, flashed with authority.

Rusanov regards himself as the "new man" produced by Soviet society, a man of culture who intelligently and resolutely strives to overcome all obstacles standing in the way of the building of the bright future. But the bright future he envisages is simply the acquisition of more comfortable living arrangements for himself and his family. Looking upon the other patients, he reflects, "How dumb they all were, how submissive, wooden almost! . . . They were not really worthy of recovery. It must have been Gorky who said the only people worthy of freedom are those prepared to go out and fight for it every day" (p. 42). His fight for freedom consists of making desperate attempts through the use of influence to get transferred to a hospital in

Moscow. As for his culture, it consists of a rote recital of quotations, often misattributed, and a contempt for the uncouth masses.

Seeing Kostoglotov reading a book, he thinks to himself that "the cutthroat" has "pretensions to culture" (p. 11). It is true that Kostoglotov, like many self-taught persons, likes to show off the knowledge he has picked up, but his pretensions are superficial compared to those of Rusanov. Rusanov is certain that he possesses the final truth on everything of importance, delivered once and for all by those who have only to be quoted to be accepted as unchallengeable authority. Kostoglotov, aware of the limitations of his knowledge, is actively searching for the truth.

The contrast between the rebel and the bureaucrat is present throughout the novel. Kostoglotov, close to death and knowing that no hotel will admit him because he doesn't have proper papers, with the tenacity he learned in the camps succeeds in being admitted into the hospital although it is full and not taking patients; Rusanov, once admitted to the hospital, decides he should go elsewhere but is unsuccessful and is convinced that he must stay and begin immediately a course of injections. He, who has been so rigorous in applying rules and regulations, tries to circumvent those of the hospital but finds that he can't.

The ups and downs in the fortunes of the two men contrast with each other. Thanks to his unusual ability to withstand the effects of a large amount of X-rays, Kostoglotov has made a remarkable recovery. Rusanov, on the other hand, perceiving his tumor growing, realizes that he is near death's door. The first effect of his injections is to send him into a delirium in which he imagines retribution coming to him.

But then the injections make Rusanov's tumor decrease in size. They leave him, however, in a weakened condition. At the same time the X-rays have caused Kostoglotov to be in a state of constant nausea. They lie there, side by side, Rusanov listless and Kostoglotov nauseous. As the line of Rusanov's fortune has ascended and that of Kostoglotov's fortune has descended, they have intersected.

At the conclusion, Rusanov, feeling well again and seeming fit, is discharged from the hospital. He feels proud of himself as a "new man" who has won out. He does not know that the doctors "still expected an outbreak of tumors in many of his glands, and it depended on the speed of the process whether or not he would live out the year" (p. 454). Kostoglotov too is discharged from the hospital, seemingly fit. He knows, however, that the X-rays have made him sexually impotent.

The ups and downs of the two men constitute a kind of hospital bedside progress chart of de-Stalinization in their society. Rusanov is depressed and Kostoglotov is elated by the evidence of the process of de-Stalinization they see in the newspaper. In the last chapter of Part I, entitled "The Shadows Go Their Way," there is a turning-point for Rusanov. His daughter Aviette, a young woman with a high degree of sophistication, tells him that, "though they talk about the 'cult of personality,' in the same breath they speak of 'the great successor.' Generally speaking, you have to be flexible, you have to be responsive to the demand of the times" (p. 279). Her last words, which conclude the chapter, are "Fight hard, get rid of your tumor, and don't worry about *anything . . . .* Everything's going to be all right, *everything*" (p. 287). But, unknown to them, Rusanov's doom in the form of his cancer awaits him, however long or short is the process by which that doom proceeds. Whatever his skill in adapting himself to "the demand of the times," the bureaucrat will not be able to retain his old position, just as, perhaps it can be said, the entire bureaucracy is doomed, however long it takes for its fate to catch up with it.

Although Kostoglotov survives, the ravages of cancer—like the ravages of Stalinism in the country at large—cannot be gotten rid of as if they had never been. But Kostoglotov is able to rise above his condition. Vera Gangart, the doctor with whom he has fallen in love, has invited him to stay in her home on leaving the hospital. Kostoglotov could ask for nothing more in life. However, his sexual desire tells him that this would not be fair to her. He would continue to feel desire for some time, he had been told, but would not be able to fulfill that desire. In a letter to her, he avows his love but says that he is sure that she will come to be thankful to him for not entangling his life with hers by coming to stay with her. In making this sacrifice for love, Kostoglotov is showing the moral strength that Nerzhin shows at the conclusion of *The First Circle.*

But, unlike *The First Circle*, *Cancer Ward* does not end with only the hope of personal salvation. Dyomka, like Kostoglotov, survives, crippled like him, to be sure, but constituting the hope for the future of Soviet society. When Dyomka told Kostoglotov that he has "a passion for social problems," Kostoglotov with prison-camp cynicism replied, "Social problems? . . . Oh, Dyomka, you'd better learn to assemble radio sets. Life's more peaceful if you're an engineer" (p. 22). But at the same time as he writes to Vera, Kostoglotov, who has undergone a process of education, writes to Dyomka, "Get better and live up to your ideals. I'm relying on you" (p. 527). Dyomka does not have the brilliance of Vadim or the self-assurance of Aviette, but it is only through young people with idealism and moral earnestness such as his that society will be regenerated.

In *August 1914* the yardstick by which characters are measured is the sense of responsibility or the lack of sense of responsibility which they feel toward Mother Russia. This is true not just of individuals but of social groups and classes.

The senior officers with the exception of a few mavericks are only concerned about the advancement of their careers, not about the fulfillment of obligations. The system of promotion by seniority has served to encourage those who "saw the army as a comfortable, highly polished, and luxuriously carpeted stairway on which awards, great or small, were distributed at every step." The consequence is that "the more important the command, the more surely and painfully you could expect to meet the same self-infatuated, careerist routineers, enthusiasts for the quiet life, interested only in eating and drinking their fill and rising effortlessly to the top" (p. 93). General Zhilinsky, an arrogant, stupidly incompetent, lying blusterer with powerful connections at court, is representative of the Russian commanders.

As against these senior officers there are a small number of captains and colonels trained in the General Staff Academy by Professor Golovin, a military genius, who, running afoul of the system, lost his post. His trainees, as a result of the system of seniority and of placement through court influence, did not receive positions of power but were dispersed throughout the army. These few junior officers are aware that what Russia needs is "modern technology, modern organization, and fast and furious thinking." They regard themselves as responsible for "the future of the Russian army" (p. 99). The keen-minded, energetic Colonel Vorontyntsev is their representative. Telling two lieutenant colonels of how their companies must fill the gap left by the reprehensible retreat of the regimental commander with the other companies of the regiment, he realizes that they are of the same breed as he and that they embody, "in refined and concentrated form, the vitality and courage of the nation" (p. 306).

Contrasted with these junior officers are the members of the intelligentsia. The intelligentsia is anti-patriotic, despising not only the regime but everything that is military. It prides itself on being progressive, but it is blind to the progressive developments taking place in Russia that are perceived only by a handful of officers and engineers. Typical of the intelligentsia is Madame Kharitonova, who runs a fashionable private school. The intellectuals in her circle sigh and dream a good deal about changing Russia but are incapable of action.

Bowled over by the sheer energy of the wealthy new-style farmer Zakhar Tomchak, so unlike her friends, Madame Kharitonova agrees to take his daughter Ksenia into her school and into her household as a lodger. But Tomchak has not understood what the effects of the school will be. Under Madame Kharitonova's tutelage Ksenia is transformed from an obedient, hard-working devout little girl into a supercilious young lady disdainful of the people of her native Ukraine and skeptical of all authority. Her sister-in-law Irina, who was in charge of Ksenia until she went away to school and loves her but deplores the change in her, tells her, "Everything around us here is much closer to the nation's roots than your enlightened Kharitonovs, who don't care about Russia at all" (p. 33).

In opposition to the skepticism of the intellectuals is the simple faith of the peasant-soldiers. Vorontyntsev, regarding the troops whom he has joined, feels "the strength of that stout-hearted and inexhaustible Russia under every Russian greatcoat which has no fear at all of Germans" (p. 217). These soldiers have no concept of Mother Russia; their respective villages and adjacent localities are all they know. But in the religious sense of the brotherhood of man they do understand what human solidarity is and, properly appealed to, are ready to die for their comrades-in-arms.

When Vorontyntsev addresses the remnants of a terribly battered regiment to urge them to fill a gap in the line and to stand firm so that other regiments will not be cut to pieces, it is this sentiment that he invokes. "Brothers!" he exclaims, identifying himself with them. "We shouldn't be wondering how we can get off lightly. We should be thinking about how to avoid letting our comrades down." He explains what is necessary and perceives the effect of his words. "When he saw those generous smiles break through, the colonel called out in a loud, commanding voice, 'Volunteers only!'" The ranks step forward as one man, and Vorontyntsev cannot forebear responding: "Mother Russia still has stout sons left!" (pp. 307–08). The men may not understand the concept of Mother Russia, but they exemplify it.

Nevertheless, it is suggested, in their failure to understand the concept, there is a danger for the future when they will be influenced by anti-patriotic forces. So too their looting of a German town, after the inefficiency of the high command has made them go without food for days and after they have, furthermore, perceived their officers taking fine things for themselves, foreshadows in its destruction of army disciplne the break-up of the army later in the war.

In developing his theme of responsibility toward Mother Russia, Solzhenitsyn makes occasional employment of some of the techniques he uses in *The First Circle* and *Cancer Ward*. He uses, for instance, parallel situations to display character and theme.

Thus Vorontyntsev's address to the remnants of the Estland regiment contasts with Artamonov's to the platoon of the Vyborg regiment. The Vyborg regiment is fresh, and the men have been joking among themselves while working, quite unlike the battle-weary Estland regiment, but Artamonov with his fatuous cheerleader questions—"What do you say, then, boys? Are we going to beat them?"—which soon degenerate into the customary hectoring, is only able to get from them automatic responses in "a ragged roar" (p. 207). Instead of replying to Vorontyntsev automatically with simulated enthusiasm, however, the Estland regiment responds with a "low murmer of assent" (p. 308).

So too Colonel Krymov's pressing vodka upon Vorontyntsev at breakfast is parallel to General Samsonov being constrained to exchange numerous toasts at dinner with the visiting English General Knox. Vorontyntsev has the un-Russian characteristic of drinking only when work has been successfully completed, but, after declining, has to join Krymov in the Russian ritual lest the frank atmosphere of their conversation be spoiled. Krymov is a blunt, tough professional officer, but he is impulsive and erratic, lacking Vorontyntsev's self-discipline. The consequence is that, despite his conscientiousness, he moves only by fits and spurts and slows down Vorontyntsev's plans. The old-style junior officer does not meet Russia's needs.

Samsonov too is conscientious, but he has the deficiencies of the senior officer even at his best. Slow-thinking and poorly trained for his position, he is unable to cope with his own limitations and the obstacles thrown in his path by the general staff and other senior officers. He needs to have a chance to sit down and ponder over his many problems but is forced to participate in the profusion of toasts dictated by protocol. The many fine wines have no savor for him, but as he imbibes them and receives the meaningless compliments on the excellence of the Russian army, he is cheered up into believing that the situation is not so gloomy, after all. Thus the rituals of the Russian army both exemplify and contribute to its inefficiency, and even those with a sense of responsibility are hamstrung by them.

But, although *August 1914* uses such devices of *The First Circle* and *Cancer Ward* as parallel situations and contrast of characters, it differs from them in many ways. For one thing, it is considerably less polyphonic than they are. The major portion of the novel, which is concerned with the front-line doings, is mostly told either by an omniscient author or seen from the point of view of the commanding officers. We do not see things from the enlisted man's point of view at all. The two enlisted men who are important characters, Arseni Blagodarev and Terenti Chernega, are exemplary figures observed almost entirely from the outside, perhaps because Solzhenitsyn is too preoccupied with describing the course of battle to enter into their minds or perhaps because he is unable to identify himself with them.

The relationship between Vorontyntsev and his good-natured, alert, devoted orderly, the peasant-soldier Blagodarev, symbolizes a technocratic elite's leadership of the people that, if it had been nationally achieved, might have harnessed Russia's spiritual strength and energy and saved it from disaster. They work closely together, and Vorontyntsev marvels at Arseni's "self-possessed dignity, his ability to remain his own man without insubordination" (p. 378).

Chernega is the sergeant major of Lieutenant Colonel Venetsky. Colonel Khristinich, the brigade commander, had shrewdly suggested the appointment to Venetsky so that Chernega, a natural leader, might supply the qualities lacked by Venetsky, who is "too soft a master," "addressed his men apologetically, and gave his orders as though they were requests." Although his education has consisted only of two years at a village school and a year at a commercial school, Chernega, with his "nimble mind" and his commanding bellow is, as he is perceived to be by the young officer, Second Lieutenant Yaroslav Kharitonov, a "splendid sergeant major" (p. 153). In battle he inspires the men with his own "reckless generosity" (pp. 349–53).

The characters of many of the officers are often only very lightly sketched, a descriptive adjective or two acting as an identifying label. The sketchiness of characterization is difficult to avoid where the list of personae is so long. "Of the numerous military figures (close to 100) identified by name in *August 1914*," says Dorothy Atkinson, who has studied Solzhenitsyn's military sources, "only a handful appear to be fictional," and, aside from Vorontyntsev, "most of these [fictional characters] are common soldiers or men of low rank."[10] The historical characters, conceived in "archival test-tubes," to recall Kopelev's expression, are all too often stillborn.

The military operations in which these characters are engaged are described, as many critics have declared, with an over-abundance of technical detail that is inert and undramatized. They squeeze, moreover, the non-military characters to the beginning of the novel, where they are introduced only to disappear or to reappear much later for just a moment, or toward the conclusion of the novel, where they are introduced only to be dropped.

Undoubtedly, some of these characters—certainly Sanya—will play significant parts in the larger design of the entire series of novels, but *August 1914*, even if we are to think of it as a huge fragment rather than a unit standing independently, should excite enough interest in itself to make us look with anticipation to the working out of the pattern. Instead, we are, in the words of Mary McCarthy, for two-thirds of the novel caught in a "dense thicket of military tactics and strategy" that is "bewildering to anybody but a military specialist."[11] *The First Circle* and *Cancer Ward*, with their multiplicity of characters and intricate weave, also make large demands upon the reader, but there are compensating rewards. In *August 1914* the rewards are much diminished.

As signposts for his narrative, which is both crowded in its detail and constantly shifting in scene, Solzhenitsyn uses a number of devices, some of them similar to those used by Dos Passos in *USA*. They include survey summaries of events set off in special type; extracts from documents, likewise set off in special type; montages of newspaper clippings with boldface headlines; "screen" sequences with different margins to represent different sets of technical instructions for such things as sound effects and camera direction; songs and proverbs, printed in italics, to conclude chapters.

These devices have been generally criticized, and with good reason. The summaries of events read like extracts from a dull textbook. The documents and the newspaper clippings are ironic in their contexts, the military orders and communiqués making empty, boastful claims at variance with the facts and the newspapers reflecting the smugness, complacency, and fatuousness of middle-class life behind the front; however, the irony of the orders and communiqués tends to be repetitious and that of the newspaper montages tends to be diffuse. The "screen" sequences are designed to convey through direct sense impressions unmediated by a narrator a sense of the chaos of war; they are partially successful, but their staccatto rhythym becomes tedious. The soldiers' songs and proverbs at chapter endings are intended to be ironic commentaries on and pithy summations of what has transpired in the chapter, but they are limp compared with the surprises, ironic twists, and climaxes that constitute the always effective and often stunning chapter endings of *The First Circle* and *Cancer Ward*. It seems as if Solzhenitsyn is constrained by being obliged to recount historical events.

The lack of success does not come, as some have said, from Solzhenitsyn using an outmoded modernism. Effectiveness does not necessarily depend on fashion. Norman Mailer in *The Naked and the Dead* made effective use of the Dos Passos device of "The Time Machine," a biographical flashback that shows how a character's past life has made him that which is revealed by the rigors of combat. This is what Solzhenitsyn did in his two earlier novels without the use of such devices, but such flashbacks are rare in *August 1914* and the development of character is not often portrayed.

This is illustrated by two important characters, Sanya Lazhenitsyn and Yaroslav Kharitonov. Sanya is earnest, thoughtful, and idealistic. Through patient persistence he has managed to persuade his father, a prosperous farmer, to permit him to go to the university although the old man had contended that Sanya's older brothers and sisters had managed well enough without it. His secret dream is to use the education he is acquiring for the benefit of the people.

Sanya is in many ways like the earnest, thoughtful, and idealistic Dyomka of *Cancer Ward*. He searches zealously for an understanding of the important truths of life and seeks to live by them. Despite his Tolstoyism, he volunteers at the inception of the war, not out of war-time excitement but because something within him tells him that this is what he has to do. To the fervent anti-Czarist and Tolstoyan arguments against his volunteering by a young girl friend, he can only say quietly and gently, "I feel sorry for Russia" (p. 11). So Dyomka quietly persists in pursuing his interest in social problems in spite of the dangers he knows he faces in Stalinist Russia.

But in the case of Dyomka we are shown what made him what he is. His father was killed in the war when Dyomka was two, and when his mother became a prostitute, his stepfather left them. His mother would bring men to their one-room unpartitioned apartment, and Dyomka grew up disgusted by what he saw. When he reached the seventh grade, he left his mother, who was glad to let him go. Dyomka became a lathe operator and went to night school. "He wasn't very good at the job, but as he wanted to be different from his devil-may-care mother, he didn't drink or yell rowdy songs. Instead he studied" (p. 121). The only pleasure he allowed himself was an occasional game of football, where ironically he got the kick in the shin that resulted in his cancer. His earnestness can, therefore, be traced to his childhood experience. We do not see, however, what made Sanya desire, unlike his brothers and sisters, to go to the university and persist in urging his father to permit him to do so. His childhood is a blank.

Yaroslav Kharitonov is a boyish, good-natured, freckle-faced lieutenant. Instead of getting a month's leave of absence after his graduation from military academy, the war causes him to be sent into the army immediately. For Yaroslav it is all very thrilling. In his family there had been constant talk about loving the peasants, but there was no contact with them, and Yaroslav could not even go to the nearby market without the permission of his mother and without washing his hands afterwards. Now at nineteen years of age he feels himself almost a father to the bearded muzhiks under his command. More than anything else, he wants to be a good officer and to serve Russia.

Yaroslav, the son of the schoolmistress Madame Kharitonova, had unexpectedly departed from her ideas.

> He had been duly steeped in the spirit of enlightenment from his earliest years, but while still in the fifth class he had developed an urge to become an officer cadet. . . . Yaroslav was a gentle boy, but this kink of his proved a stubborn one. His mother wrestled with him and nagged him for three years, . . . but she could not bring enough

authority and logic and anger to bear, so Yaroslav left home for Moscow and entered the Aleksandrov Military School (pp. 791–92).

Yaroslav's unexpected decision does not seem to be the normal revolt against a domineering mother. It occurs before his adolescence and is described as an aberration from his usual pliability. Even as an officer he is said to have "neither moustache nor beard, and as yet his lips lacked character, showed nothing but extreme youth and good nature. He had the innocence and good manners of one brought up in a female household" (pp. 296–97). His decision to enter military academy and his patriotic feeling are not, therefore, really explained.

With Yaroslav we may compare *Cancer Ward*'s Kostoglotov, who rebels against Stalinist conformism, as Yaroslav deviates from fashionable radicalism. Kostoglotov's revolt, he tells the nurse Zoya, took place when he was a first-year university student. The critical spirit that has remained a central part of him came to him from a current of feeling that manifested itself among the student youth in the period immediately after the war. "We used to meet, flirt with the girls, dance, and the boys used to talk about politics. . . . We weren't, so to speak, ecstatic about everything. Two of us had fought in the war, and afterwards we expected things to be different somehow" (p. 165). Yaroslav, on the other hand, at the age of twelve inexplicably goes counter to what Solzhenitsyn represents is the virtually unanimous feeling among the educated élite of which his family is representative.

In opposition to Yaroslav Kharitonov is Sasha Lenartovich. The extended contrast between the two recalls similar contrasts of character in *The First Circle* and *Cancer Ward*, but here the contrast all too often rings false because the character of Lenartovich is perceived to be a hollow counterfeit. This is sensed by Mary McCarthy, who writes, "The shallowness of Lenartovich (even granting that he is conceived as a shallow person) shows a failure of justice on the author's part—understandable, God knows, humanly after what he has suffered, but in the author-as-novelist, a shortcoming nonetheless," and by Kathryn B. Feuer, who writes, "[T]he wisdom of all the patriots, and the shallowness of all the oppositionists, is disquieting."[12]

Lenartovich is a twenty-four-year-old lawyer who was drafted and, being a university graduate, commissioned as an ensign. He is dedicated to the revolutionary cause and therefore opposed to the war.

Whereas Kharitonov, in hospital with a severe concussion as a result of having been exposed with his men to an intense shelling, begs Vorontyntsev to have the administrators release him because the hospital is about to be captured by the advancing Germans and he does not want to be a prisoner of war, Lenartovich seeks to desert and give himself up to the enemy. He tells himself that saving himself for the revolutionary cause is not at all reprehensible.

That this is a rationalization for cowardice is made clear by the fact that, after his kneecaps had quivered violently when his troops had come under heavy fire, he thought on the cessation of firing, "His knees had stopped trembling. Anyway, it wasn't from fear. He wasn't frightened at all. He just felt that this was not *it*, that this was not the place, that this was most certainly not where he should be laying down his life" (p. 288). The absurdity of the rationalization, however, is so gross that it seems overdrawn: could any rational person, let alone the highly intelligent man Lenartovich is represented as being, seriously entertain the idea that his kneecaps have been so educated by his brain that they quiver only when the fighting is for the wrong cause?

When, having deserted, Lenartovich meets Vorontyntsev and Kharitonov, who are intent on breaking through the German lines to find their way to the Russian army, he joins them. He had been pinned down by German machine-gun fire, and now he "was truly glad that he had fallen into what were obviously safe hands. . . . Trying to give himself up had proved even more dangerous than fighting . . ." (p. 383). In the company of Kharitonov, he proves himself to be the opposite of him in every way. Kharitonov boyishly worships Vorontyntsev; Lenartovich knows that only Vorontyntsev can get them out, and this is his only concern. Kharitonov is moved by the simple heroism and religious belief of the men in their little band, who at the risk of their own lives are carrying their wounded lieutenant and the dead body of their colonel to give him Christian burial on Russian soil; Lenartovich despises them as superstitious peasants who are endangering him because of their stupid beliefs.

Sasha Lenartovich is not just an intellectual who happens to be a rationalizing coward. He is representative of the socialists opposed to the war. He thinks to himself that the "most sensible thing would have been to emigrate but he had let that blessed opportunity slip when many of his friends had taken it. Out there in Switzerland and France, party politics, the exchange of ideas, the serious business of life, went unhindered in spite of the war" (p. 364). If he were in exile, he thinks on another occasion, "he would have been among his own kind, he would beyond doubt have been preserved for the coming revolution. All decent revolutionaries were there, if they had not emigrated" (p. 286).

In *Lenin in Zurich* it is seen that "decent revolutionaries," to use Solzhenitsyn's ironic phrase, are indeed draft dodgers playing happily at politics in the safe harbor of Switzerland. Lenin's associates Munzenberg and Radek are characterized as "deserters from the German and Austro-Hungarian armies" (p. 60). Lenin, who is contemptuous of anything smacking of pacifism, regards the conferences of socialists opposed to the war as "conferences for women and deserters" (p. 185).

Lenin himself, however, enraptured though he is by visions of bloody civil wars, is a coward who is terrified of leaving the Swiss sanctuary. When he is in the Austro-Hungarian city of Cracow and sees the war slogan on the train station wall, "A bullet shot for every Russian!" he can't "suppress a shudder" (p. 33). When he sees a commemoration of a nineteenth-century battle in which the Russians fought the French for Zurich, it is "a frightening thought" for him "that Russian troops had been there" and that Switzerland is not beyond the reach of the Czar's government. When he hears a rumor that Switzerland will soon be drawn into the war, he finds it "spine-chilling" (p. 198). When, therefore, at the Zimmerwald Conference, he is taunted, "You can put your name to it here, because you're safe—why don't you go to Russia and *send* your signature?" we see the validity of the taunt (p. 52).

Lenartovich's doctrine of "the worse, the better" (p. 122), which causes him to rejoice in every defeat of the Russians (except for those in which his own safety is endangered), is an anticipation of the doctrine that Solzhenitsyn's Lenin develops. It is, however, a distortion of the doctrine of the historical Lenin. This distortion tends to make Lenartovich, as its expounder and exemplifier, merely a straw man to be knocked down.

Lenin's policy was encapsulated in his statement, "Defeat is the lesser evil." Military defeat is an evil not to be sought for, but it is preferable to a military victory gained by a "civil peace" that suppresses the struggle against the regime and its war. Revolutionists should not therefore discontinue their agitation on the ground that it weakens the war effort. In carrying out this effort, revolutionists in opposing countries give strength to each other and thus enable the imperialist war to be ended sooner.[13] Indeed, this was how it actually happened: revolutionary example caused German workers and soldiers to rise up against their masters so that Ludendorff, writing in his memoirs of the Russian Revolution and seeking to justify having allowed Lenin to go to Russia, said, "I could not suppose that it would become the tomb of our own might."[14]

Lenartovich is represented as a kind of proto-Bolshevik who no doubt in a future volume will join the Bolshevik forces. However, he has no international perspective and his only concern is to seek the defeat of Russia as a desirable end in itself. It is easy enough, therefore, for him to rationalize his desertion. The words the historical Lenin used to describe his policy to his followers in Russia, however, were "not by sabotage of the war effort, not by isolated interventions, but by propaganda among the masses."[15] Just as a Bolshevik working in a factory under difficult conditions does not quit his job under the pretext that he is not going to allow himself any longer to be exploited by his boss but seeks to organize his fellow-workers to take collective action, so the Bolshevik in the army does not by deserting abandon the struggle to influence his fellow-soldiers against the war, a struggle which entails gaining their respect by his courage, competence, and concern for their common welfare.

Lenartovich had tried to carry out agitation in his platoon but to no avail: the supercilious intellectual could not make contact with the soldiers. "Their obtuseness and meek subservience drove him to despair" (p. 287). This is quite contrary to the adjurations of the historical Lenin, who frequently reiterated that the first virtue of a Bolshevik is patience.

It would seem self-evident that revolutions cannot be led by those who cannot make contact with the masses, who are cowards, and who shirk responsibility. The Bolshevik Party was made up of individuals, each with his or her strengths and weaknesses, but its members did tend to have some common traits. Albert Rhys Williams, one of the two Americans who wrote fine eye-witness accounts of the Russian Revolution—the other, of course, was John Reed—stated: "The Bolsheviks were mostly young men not afraid of responsibility, not afraid to die, and, in sharp contrast to the upper-classes, not afraid to work."[16] Each of these traits is foreign to Lenartovich, who fobs off his duties on his sergeant and who, in charge of putting out a fire, supervises the inept firefighting with "little interest in the work" and with "languid movements" (p. 120). But Lenartovich is presented not as a dilettante in revolution but as one who was dedicated to it from childhood and who had been arrested three times. Yet his character is scarcely that of a revolutionist. It is no wonder that McCarthy and Feuer have the feeling that Solzhenitsyn has not played fair in his depiction of Lenartovich.

There are indications that Solzhenitsyn intended to make Lenartovich a more complex character than he is but did not succeed in doing so. Vorontyntsev, a fine judge of character, thinks that "even this student with his contempt for military service could with proper training be turned into an excellent soldier," and later he tells himself, "[S]omething might yet be made of him, but time was short" (pp. 383, 428).

But Vorontyntsev has surmised that Lenartovich is a deserter and knows that he has to give him a direct order to make him join him in taking his turn carrying the stretcher of the wounded lieutenant. It is evident that the immature but conscientious Kharitonov under the pressure of war and the tutelage of Vorontyntsev will be molded into an excellent officer, but how could anyone with the character deficiencies Lenartovich exhibits become one? It would seem that in having Vorontyntsev speak of Lenartovich's potential Solzhenitsyn was seeking to sound the theme of *The First Circle* of the possibilities of good and evil in each of us but that he could not bring himself to show good qualities in him.

The only reason Vorontyntsev gives for his belief in Lenartovich's potential is that he is "well built and held his head high" (p. 383). This is so superficial a criterion that it does not seem appropriate for the intelligent Vorontyntsev to be guided by it. After all, General Martos, "lean, quick, sharp-tongued," looking "less like the ordinary ponderous Russian general than a masquerading civilian," with his unbuttoned greatcoat and his pointer in his hand, happens to be one of the rare good generals in the army (p. 245). Nor does Kharitonov, who is short and slight and has a most un-officer-like boyish exuberance, seem very military in his bearing, but he has Vorontyntsev's approval.

It is also true that Vorontyntsev regards Lenartovich, who is described as having a "keen, clever face" (p. 122), as intelligent. In action, however, Lenartovich does not show himself as very clever. In fighting the fire, he displays not only a lack of concern but a lack of resourcefulness. When a higher-ranking officer upbraids him for exhausting his men by having them carry buckets of water for long distances instead of finding a pump, he can only meekly reply that the battalion doesn't have a pump. "So use your brains for once," raps out the officer. "You're not at the university now, you know. . . . Follow me, I'll show you where you can get a pump and a hose. You should have looked around some of the barns" (p. 126). And when he seeks to surrender, he does not, as we have seen, anticipate the dangers he will face and is glad to let Vorontyntsev, whom he perceives to be a "strong and clever man" (p. 403), make the decisions. The university-educated Lenartovich does not seem to be so smart, after all.

The face of Lenartovich is likewise described as having "a set determination, unusual for one of his age" (p. 120), which contrasts with Kharitonov's look of immaturity. Lenartovich's sureness of himself, however, appears only in his political argument with the medical officer, in which he speaks with "a youthful certitude" (p. 124). When he is about to desert, he is not so decisive. "An hour went by, two hours, and Sasha had still made no move. . . . He found it difficult to pull himself together and get started. Yet all he need do was walk away" (p. 365). He may be self-confident in his political argument with the medical officer, but after his encounter with the German machine-gunners he is happy to be "cushioned against alarming reality" by placing himself in the hands of Vorontyntsev—"no need to plan, no need to worry, just do what, and go where, he was told" (p. 403).

In none of his actions, therefore, does Lenartovich reveal the potential of a good officer. In general, it may be said, in *August 1914* courage and intelligence go together with integrity. The exception is Samsonov, who is brave and honorable but of only limited competence. Even he, however, is not downright stupid, as most of the other Russian generals are. Nevertheless the fact that Samsonov is not an exemplary character but one who strives to do the best he is capable of makes his defeat, as many have pointed out, the most moving part of the book.

There are no characters of mixed hues in *Lenin in Zurich*, the chapters from *The Red Wheel* that Solzhenitsyn has published separately from *August 1914*. Lenin's associates are all either utter fools and dupes like Platten and Bronski or complete rogues and scoundrels like Radek and Münzenberg. Lenin himself not only, as we have seen, bears little resemblance to the historical Lenin but is psychologically inconsistent because Solzhenitsyn seeks at one and the same time to diminish his stature and to portray him as a mighty demonic force.

To begin with a trivial example, Lenin is upset on board the train to Cracow because his mother-in-law discovers that she has left one of their suitcases behind. "It might sound comic, but an orderly household was itself a contribution to the party cause. He didn't dare tell the older woman off. She could give as good as she got, and anyway, they respected each other—he even gave her little presents to stay on her good side. But he reprimanded Nadya" (pp. 23–24). The "It might sound comic" is of course a signal to the reader to laugh at the fussy, excitable little man who is too cowed by his feisty old mother-in-law to upbraid her and takes it out on his wife.

But how is Lenin's conduct toward his mother-in-law compatible with that of the political leader who, if any of his followers "ceased to understand why his duties were essential and urgent, began to mention his mixed feelings or his own unique destiny," was immediately ready to "abuse and anathematize him" (p. 19)? "In all his personal relationships," we are told, "Lenin was careful to assert his superiority, was always on his dignity" (p. 78)—all except in his relationship with his mother-in-law, where Solzhenitsyn for the sake of his mother-in-law joke violates consistency of characterization.

Thus also Solzhenitsyn, always eager to show how wrong Lenin could be, recalls the historical fact that he was so disbelieving that German Social Democrats could betray their internationalism by voting war credits for their government that he thought it must be a government fabrication. Lenin's conviction that to serve German imperialism was for socialists an incredible height of perfidy contradicts, however, Solzhenitsyn's portrayal of him as a German agent.

So too he has Lenin admit to himself that he was an "apathetic and ineffectual spectator during the First Revolution [of 1905]" (p. 32), that he is a man who has studied revolutions in the library but proved unable to act at a crucial time. On another occasion, however, when he thinks of how the war and the Czarist government have fragmented and scattered the Bolsheviks and he has been left a leader without forces, he says to himself, "What he had was a . . . tiny group, calling itself a party, and he could not account for all its members. . . . What he had was—a head, capable at any moment of providing a centralized organization with decisions, each individual revolutionary with detailed instructions, and the masses with stirring slogans" (p. 183). But a man who is capable at any moment of providing decisions, instructions, and slogans can scarcely be said to be one who is incapable of action.

The contradiction does not stem from Lenin's varying moods in appraising himself. Parvus intimates that 1905 revealed a fundamental defect in Lenin; on the other hand, we see Lenin, "his leaping passion to enter the fray almost bursting his rib cage," providing a "program of action" to the Bolsheviks in March 1917 (p. 243). The contradiction rises from Solzhenitsyn's confused double view of Lenin as an ineffectual student of revolution and as a dynamo of demonic energy driving a party of automatons.

Deutscher says of Lenin's role in 1905 that he "was still experimenting in the laboratory of revolutionary politics when the revolution, not waiting for the results of his work, knocked at his door." Not he alone but all of "the great leaders of Menshevism and the lesser lights of Bolshevism"—for the leaders of the Bolshevik Party were not, as Solzhenitsyn would have it, automatons mechanically obedient to Lenin but bold, independent thinkers who constituted a brilliant galaxy—were "stranded on the shoals" by "the powerful tide of 1905." "The leaders of 1905" were almost entirely "nameless rankers swept forward by popular enthusiasm or indignation but possessing little revolutionary training or technique." The sole exception was the twenty-six-year-old Trotsky, who, however, displayed an "inspired amateurishness that was not to be found in the Trotsky of 1917." In all of this was revealed "the 'immaturity' of the First Revolution."[17] For Solzhenitsyn in *Lenin in Zurich*, however, the 1905 revolution was brought about by the conspiratorial machinations of Parvus, as the 1917 revolution was brought about by the conspiratorial machinations of a Lenin who, without having developed in any way, was somehow no longer apathetic or ineffectual.

Solzhenitsyn's vision of the history of the Russian Revolution, then, is a fabrication that can only result in an increasing stultification of his art.

## NOTES

1. Rosa Luxemburg, "Introduction to Korolenko's *History of a Contemporary*," *Marxism and Art: Essays Classic and Contemporary*, ed. Maynard Solomon (New York: Knopf, 1973), p. 152.
2. *Khrushchev Remembers*, p. 246.
3. Norman Mailer, *The Naked and the Dead* (New York: New American Library, n.d.), p. 139.
4. Leon Trotsky, *Portraits: Political and Personal* (New York: Pathfinder Press, 1977), p. 215.
5. Trotsky, *Portraits: Political and Personal*, p. 218.
6. Trotsky, *Portraits: Political and Personal*, pp. 215, 219.
7. Werth, p. xvii.
8. Trotsky, *Stalin: An Appraisal of the Man and his Influence* (New York: Stein and Day, 1967), p. 393.
9. Cf. Trotsky, *Portraits*, p. 215, on the impression Stalin gave in his early years to many: "On ingenuous people hardness often produces the impression of sincerity. 'This man does not think slyly, he says openly everything he thinks.' " Cf. also Deutscher, *Stalin*, pp. 274–75: "Himself taciturn, he was unsurpassed at the art of patiently listening to others. . . . This was one of his qualities that seemed to indicate a lack of egotism. . . . To party audiences he appeared as a man without personal grudge or rancour."
10. Dorothy Atkinson, "*August 1914*: Historical Novel or Novel History," *Aleksandr Solzhenitsyn: Critical Essays*, p. 412.
11. Mary McCarthy, "The Tolstoy Connection," *Aleksandr Solzhenitsyn: Critical Essays*, pp. 332–33.
12. McCarthy, p. 338 and Kathryn B. Feuer, "*August 1914*: Solzhenitsyn and Tolstoy," *Aleksandr Solzhenitsyn: Critical Essays*, p. 381.
13. Deutscher, *The Prophet Armed*, p. 236.
14. Trotsky, *History of the Russian Revolution*, II, 109.
15. Liebman, *The Russian Revolution*, p. 95n.
16. Albert Rhys Williams, *Through the Russian Revolution* (New York: Monthly Review Press, 1967), p. 21.
17. Deutscher, *Stalin*, pp. 65–66.

# GLOSSARY OF CHARACTERS IN SOLZHENITSYN'S NOVELS

This glossary of the characters discussed in Chapters 2 and 6 is appended as an aid to readers who may have difficulty in recalling the unfamiliar-sounding Russian names.

## The First Circle

**Adamson, Grigory Borisovich,** a zek survivor of the early revolutionary opposition.

**Agniya,** fiancee of Yakonov in his youth.

**Doronin, Rostislav (Ruska),** zek disciple of Nerzhin, in love with Clara Makarygin.

**Galakhov, Dinera,** the wife of Nikolai Galakhov and daughter of Pyotr Makarygin.

**Galakhov, Nikolai,** a popular novelist.

**Gerosimovich, Illarion,** a zek specialist in optics.

**Kagan, Isaak Moiseyevich,** a Jewish informer among the zeks.

**Klimentiev, Ilya,** a lieutenant colonel who is the head of Mavrino, a special camp for scientists.

**Kondrashev-Ivanov, Hippolyte,** a zek mystical painter.

**Lansky, Alexei,** a young literary critic and suitor of Clara Makarygin.

**Lyubimichev, Victor,** a handsome, engaging young informer among the zeks.

**Lyuda,** a frivolous, cynical university student living in the women's dormitory.

**Makarygin, Clara,** a free employee at Mavrino, daughter of prosecutor Makarygin.

**Makarygin, Pyotr,** thirty years a prosecutor for political crimes, fought in the Civil War.

**Muza,** a graduate student in the humanities who is asked to be an informer.

**Nadelashin, Lieutenant,** a junior officer at Mavrino, popular among zeks but a spy.

**Nerzhin, Gleb,** a seeker for truth, an autobiographical character.

**Nerzhin, Nadya,** his wife, a graduate student.

**Potapov, Andrei,** a zek electrical engineer, formerly a POW of the Nazis.

**Radovich, Dushan,** an orthodox Marxist who has survived the purges, formerly a comrade-in-arms of Makarygin during the Civil War.

**Roitman, Adam,** a major who is a Jewish CP member and deputy to Yakonov.

**Rubin, Lev Grigoryevich,** a Stalinist zek, but intelligent and good-hearted, a character based on Solzhenitsyn's prison-camp friend Lev Kopelev.

**Shikin,** a major who is the security officer at Mavrino.

**Sologdin, Dmitri,** a zek who is a rather eccentric individualist, based on Solzhenitsyn's prison-camp friend Panin.

**Spiridon.** See "Yegorov."

**Volodin, Innokenty,** son-in-law of Makarygin, a diplomat who is sentenced to labor camp after being arrested.

**Yakonov, Anton,** colonel who is chief of operations at Mavrino, formerly a prison-camp inmate.

**Yegorov, Spiridon Danilovich,** a peasant zek, janitor at Mavrino. Usually referred to by his first name.

*Cancer Ward*

**Ahmadjan,** a Uzbeck patient, formerly a prison-camp guard.

**Asya,** a seventeen-year-old patient, suffering from cancer of the breast.

**Chaly, Maxim Petrovich,** a black-market operator, suffering from cancer of the stomach.

**Dontsova, Ludmila Afanasyevna,** radiologist who develops cancer.

**Dyomka,** a sixteen-year-old idealistic and earnest student suffering from cancer of the leg.

**Podduyev, Yefrem,** construction foreman, suffering from cancer of the tongue. Generally referred to as "Yefrem."

**Kostoglotov, Oleg,** a patient, former zek, an autobiographical character.

**Rusanov, Pavel Nikolayevich,** a high-ranking bureaucrat, suffering from cancer of the neck.

**Shulubin, Alexei Filippovich,** a librarian, suffering from cancer of the rectum.

**Vadim.** See "Zatsyrko, Vadim."

**Zatsyrko, Vadim,** a young geologist who thinks to complete his work before he dies of cancer.

**Yefrem.** See "Podduyev, Yefrem."

*August 1914*

**Arkhangorodsky, Ilya Isakovich,** an industrialist.

**Arkhangorodsky, Sonya,** his radical daughter.

**Blagodarev, Arseni,** a peasant-soldier, Vorotyntsev's orderly.

**Chernega, Terenti,** a sergeant major, poorly educated but nimble-minded.

**Kharitonov, Yaroslav,** son of the schoolmistress Madame Kharitonova, a young lieutenant.

**Kharitonova, Aglaidi Fedoseevna,** a fashionably radical head of a girl's school.

**Kotya,** Sanya Lazhenitsyn's friend, a student war volunteer.

**Krymov, Colonel Aleksandr Mikhailovich,** a blunt, tough professional officer.

**Lazhenitsyn, Isaaki (Sanya),** a university student volunteer. An autobiographical character.

**Lenartovich, Sasha,** a lawyer drafted into the army as an ensign, devoted to the revolutionary cause.

**Naum,** a student radical, friend of Sonya Arkhangorodsky.

**Obodovsky, Pyotr Akimovich,** an engineer, formerly a revolutionist.

**Samsonov, General Aleksandr Vasilievich,** slow-thinking but conscientious.

**Tomchak, Ksenia,** a fashionably radical and superficially cultured young woman, daughter of Zakhar Tomchak and pupil of Madame Kharitonova.

**Tomchak, Roman,** a fashionably radical pseudo-intellectual, son of Zakhar Tomchak.

**Tomchak, Zakhar,** a wealthy new-style farmer.

**Vorotyntsev, Georgi,** a keen-minded, energetic, patriotic colonel.

**Varsonofiev, Pavel Ivanovich,** a philosopher and scholar at the Rumyantsev Museum Library.

# BIBLIOGRAPHY

Atkinson, Dorothy. "*August 1914*: Historical Novel or Novel History," *Aleksandr Solzhenitsyn: Critical Essays and Documentary Materials*, ed. John B. Dunlop, Richard Haugh, and Alex Klimoff. Belmont, Mass.: Nordland Publishing Co., 1973.

Bailyn, Bernard. *The Ideological Origins of the American Revolution*. Cambridge, Mass.: Harvard Univ. Press, 1967.

Balabanoff, Angelica. *Impressions of Lenin*. Ann Arbor: Univ. of Michigan Press, 1965.

Barker, Francis. *Solzhenitsyn: Politics and Form*. New York: Barnes & Noble, 1977.

Belden, Jack. *China Shakes the World*. New York: Monthly Review Press, 1970.

Carlisle, Olga. *Solzhenitsyn and the Secret Circle*. New York: Holt, Rinehart and Winston, 1978.

Cohen, Stephen F. *Bukharin and the Bolshevik Revolution: A Political Biography 1888–1938*. New York: Oxford Univ. Press, 1980.

Chomsky, Noam and Herman, Edward S. *The Washington Connection and Third World Fascism*. Boston: South End Press, 1979.

Deutscher, Isaac. *Stalin: A Political Biography*. New York: Oxford Univ. Press, 1949.

_____ *The Prophet Outcast*. New York: Oxford Univ. Press, 1963.

Deutscher, Tamara. *Not By Politics Alone . . . the other Lenin*. London: Allen & Unwin, 1973.

Djilas, Milovan. *Conversations with Stalin*. New York: Harcourt, Brace & World, 1962.

Engels, Frederick. *The Origin of the Family, Private Property and the State*. New York: International Publishers, 1972.

Feuer, Kathryn B. "*August 1914*: Solzhenitsyn and Tolstoy," *Aleksandr Solzhenitsyn: Critical Essays and Documentary Materials*, ed. John B. Dunlop, Richard Haugh, and Alex Klimoff. Belmont, Mass.: Nordland Publishing Co., 1973.

Fromm, Erich, ed. *Marx's Concept of Man*. New York: Frederick Ungar, 1961.

Goldstein, David I. *Dostoyevsky and the Jews*. Univ. of Texas Press, 1980.

Gorky, Maxim. *Lenin*. Edinburgh: University Texts: 1, Oxford Univ. Press, 1967.

Hallett, Richard. "Beneath a Closed Visor: Dimitry Panin and the Two Faces of Sologdin in Solzhenitsyn's 'The First Circle,' " *Modern Language Review*, 78 (1983).

Hill, Christopher. "The English Civil War Interpreted by Marx and Engels," *Science and Society*, 12 (1948).

Inkeles, Alex and Bauer, Raymond A. *The Soviet Citizen: Daily Life in a Totalitarian Society*. Cambridge, Mass.: Harvard Univ. Press, 1959.

Katkov, George. *The Trial of Bukharin*. New York: Stein and Day, 1969.

Kern, Gary. "Solzhenitsyn's Self-Censorship: The Canonical Text of *Odin den' Ivana Denisovicha*," *Slavic and East European Journal*, 20 (1976).

Khrushchev, Nikita. *Khrushchev Remembers*. Boston: Little, Brown, 1970.

Kopelev, Lev. *Ease My Sorrows*. New York: Random House, 1983.

Krasnov, Vladislav. *Solzhenitsyn and Dostoevsky*. Univ. of Georgia Press, 1980.

Krupskaya, N. K. *Reminiscences of Lenin*. Moscow: Foreign Languages Publishing House, 1959.

Lashkin, Vladimir. *Solzhenitsyn, Tvardovsky, and Novy Mir*. Cambridge, Mass.: MIT Press, 1980.

Lenin, V. I. *Imperialism: The Highest Stage of Capitalism*. New York: International Publishers, 1939.

Lewin, Moshe. "The Social Background of Stalinism," *Stalinism: Essays in Historical Interpretation*, ed. Robert C. Tucker. New York: W.W. Norton, 1977.

Liebman, Marcel. *The Russian Revolution*. New York: Random House, 1970.

_____ *Leninism Under Lenin*. London: Merlin Press, 1980.

Loftus, John. *The Belarus Secret*. New York: Knopf, 1982.

Löwy, Michael. *The Politics of Combined and Uneven Development: The Theory of Permanent Revolution*. London: Verso, 1981.

Lukacs, Georg. *Solzhenitsyn*. Cambridge, Mass.: MIT Press, 1969.

Lunacharsky, Anatoly Vasilievich. *Revolutionary Silhouettes*. New York: Hill and Wang, 1967.

Luxemberg, Rosa. "Introduction to Korolenko's *History of a Contemporary*," *Marxism and Art: Essays Classic and Contemporary*, ed. Maynard Solomon. New York: Knopf, 1973.

Mailer, Norman. *The Naked and the Dead*. New York: New American Library, n. d.

Malinowski, Bronislaw. "War—Past, Present, and Future," *War as a Social Institution*, ed. Jesse D. Clarkson and Thomas C. Cochran. New York: AMS Press, 1966.

Mandel, Ernest. *Marxist Economic Theory*, vol. 1. New York: Monthly Review Press, 1970.

_____ "Solzhenitsyn, Stalinism and the October Revolution," *New Left Review*, no. 86 (July-Aug. 1974).

_____ "Peaceful Coexistence and World Revolution," *Revolution and Class Struggle*, ed. Robin Blackburn. Atlantic Highlands, N.J.: Humanities Press, 1978.

Marx, Karl. *Selected Works*, vol. 1. New York: International Publishers, n. d.

Marx, Karl and Engels, Frederick. *The Communist Manifesto*. New York: Pathfinder Press, 1978.

McCarthy, Mary. "The Tolstoy Connection," *Aleksandr Solzhenitsyn: Critical Essays and Documentary Materials*, ed. John B. Dunlop,

Richard Haugh, and Alex Klimoff. Belmont, Mass.: Nordland Publishing Co., 1973.

McNeal, Robert H. *Bride of the Revolution: Krupskaya and Lenin.* Ann Arbor: Univ. of Michigan Press, 1972.

Medvedev, Roy. *Let History Judge: The Origins and Consequences of Stalinism.* New York: Knopf, 1971.

_____ "Solzhenitsyn's *Gulag Archipelago: Part Two*," *Dissent*, 23 (1976).

_____ *The October Revolution*, tr. George Saunders. New York: Columbia Univ. Press, 1979.

Medvedev, Zhores. *A Question of Madness.* New York: Knopf, 1971.

_____ "Russia and Brezhnev," *New Left Review*, no. 117 (Sept.-Oct. 1979).

Mintz, Morton and Cohen, Jerry S. *America, Inc.* New York: Dial, 1971.

Montagu, M.F. Ashley. "The New Litany of 'Innate Depravity' or Original Sin Revisited," *Man and Aggression*, ed. M.F. Ashley Montague. New York: Oxford Univ. Press, 1968.

Navrozov, Lev. "Solzhenitsyn's World History: *August 1914* as a New *Protocols of the Elders of Zion*," *Midstream*, June-July 1985.

Orlov, Alexander. *The Secret History of Stalin's Crimes.* New York: Random House, 1953.

Pasternak, Boris. *Doctor Zhivago.* New York: New American Library, 1958.

Perakh, Mark. "Solzhenitsyn and the Jews," *Midstream*, 23 (1977).

Reisner, Larissa. "Svyazhsk," *Leon Trotsky: The Man and His Work.* New York: Merit Publishers, 1969.

Rosenberg, Edgar. *From Shylock to Svengali: Jewish Stereotypes in English Fiction.* Stanford, Calif.: Stanford Univ. Press, 1960.

Scammell, Michael. *Solzhenitsyn: A Biography.* New York: W.W. Norton, 1984.

Schapiro, Leonard. "Lenin After Fifty Years," *Lenin: The Man, The Theorist, The Leader: A Reappraisal*, ed. Leonard Schapiro and Peter Reddaway. New York: Praeger, 1967.

Selsam, Howard and Martel, Harry, eds. *Reader in Marxist Philosophy*. New York: International Publishers, 1973.

Shafarevich, Igor. "Socialism in Our Past and Future," *From Under the Rubble*, ed. Aleksandr Solzhenitsyn. Chicago: Regnery Gateway, 1981.

Siegel, Paul N. *Revolution and the Twentieth-Century Novel*. New York: Monad Press, 1979.

_____ "Solzhenitsyn's Political Evolution Reflected in His Novels," *Clio: A Journal of Literature, History and the Philosophy of History*, 12 (1983).

_____ *The Meek and the Militant: Religion and Power Across the World*. Atlantic Highlands, N.J.: Zed Books, 1986.

Singer, Daniel. *The Road to Gdansk*. New York: Monthly Review Press, 1981.

Solzhenitsyn, Aleksandr. *One Day in the Life of Ivan Denisovich*, tr. Max Hayward and Ronald Hingley. New York: Praeger, 1963.

_____ *Cancer Ward*, tr. Nicholas Bethell and David Burg. New York: Bantam, 1969.

_____ *The First Circle*, tr. Thomas P. Whitney. New York: Bantam, 1969.

_____ *Letter to the Soviet Leaders*. New York: Harper & Row, 1974.

_____ *The Gulag Archipelago 1918–1956: an Experiment in Literary Investigation I–II*, vol. 1, tr. Thomas P. Whitney. New York: Harper & Row, 1974.

_____ *The Gulag Archipelago*, vol. 2, tr. Thomas P. Whitney. New York: Harper & Row, 1975.

_____ *Lenin in Zurich*, tr. H.T. Willetts. New York: Farrar, Straus and Giroux, 1976.

_____ *Warning to the West*, tr. H.T. Willetts. New York: Farrar, Straus and Giroux, 1976.

_____ *The Gulag Archipelago*, vol. 3, tr. Harry Willetts. New York: Harper & Row, 1978.

_____ *The Oak and the Calf: Sketches of Literary Life in the Soviet Union*. New York: Harper & Row, 1980.

_____ *Solzhenitsyn at Harvard: The Address, Twelve Early Responses, and Six Later Reflections*, ed. Ronald Berman. Washington, D.C.: Ethics and Public Policy Center, 1980.

_____ *Detente: Prospects for Democracy and Dictatorship*. New Brunswick, N.J.: Transaction Books, 1980.

_____ *The Mortal Danger: How Misconceptions About Russia Imperil America*. New York: Harper & Row, 1980.

_____ , ed. *From Under the Rubble*. Chicago: Regnery Gateway, 1981.

_____ *Victory Celebrations: A Comedy in Four Acts*. London: The Bodley Head, 1983.

_____ "An Interview on Literary Themes with Nikita Struve, March, 1976," *Solzhenitsyn in Exile: Critical Essays and Documentary Materials*, ed. John B. Dunlop, Richard S. Haugh, and Michael Nicholson. Stanford, Calif.: Hoover Institution Press, 1985.

_____ *Victory Celebrations; Prisoners; The Love-Girl and the Innocent*. New York: Farrar, Straus and Giroux, 1986.

_____ *August 1914*, tr. H.T. Willetts. New York: Farrar, Straus and Giroux, 1989, revised and expanded edition.

Souvarine, Boris. "Solzhenitsyn and Lenin," *Dissent*, 24 (1977).

Struve, Gleb. "Behind the Front Lines: On Some Neglected Chapters in *August 1914*," *Aleksander Solzhenitsyn: Critical Essays and Documentary Materials*, ed. John B. Dunlop, Richard Haugh, and Alex Klimoff. Belmont, Mass.: Nordland Publishing Co., 1973.

Swingewood, Alan. *The Novel and Revolution*. New York: Barnes & Noble, 1975.

Trotsky, Leon. *My Life*. New York: Charles Scribners Sons, 1930.

_____ *The History of the Russian Revolution*. 3 vols. New York: Simon and Schuster, 1937.

_____ *The Revolution Betrayed: What Is the Soviet Union and Where Is It Going?* Garden City, N.Y.: Doubleday, Doran, 1937.

_____ *Their Morals and Ours.* New York: Merit Publishers, 1969.

_____ *Stalin: An Appraisal of the Man and His Influence.* New York: Stein and Day, 1970.

_____ *Lenin: Notes for a Biographer.* New York: Putnam, 1971.

_____ *The Young Lenin.* Garden City, L.I.: Doubleday, 1972.

_____ *Portraits: Political and Personal.* New York: Pathfinder Press, 1977.

_____ *"The Communist Manifesto* Today," Introduction to *The Communist Manifesto.* New York: Pathfinder Press, 1978.

_____ *The Permanent Revolution and Results and Prospects.* New York: Pathfinder Press, 1978.

Tucker, Robert C. "Introduction," *The Great Purge Trial,* ed. Robert C. Tucker and Stephen F. Cohen. New York: Grosset & Dunlap, 1965.

Valentinov, Nikolay. *Encounters with Lenin.* New York: Oxford Univ. Press, 1968.

Werth, Alexander. *Russia at War 1941–1945.* New York: Dutton, 1964.

Williams, Albert Rhys. *Lenin: The Man and his Work.* New York: Scott and Seltzer, 1919.

_____ *Through the Russian Revolution.* New York: Monthly Review Press, 1967.

Wise, David. *The American Police State.* New York: Random House, 1976.

Wolfe, Bertram D. *Three Who Made a Revolution.* Boston: Beacon Press, 1960.

_____ *Strange Communists I have Known.* New York: Stein and Day, 1965.

_____ *The Bridge and the Abyss: The Troubled Friendship of Maxim Gorky and V.I. Lenin.* New York: Praeger, 1967.

_____ *Lenin and the Twentieth Century*. Stanford, Calif.: Hoover Institution, 1984.

Zeman, Z.A.B. and Scharlau, W.B. *The Merchant of Revolution: The Life of Alexander Israel Helphand (Parvus) 1867–1924*. New York: Oxford Univ. Press, 1965.

# INDEX